PRAISE FOR *A FAMILY, MAYBE*

"I loved this riveting, well-paced, moving account of two gay men persevering in their determination to create a family through the foster-to-adoption process. The ups and downs as they work their way through the maze of the foster system had me turning pages long after bedtime. The cruelty of a haphazard legal system comes through loud and clear. But those two little girls, a toddler and her baby sister, could not have found better heroes. An inspiring portrait of steadfast love under pressure."
—Janet Fitch, author of *White Oleander,* an Oprah's Book Club selection and a New York Times bestseller

"Lane and Jon's story brings attention to the still existing barriers to supporting children in need of a loving home. It helps to guide and comfort future parents through the challenging foster and adoption processes and shines a bright light on why we fight. I hope everyone who cares about justice and fairness reads this important memoir. It's a story of hope and perseverance."
—Alan Lowenthal, US Congressman (CA-47, 2013-2023)

"*A Family, Maybe* is a breathtaking exploration of the intricacies and challenges that adults and children face when navigating the path through foster care adoption. With heartfelt compassion, Lane thoughtfully unravels the layers of societal perceptions, system bureaucracies, legal delays, and paralyzing fears that can hinder the path to building or growing a loving family. His powerful storytelling reminds us that love knows no boundaries, that love is love, and that every child deserves a loving family and a safe home."
—Rita L. Soronen, President & CEO, Dave Thomas Foundation for Adoption

"The fost-adopt process . . . can look incredibly complex, cumbersome, and even biased. Seeing that there can be a happy ending should inspire hope and help everyone involved understand the complexity of the process, and the possibility of forging greater love in a chosen family . . . we, as a system and a society, are grateful for families like Lane's that show up for these children."
—Jenny Serrano, Children's Services Administrator, Los Angeles County Department of Children and Family Servic⸍

"*A Family, Maybe* is an important lesson from a difficult, but, ultimately, transformative era when California's LGBTQ+ community was struggling to gain acceptance, respect, and equal rights, as gay and lesbian families were moving out of the darkness and into the national spotlight. Thankfully, through decades of organizing, much has changed. While the struggles of Lane's generation of gay men are beginning to fade, this memoir preserves a record of what it took to make a family in those pre-equality days: the joys, the perils, and the costs."
—Sheila Kuehl, California State Senator, the state's first openly gay legislator and a founder of the California Legislative LGBTQ Caucus

"Remarkably honest and timely, *A Family, Maybe* personalizes the experience of the surging number of LGBTQ+ adoptive parents who came of age in the 2000s. They pushed the boundaries of both the LGBTQ+ and adoptive-parent movements, battling discrimination and a broken child welfare system . . . Lane's memoir shows a thriving, multiracial and multicultural family based on love, stability, and an infinite devotion to their kids. At a time when foster care and adoption agencies have again been given a license to discriminate against LGBTQ+ perspective parents, the story of Lane and Jon's family needs to be told and shared."
—Stacey Stevenson, CEO, Family Equality, the nation's LGBTQ family advocacy organization

"Lane Igoudin's *A Family, Maybe* is an important addition to the adoption-memoir canon. With great compassion and masterful storytelling, Lane recounts his struggle to create a family amid crushing, often mind-boggling bureaucracy of the foster system, ever complicated by the birth parents' heartbreaking and earnest attempts at reunification. However murky the fates of their parenthood seemed sometimes, the unbridled, steadfast love Lane and his partner bestowed on their girls can serve as a clear beacon for all of us."
—Vanessa McGrady, author of the critically acclaimed *Rock Needs River: A Memoir About a Very Open Adoption*

"In this tumultuous time of anti-LGBTQ+ attacks, it is rare to find the brave soul willing to tell the complicated, tender story of building a family. Yet Lane does so here, finding the unique threads of trans-racial adoption in and among the universal fabric of parenthood. Despite cultural forces wishing us ill, Lane unites the LGBTQ+ community by sharing his family-building journey with the world—shining a much-needed light upon the kids and families that make us whole."

—Trystan Reese, author of *How We Do Family*, a 2021 Foreword INDIES Winner

"*A Family, Maybe* is an honest and inviting first-hand account of one father's journey toward adoption. Written with clarity, honesty, and love, Lane's memoir captures the longing for children that any parent or would-be parent can relate to. Keep this book by your bedside table. It will build your resilience and give you hope!"

—Dasee Berkowitz, parent educator and author of *Becoming a Soulful Parent: A Path to the Wisdom Within*

"*A Family, Maybe* opens with an emotional hook to the heart . . . The people who populate the pages of the book are well-drawn. We know them. They are our family members and our neighbors, which makes the story both poignant and compelling."

—Greta Boris, a *USA TODAY* bestselling author

A FAMILY, MAYBE

A FAMILY, MAYBE

Two Dads, Two Babies, *and the* Court Cases *That* Brought Us Together

LANE IGOUDIN

Ooligan Press | Portland, Oregon

A Family, Maybe: Two Dads, Two Babies, and the Court Cases That Brought
Us Together
© 2024 Lane Igoudin

ISBN13: 978-1-947845-45-9

Ooligan Press
Portland State University
Post Office Box 751, Portland, Oregon 97207
503.725.9748
ooligan@ooliganpress.pdx.edu
www.ooliganpress.com

Library of Congress Cataloging-in-Publication Data
Names: Igoudin, Lane, author.
Title: A family, maybe : two dads, two babies, and the court cases that
  brought us together / by Lane Igoudin.
Description: Portland : Ooligan Press, 2024. | Includes bibliographical
  references.
Identifiers: LCCN 2023017339 (print) | LCCN 2023017340 (ebook) | ISBN
  9781947845459 (trade paperback) | ISBN 9781947845466 (ebook)
Subjects: LCSH: Adoption. | Adoption--Law and legislation. | Foster
  children. | Gay fathers.
Classification: LCC HV875 .I46 2024 (print) | LCC HV875 (ebook) | DDC
  362.734--dc23/eng/20230624

LC record available at https://lccn.loc.gov/2023017339
LC ebook record available at https://lccn.loc.gov/2023017340

Cover design by Elaine Schumacher
Interior design by Eva Sheehan

Images from Lane Igoudin

Printed in the United States of America

Ooligan
PRESS

Portland State
UNIVERSITY

Disclaimer
This book is a memoir. It reflects the author's present recollections of experiences over time. The names of the birth parents and their family members, as well as those of the judge, social workers, lawyers, neighbors, and the foster/adoption agency have been changed. Some events have been compressed, and some dialogue has been recreated.

Content Warning
The book contains references to alleged domestic violence and statutory rape, as well as loss of life.

To my husband Jonathan,

the heart and soul

of our family

Part 1

A Baby and a Bag

Jon holding Gaby, June 2006
© Lane Igoudin, 2006

Curbside Delivery

It was on a hot, early summer afternoon, just before the breezes would begin blowing inland from the ocean that Jonathan shot me an irritated sideways glance.

"Where is she? Didn't she say 'early in the morning?' That was hours ago. What's taking her so long?"

A 6'3" athlete with the face of the *Bridgerton* lead, my partner Jon was lining up daisy-patterned onesies and burp cloths by the bassinet in the baby room. I'd heard him vacuuming this room earlier, and before that tidying up the crib and the toys in the green bedroom upstairs.

"Patience, dear," I sighed, "give her a few more minutes. She should be on her way."

Like Jon, I was trying to control my anxiety by being useful, yet I couldn't help rushing to the window every time I heard a car drive by. Jackie Willis, our designated Los Angeles County social worker, was neither here nor responding to my calls. Did the county change its mind? Did they release the baby to her mother, Jenna?

Every day, thousands of parentless children are shuffled around the county between foster homes, schools, courtrooms, and family visits. A foster child may be in the freeway lane next to yours; or in the car behind you at the gas station while a social worker like Jackie is pumping gas; or at a nearby table at an In-N-Out, freshly removed, hungry, disoriented, and being fed. These children used to be invisible to us, yet that day, June 6, 2006, somewhere on one of LA's freeways, their traffic hardening like arteries in the hot afternoon air, one particular car was supposed to be heading to our house to deliver a baby. And yet it wasn't there.

We'd been living with this uncertainty for months. Jenna was due around Memorial Day, but with office closures and Jackie out on medical leave, the baby could have gone to the wrong home. But that Memorial Day, I received a call—Babushka, my paternal grandmother.

"*Mazel tov!*" she announced. "Your Jenna gave birth today."

"How on earth do you know that?" I scoffed at her. "We've heard nothing."

"I just know," she said in her raspy, confident voice, "*Tak shto ne volnuisya, sam uvidesh* (Don't worry, you'll see it for yourself)."

I relayed her announcement to Jon. He chuckled at my dear 84-year-old grandma, our closest ally in the family. I chuckled with him, but deep down I felt even more anxious. What if she was right? I had no experience raising a newborn, nor did Jon. Zero. We'd been trained and certified, but that was all just textbook learning. Were we really about to become caretakers of a tiny, fragile life, 100 percent, 24/7? What were we getting ourselves into?

§

The county was back in business the next day, May 30. I left messages everywhere. None were returned.

Three days later, a social worker called from the hospital with the news that the baby had been born on Memorial Day at noon, just as Babushka had said, but couldn't be released yet. She had sepsis, a potentially fatal blood infection, likely from the Cesarean, and had to be put on medication.

Other arrangements had already been made by Jackie's Department of Children and Family Services (DCFS) between the county Juvenile Dependency Court (Children's Court), the hospital, and Our Bright Futures, the non-profit agency that represented us in this foster-to-adopt process.

The newborn would not be released to her mother. Instead, she would be *detained*—that is, put in the court's protective custody, and placed with us as an emergency foster home.[1] Afterwards, if cleared by the DCFS, the baby would be reunited with Jenna. But in the most likely scenario, the baby would remain with us as her long-term foster parents, while Jenna would be given an opportunity and resources to reunify with her child. Should she fail to complete her court-ordered reunification services, her parental rights would be cut, and the baby would become available for adoption. This two-pronged—reunification vs. foster-to-possible-adoption—approach is known as *concurrent planning*.[2]

Sepsis actually made it easier for the county to carry out its plan. Jenna recovered quickly and was discharged home to continue, as we were told, with her drug rehab and counseling. Meanwhile, the baby was improving on antibiotics, while the court, on the DCFS request, formally detained her.

But Jenna came back to breastfeed, and the nurse leaked the secret. Devastated and desperate, Jenna refused to leave, pleading with the staff to let her take her baby home.

That's when the hospital social worker called me.

"You're the foster parents. So come and get the baby. We have her ready for you."

Not so fast. Why should I, I reasoned, be the one to pry her from her mother's arms, from the one who'd carried her for nine months, loved her, and pinned her entire future on her? Why me when it's really the county and the court's decision?

"You called the mother's social worker, Jackie Willis?" I asked the woman on the phone.

"She's out sick," she replied.

"Well, what about Our Bright Futures—our foster-adoption agency? They could pick her up and bring her here."

"They said they couldn't. Apparently it's too far for them."

That made sense. The agency was in Echo Park, west of downtown Los Angeles. The baby was on the other side of downtown, plus another twenty miles to the east.

"Could you wait a little?" I asked. "I'm sure Jackie will be back in a day or two."

"Fine, we can keep the baby here a couple more days, but no more than that. She has to go."

§

On June 5, Jackie returned to work and called me.

"I heard you refused to pick up the baby yesterday."

"Given the situation," I paused, "don't you think it would be more appropriate if you handled it?"

Jackie sighed noisily. "Fine, I'll do it first thing tomorrow."

That fateful next day, June 6, the phone rang again.

"I'm on my way to the hospital. Hope you're happy," Jackie yelled over the freeway hum in the background.

"Jenna still there?"

"Oh, yes," she sighed, "still there, camped out, refusing to leave. She knows I'm coming to get the baby."

Poor Jenna. I couldn't imagine how she would feel or what she would do once Jackie got there. My chest tightened. And it was becoming real for us too, after all these months, really real. Our life was going to split into before and after.

At 4:30 p.m., a black SUV pulled up to the curb in front of our house. Jackie?

Jon ran out the front door. I followed him out onto the porch into the blindingly bright afternoon.

Jackie didn't hand the baby over, but waited for Jon to take her out of the car seat inside her vehicle—liability reasons, I assumed.

In Jon's hands, the baby looked small, like a delicate, light brown doll, her face no bigger than Jon's palm. All she had on was a pink onesie with the word *BABY* embroidered in white across the chest.

Despite my hesitations, a strong affection washed over me the moment I saw her—barely awake, helpless, innocent.

Jon just melted. Eyes on the baby, breathlessly, he carried her into the house.

Jackie looked a bit shaken; Jenna had confronted her in the parking lot, yelling, accusing her of betrayal.

Jackie handed me the cooler bag with several formula bottles and a three-inch binder with medical information and placement papers.

The baby and the bag. No baby blanket. Nothing else.

Then Jackie glanced at her watch and said, "I've got to go, guys. I'm trying to beat the rush hour."

I thanked her. She got back into her SUV and left. It was done.

I found Jon inside in the hallway, standing still with the baby in his arms, awestruck. Keeping his eyes on her, he passed the infant to me. Then he picked up his car keys from the dining room table and headed out. I knew he'd be back in a few minutes, and not alone.

§

In my arms, the baby felt warm and heavy, an unfamiliar weight. And she was whimpering. She was hungry, I assumed, so I sat down on the couch and, cradling the little girl, gave her a feeding from one of the disposable formula bottles left by Jackie.

While she sucked on a blue bottle nipple, I moved, with my index finger, a slick lock of her hair to the side of her forehead.

What a lovely baby. She had a full head of raven-black, curly hair that receded into velvety fuzz on her forehead and chin. Bumpy rosacea spots dotted her plump cheeks. Her eyes, as dark as Jon's, had almost no eyelashes, and a scarlet birthmark smudged her left eyelid. Her gaze seemed unexpectedly focused and introspective, as if while looking at me, she was thinking of something else.

How long will she be with us? What will the court do with her and her mother? I wondered.

I was still feeding the baby when the front door opened, and in walked Jon with a toddler holding him by the index finger, her cheeks rosy after a day of play at her pre-school—the baby's older sister, Marianna.

Gabriella

Jon went upstairs to change. Marianna remained with me in the living room. The toddler stood by the side of the coffee table, gripping its side, wobbling slightly, staring at me feeding the baby. Her gaze was somber; I'd never seen her look at me that way. In it was a mixture of incredulity, jealousy, and sadness.

Jon returned to the living room and sat down in the armchair next to Marianna. I knew he really wanted to hold the baby but, noticing Marianna's expression, he picked her up and sat her on his knee.

"See that baby, sweetie? She's your baby sister."

"Ba-by," said Marianna, stressing hard each syllable.

"Yes, ba-by, your baby sister. Remember how we used to watch the baby movie, and I always told you, 'That's your baby sister, your baby sister's coming?'"

Marianna shook her head.

The baby felt strange, an alien in our home, disrupting our three-person balance, becoming its center of gravity.

"I guess I'm supposed to burp her now," I said after she finished her bottle. "Except I don't know how."

I panicked slightly. A burp cloth. I recalled the "baby movie," our family phrase for the parent training DVD supplied by the county.

I needed a burp cloth. There was a stash of them somewhere, but where? Oh, well. Quickly grabbing a kitchen towel, I threw it over my shoulder and gave the baby a light pat on the back. No effect. I tried again, a bit harder. Still nothing; her face squirmed, but no air escaped her chest. I put more force in my slap.

"Papa hit baby," said Marianna.

"Papa burp baby," Jon corrected her.

It worked. The baby emitted a creaking whoosh and spurted out, along with the air, some milk onto the towel. I massaged her back, which was no wider than my hand, in a circular motion and felt the tension gradually leaving her little body.

The doorbell rang. The first visitors to see the baby were our neighbors: Inga, a Lithuanian beauty; Roger, her American husband; and their son Tommy, sitting high in his father's arms.

Inga didn't come empty-handed; packed in two plastic bags was a homemade dinner: a pot of roasted chicken *au jus,* and potatoes sprinkled with dill, a touch of her native land. We hugged, and she immediately took over the baby girl, cooing to her softly. Our neighbors didn't stay long, but before leaving, Inga showed us how to swaddle the child— her parting gift.

The next time the doorbell rang, it was my sister, Natalie, stopping by in her smart suit and high heels on her way home from the law firm. When she took the infant, still wide awake, into her arms, I recalled seeing Natalie brought home from the hospital in a blanket 28 years earlier. *What's going through her head?* I wondered while she was holding the newborn. *Will the next baby be hers and her fiancé Devlon's?*

After the second bottle of formula, the baby was finally getting sleepy. We swaddled her, mimicking Inga's instructions— wrapping her tightly in a blanket envelope so she wouldn't somehow roll over during sleep—and put her down carefully in the bassinet in the guestroom.

Then we sat down to Inga's dinner.

"She's so, so adorable! What's her name?" Natalie asked.

"They've got one for her in the file, yep," said Jon, "not a common name, but one of those fanciful concoctions a teenager might like. In public, we'll call her by that name, but at home, since she'll be staying with us all the way to the adoption, we'd rather use something we're comfortable with. Jackie said it's fine."

"I like Camille," I said. "I think it's pretty, a beautiful flower." Jon made a face. "But his favorite is Zhanna, which to me sounds like a Russian peasant name. He must have picked it up from one of those figure skating competitions on TV."

"Zhanna? Nah, she doesn't look like some Zhanna from Siberia." said Natalie. "Believe me, Jon, I know."

"Well," Jon replied, "you think that Camille, like Camilla Parker Bowles, is better?"

He was splitting roasted potatoes on Marianna's plate with the side of his fork. She lifted each bite-size chunk with her own fork, then, halfway to her mouth, delicately took it off with her fingers and shoved it in.

"But I also wouldn't mind Danielle, Dani for short," I said.

Jon shook his head; negative.

"How about Gabrielle?" asked Natalie.

I looked at Jon. I liked the sound of it: sparkling, refined, yet light-hearted. And it was Jewish: Archangel Gabriel's name, *Gevurah + El,* which means "strength of God."

"It's not bad, 'Gabrielle,' 'Gaby,'" said Jon pensively. "Sounds pleasant, cozy."

"What if we add an *a* at the end so that it sounds like her sister's name?" I proposed.

"You mean *Gabriella?*"

"That's right, Gabriel-la, like Marian-na."

"I suppose it's fine," said Jon.

With that, the name issue was settled.

§

I stayed home for two weeks, using up the rest of my eight-week parental leave from Cal Poly Pomona, where I worked as the public affairs officer of the business school. I'd spent the first six weeks with Marianna six months earlier. The union contract allowed to split it between children.

Gaby woke up at irregular hours, hungry. I was getting used to rocking, changing, and feeding her while fighting off drowsiness. In her sleep, she'd cry or make other vocal noises, to which I'd wake up instantly, ready to respond.

Difficult as our life was, it would've been even harder without friends. Inga came back to teach us how to bathe the newborn and clip her tiny toenails. Another friend, Fiona, dropped off a baby tub, blankets, bags of infant clothes, and a portable infant swing. From George and Jorge, who were foster-adopting Jack, Marianna's daycare playmate, came a grand bassinet and a brand-new infant car seat. They were hoping to adopt a second child, a baby, but were too far down the county waitlist.

Natalie aside, all my family was living in the Bay Area. My father called daily. So did Babushka, sometimes several times a day, always hungry for details. She kept offering to fly down to help, but at 84 and in poor health, it would've been madness. I politely refused her offer.

Jon's parents had passed away, but he'd call his sister often, asking for advice.

My mother didn't call until Sunday, our regular day for swapping news, five days after the baby's arrival.

"I heard from Natalie that you got the baby," she said matter-of-factly.

"Yep, we did. She's so beautiful! We just named her—Gaby, Gabriella."

"That's pretty. So how is it—with the two?"

"Hard, Mom, very hard . . . the baby cries at odd hours. The feedings are every three hours, around the clock, so I'm up every night, and then I'm off to work. I'm supposed to be out on parental leave, but I'm still Commencement Director at my college, leave or no leave. This week, I went in every day for rehearsals, equipment delivery, and so on . . . so yeah, it's a *sumashedshii dom* (madhouse) out here."

"Yeah, well, you wanted it, so . . ." Then, with halting hesitation, my mother asked, "You want *me* to come down?"

"Oh, Mom, that would help us so much. It's not just the baby—we have a toddler too, with all her needs and schedules."

My mother paused.

"Well, I can't. I'm busy taking care of Mark, and he's taking care of his mother."

Ah, taking care of Mark, her husband—Mark, brimming with energy, playing accordion, smoking a pack a day, driving my early-retired mother around town to stores, to her yoga classes, to her swimming practices—taking care of Mark, right.

"But I can send you some money," she added.

"Money? Money isn't so much of an issue, we're both working. The help we need is hands-on, especially at night."

Did I really have to explain it to a 60-year-old woman, a mother of two, what it's like to care for babies?

"Well, if things get really hard, I'll get on the plane."

If things get really hard . . . I sucked in the air through my nostrils. "That's okay, Mom. We'll manage."

This was the first time in the 35 years of my life that I asked my mother for help. And now I felt nauseous, defeated, and foolish to have asked. Was she unwilling to help because I was gay and our children weren't biologically ours? Or was it just too much of an inconvenience?

I had no time to ponder my mother's motives. Gaby was crying; she probably needed to be changed.

I handed the phone over to Jon. "You talk to her—I can't."

A Tree of Many Roots

I was now a parent of two kids, just like my mother, except without the luxury of support she had from her own mother, my grandmother Maryam, and her mother-in-law, my grandmother Tamara, i.e., Babushka.

But parenting isn't just about giving feedings or changing diapers. You pass on to your children your identity, your history. You may take pride in, or struggle with, the values and traditions you grew up with but ultimately, they carry forward in the way you raise your kids. They guide your parenting decisions, move your hand when you help your child put up the ornaments on the Christmas tree or on the walls of a *sukkah*. So where did Jon and I come from?

I arrived in California as a 21-year-old refugee from the Soviet Union with two suitcases and a hundred dollars, as part of my father's family. My mother's family (Mom, stepdad Leonid, Natalie, and Grandma Maryam) stayed behind in Moscow.

Landing in the Golden State in the middle of the prolonged recession which preceded the 1990's dot-com boom, the six of us found ourselves crammed into a small, freeway-facing apartment on the edge of Palo Alto. The two grandmothers' benefits, a small welfare check to my dad, stepmom, and six-year-old sister Rina, and my earnings were barely enough to pay the rent in one of the most expensive pockets of America. Sleeping in the breakfast nook, I'd get up at 4:30 a.m., as the sun was rising over the river of cars flowing outside our windows, and bike to El Camino Real to catch the first bus to a job in San Francisco, a two-hour trek each way.

I remember getting off the bus one boiling day, thirsty and broke after paying the bus fare. I parked my bike on Palo Alto's ritzy University Avenue, and ducked into a café to cool off, where I overheard a young waitress say something to a customer in Russian. We struck up a conversation. She took one look at me and, asking no questions, handed me a Coke, taking out the change from her tip jar and dropping it into the register. Somehow, she knew I had nothing. I never forgot the kindness of that gift of Coke.

That's where I started. Jonathan, my Black husband, was raised dirt poor on a grape farm in California's Central Valley, the ninth out of ten children. His mother, Tommie-Lee, and her family had escaped from the Arkansas Delta, a slice of eastern Arkansas bordering Mississippi, the land defined by severe oppression, poverty, and violence. The race and class tensions in the Delta culminated in the 1919 Elaine Race Riot, one of America's deadliest. What started out as a labor dispute ended as an all-out massacre, in which at least 200 Black people were murdered by vigilante gangs, local police, and 500 soldiers sent in by the state governor. Dozens more Black men were rounded up and sentenced, including twelve condemned to death.[3]

Lynchings in Arkansas continued until 1936 but by then, Tommie-Lee's family had been long gone. Following relatives who'd fled before them, they moved first to a similarly rural, poor, segregated, but safer town of El Centro, a railroad junction on the California/Mexico frontier, into a neighborhood shared by Black and Latino people, and later up the Southern Pacific train tracks to Fresno.

But even in California's multi-racial Central Valley, Jim Crow lurked in the shadows. Vigilance committees and lynchings here were recent history, and exclusionary legislation was still in force. School segregation remained legal in California until 1947, interracial marriage prohibited until 1948, and the race restrictions on residential property rental and ownership—entire neighborhoods and cities off-limits to Black families like Tommie-Lee's—continued well into the 1960s, until the state legislature, in 1963, passed the Rumford Fair Housing Act.

But the following year, California voters overturned the Rumford Act two-to-one via Proposition 14, with support coming from the California Republican Assembly and the future state governor, Ronald Reagan. It took the federal government's cutting off all housing funds and the state Supreme Court declaring Prop 14 unconstitutional to finally bring housing equality to California in 1966.

1966—it wasn't that long ago. Jonathan was three then.

Let's turn the clock back one more time, to 1941. Tommie-Lee and her sister's high school was far from the outskirts of Fresno. One day they were waiting at dawn for the school bus when, seeing them for the first time, a new bus driver told the light-skinned Tommie-Lee to get on but "You," he pointed at her darker-complexioned sister, "gonna have to walk."

Tommie-Lee refused to get on the bus without her sister. That ended her high school career.

The war was on—World War II, which would also become part of the family lore: Jon's future father, Louis Clark, fighting in Europe, his soon-to-be wife washing soldier's uniforms at the army base in Fresno.

"Hard work in this heat," Tommie-Lee told me, "but there wasn't any other for a young girl like me."

In 1946, Tommie-Lee Taylor married Louis, now a war veteran. A religious woman, she was strict about keeping order and stability at home, though not without a good measure of acceptance, especially for her gay son, and a curiosity about other cultures. *Enchiladas con salsa verde,* which Tommie-Lee learned to cook in El Centro, were as much of a dinner staple as the traditional, Southern mac 'n' cheese, potato salad, and the unparalleled (in Jon's memory) pineapple upside-down cake.

But before anything else, there was an underlying belief in hard work and self-reliance in Jon's childhood home, as in, "God helps those who help themselves." A corporate executive, Jon still gets up at 5:00 a.m. and leaves for work at 5:30 a.m. because that's what his father, a grape farm manager, did for 40 years.

As a child, Jon worked on that grape farm. All the kids did; hiring outside help was just too expensive. His school counselor, in an overwhelmingly white school, told him he possessed "the intellectual promise to dig ditches" for the rest of his life. Undeterred, Jonathan found his way into a local community college, a state university, and, eventually, corporate finance and insurance.

His family admired him, but they couldn't help him. He had to do it all on his own.

§

Across the globe in Moscow, my parents divorced when I was five and soon remarried, leaving me with my maternal grandparents, Maryam and Yosif. A child living with retired folks grows up in a strange time warp. My parents were the children of the urban, Soviet 1960s: the Beatles, cool jazz, cigarettes, beehives and sideburns, mini-dresses and bell-bottoms. Like most of their friends, they went to college and later morphed seamlessly into the educated, disenchanted Soviet middle class.

The 1960s were of little relevance in my childhood home. The main points of reference were the years of my grandparents' youths, the tumultuous 1920s–40s: the era of the Bolshevik Revolution, the full emancipation of women and Jews, WWII—the decades of great hopes and of enormous suffering.

The social order of centuries broke down during that time, and yet the domestic side of it continued to live on. The way of life, the values, the ways of running the household I absorbed from my grandparents—an ethos more indicative of the nineteenth than the twentieth century—reflected their *shtetl* childhood and pre-WWII life in St. Petersburg and Moscow.

The world is a hard place for a Jew. Education is the only way to a secure future. Family ties, near and far, never break. Music and theater are essential to a child's development. Only a fool wastes his money on things that are not absolutely necessary. The chicken stock must be boiled with onions and then clarified.

Scores of my grandparents' relatives in Poland and Ukraine perished in the Holocaust. My grandfather's teenage cousins, the only two members of his family to survive the Nazi occupation of his *shtetl*, swam across the wide Dniester River, fleeing the oncoming German troops. When the soldiers overran them, the two girls continued their perilous journey eastward by night. During the day, the younger one with olive skin and dark hair would hide in the forest, while her fair-complexioned older sister, able to pass for a Slav, would beg for food in the villages. Eventually they made it to the Soviet side, and that's why I know their story.

My grandfather, Yosif, like Jon's father, Louis, fought in that war. Wounded in the Battle of Kursk, he came home with a medal and a palm-size carriage clock he picked up somewhere along the front. Today it stands as tranquilly on our dining room buffet as it did on my grandparents'. It still runs.

Jon and I came from resilient cultures. We expected things to be hard, though never hopeless. We were proud and unapologetic for who we are.

With these basic understandings, we set off on a path to build our family, and some new lessons we would learn along the way are:

Raise your kids with the best of what you know.

Don't be afraid to improvise when you don't know.

Tackle each task together, and, as my mother proved to me, expect to have only each other to rely on.

Throw all the resources you have—spiritual, social, financial—at the issues you are going to face. Do it now, not later, because there might not be that "later."

Listen to others, but trust your own instincts because these kids have no one else to care for them, except you.

The Sweetest Trap

Gaby's bassinet was bathed in the soft, golden glow of a torchiere. We kept her bedroom semi-dark on purpose, "staging" her for the night. Gaby was in my lap, sucking rhythmically from the bottle, her head resting on the bend of my arm.

In ten days, she had gained a pound of weight, and her face had started to fill out along with the rest of her body. The biggest change was in her legs; those chicken drumsticks, bruised by the forceps, were now padding out. A pronounced chin and a small potato nose bore some resemblance to her mother. Her brown eyes, olive skin, and jet-black hair had to have come from a different source.

"I put in two ounces of formula," I whispered.

"She'll need it," Jon whispered back. "She only drank two ounces two hours ago, less than her usual."

"'Don't bother me, I'm eating!'" I quoted a Carl's Jr. commercial popular at the time, smiling in Jon's direction. Bending over, I kissed Gaby's forehead. We'd just given her a bath. She smelled of vanilla-scented baby shampoo.

"Can you imagine what she's going to look like at one?"

"Tall, pretty, like a baby Halle Berry," Jon smiled.

My hand registered the rejection of the bottle; Gaby's tongue was pushing it away, a signal that she was full. Setting the bottle aside, amidst her fast, discomfited cries, I picked her up and leaned back, laying her directly on my stomach, her head against a burp cloth.

"C'mon, c'mon, where is it? Where is that belch?"

Gaby quacked, swinging her head around as I patted her on the back. She finally emitted a low growl.

"There we go . . . whew," I grinned, waving away the cloud from my face.

Our communication with Gaby was developing as we went along. A fast suck on the bottle's nipple, for instance, showed hunger, as did a low alto cry. A high-pitched cry signaled physical irritation, as in asking to be changed or moved. Some cries weren't cries at all. They sounded uncertain, passing like clouds. Others seemed to be attempts at conversation; she'd hear us talk and want to join in.

Now it was time for bed. Her eyes were already half-closed, but her face relaxed around the mouth in a contented smile. Even in simple jammies, she looked adorable; Buddha-like peace and kindness were radiating from her. Amid all the drama pervading our life, around her spread an oasis of calm.

Just as I'd told my mother, it was rough handling a newborn and a pre-toddler: completely different needs and schedules, yet both have to be constantly watched. We had to figure out ways to manage it while working full-time.

Before Jon's two-week vacation time ran out, we hired a daytime nanny, Gloria, a feisty, rotund Peruvian who'd raised the kids of our Bangladeshi neighbors. She took over the daytime with both kids, which allowed us both to go back to work and care for them during the evenings, nights, and weekends.

The Commencement I'd been organizing at my college, my fourth, went off perfectly. The 1,200 graduates received their diplomas, speeches were made, mortarboards flew up in the air, and 10,000 guests made it back to the parking lot safely.

And I graduated as well. This new degree, a master's in linguistics with the English as a Second Language (ESL) teaching option, completed at Cal Poly's sister campus, CSU Long Beach, followed, in a roundabout way, my Stanford doctorate earned a decade earlier. There was no time to attend the graduation ceremony, but the path to my future was now laid open: I would soon be leaving the world of public relations for good.

§

"There have been some developments," said Suzanne Cohen, the adoption director at Our Bright Futures and our formal liaison with the Los Angeles County, guiding our foster-to-adopt process.

I stopped wheeling the supermarket cart and pushed the phone closer to my ear.

"Jenna's been trying to get the baby. There was a hearing sometime early last week, let me see . . . on June 22, where she presented the proof of completion of her rehab and parenting classes. Judge Hooke ordered to move the baby in with her and gave her six months of reunification services."

Pow! A sharp pain, like a prick from a handful of needles, struck me in the chest. I grabbed the aisle shelf, trying to control my heartbeat.

"Hold on," I whispered coarsely, "hold on . . ." Breathing in, breathing out. A few more breaths. "It's nothing, Suzanne, I'm alright now. Move her where?"

"Into Jenna's foster home. Placed together, they can be cared for by the same foster parents, while Jenna could have what the order calls, 'unmonitored access to the child in the home.'" Outside, Jenna and the baby must be accompanied by their foster parent. On the only incomplete requirement, counseling, the judge gave Jenna an extension."

"I don't get it, Suzanne. These compliance orders were for reunification with Marianna, yet it's not Marianna but her newborn sister the judge is sending to her."

"I hear you; it makes no sense. DCFS did point out the fact that Jenna hasn't been able to reunify with Marianna, but the judge said it wasn't relevant to the status of the new baby and dismissed their objections."

"How can it not be relevant? If she isn't able to safely parent Marianna, what makes her able to take care of the baby?"

"I know . . ."

"When did you find out?"

"Just this morning. DCFS actually knew about the court decision but decided to keep you in the dark, as they told me, 'so as not to disturb the infant's foster placement.'"

The deepest remorse I felt was for Jon. In one month, he'd gotten so profoundly attached to Gaby. Natalie called him "the extension of the womb" because of the way he'd carry Gaby around the house, her head resting on his broad biceps, her body cradled over his heart in the crook of his arm; the way he'd coo to her while cooking, cleaning, popping out his Nina Simone CDs, making the kids' beds. Even when Gaby rested in the playpen in the living room, Jon would lie down next to her on the carpet. He was watching the baby; she, twisting her head to one side, was watching him.

Of course, Jon knew the risks. But in his eyes, from the day he opened the door of Jackie's SUV on that hot June afternoon, Gaby was perfect. Nothing less than perfect.

"I asked God for a baby like me, and He sent her to my doorstep," he'd say to me.

Loving a child is the sweetest trap. Having fallen into it once with Marianna, I had my guard up the second time around. I liked this new baby; I liked her dearly. I cared for her around the clock, and yet I stayed somewhat detached. I felt I couldn't allow myself to get too deeply involved with a child whom we might lose at any moment.

I shared the news with Jon while we were fixing dinner. Marianna was erecting a Tupperware pyramid in the middle of the kitchen floor, and Gaby was sleeping peacefully in the swing a couple of feet away from us.

Jon burst out crying.

"I can't believe that this child will be going to her! Her! She's a freaking child herself!"

I pulled him into my arms. Fervently, with a sudden rush of

confidence, I assured him, "It'll be alright, dear. We'll make it through, I promise. Okay? Okay?"

He let me hold him.

§

He could leave me over this, I realized with sobering certainty. I'd been shielding Jon from the drama, the never-ending calls, the visits, the court decisions, not just because of our schedules, but exactly because of this. He wouldn't be able to take it—Gaby being taken away from us, and then the perpetual limbo with Marianna. He would want to get out of this whole process, and if I didn't let go, it would destroy our relationship.

I didn't blame Jon. Not everyone can make it through. I thought of our friends, a couple who, after six drama-filled weeks, returned the foster child they intended to adopt to the county. They couldn't handle the turbulence. I was just hoping we'd have the strength to make it to the end, whatever that end might be.

When the County is the Parent

In late June, the DCFS called a special *team decision meeting* (TDM). The meeting's purpose was ostensibly "to collaborate in the decision-making process regarding a child's placement, removal, or reunification"—Gaby's removal in our case.

So here we were in a windowless conference room: three DCFS social workers, a Children's Court rep, and Jon and I, downhearted, waiting for Jenna and her foster parent, Farzana.

Twenty minutes late, Jenna walked in with her head up high, followed by Farzana. Jenna was wearing a baggy sweatsuit, soiled on the stomach and thighs, her unwashed hair tied in a messy bun.

The meeting headed down a path I hadn't expected. Judge Candace Hooke, presiding over Jenna's, Marianna's, and Gaby's cases, ordered that Gaby be placed with Jenna. DCFS, while not openly disputing the court order, wasn't encouraging the placement. Jackie Willis and her supervisor Sandra Ruiz laid everything hidden about their long-term client on the table: Jenna's alleged psychiatric diagnosis, the meager six and a half credits completed in her freshman year of high school, the drugs taken during her three-month AWOL from foster care, and the frequent altercations with foster parents and other kids at the homes she'd lived in.

As the negative facts mounted, Jenna stubbornly stood her ground: "I didn' wanna . . . I wasn' gonna...but you promised... so my attorney says."

Jenna's speech grew slurred, muffled. Something seemed off with her diction.

"What about the birthfather, this Guerrero guy?" asked the court rep.

"She *thought* it was Jorge Guerrero," said Jackie.

Thought? That startled me. Guerrero was the last name inscribed on Gaby's birth certificate, MediCal insurance card, and all other documents we'd been given.

"We managed to track him down. Our former client," Jackie gave the rep a meaningful look. "He swore the child isn't his. Of course, we didn't believe him and had to get him tested. It's not him."

"Not him? Who else can it be then, if not Guerrero?"

"Well, you know Jenna was with a few men during the time she ran away. Any one of them could be the dad. We're checking out several paternity leads."

Jon threw me an incredulous glance. Then he leaned over to my ear and whispered, "How did we end up here?"

It was a metaphysical question that would continue to haunt me for the rest of our saga. I knew what he meant—the teenage mother, the question mark for the father, the oppressive intrusion of social services, the pain of losing Gaby, and, possibly, Marianna.

The truth was that we were exactly where we were supposed to be. No one made us take this newborn and her sister. Our fate wasn't a game of chance. We were there because everything we had believed, everything we had dreamed, everything we had done—from our desire to be parents, to our idealism in fostering kids rather than choosing a surrogate, to the luck of living in a liberal state that allowed gay men to adopt—had led us, inevitably, to that conference room.

"What do you think of yourself as a parent?" Jackie asked Jenna in a soft voice.

"I'm a good parent," Jenna replied without blinking an eye. "I've raised my older daughter, Marianna, since she was a baby."

"But Jenna, dear," Jackie replied, "you put that baby, out of your own will, in foster care."

"So?" Jenna retorted.

"You knew you couldn't take care of her. How're you going to take care of this baby?"

"I just need a little help, that's all."

"Oh, yes, you do. You need *a lot* of help," Jackie nodded her head.

Sandra, the supervisor, cast a mischievous glance at us. "Since you two are taking such good care of both kids, maybe you should take Jenna in as well? All three of them would be in one foster home. That would solve all our problems."

I didn't know what to say. The joke, if that's what it was, was insensitive at best, to both Jenna and us. But before I could figure out the right sort of reply, Jenna burst out, "Totally, why not? I could live there and provide all the breast milk the baby needs."

"Ah . . . sounds like a win-win," Sandra said wryly, and the court rep rolled his eyes.

"It's neither here nor there, Jenna," said Jackie, gently closing the discussion.

"Okay, now," Sandra put her hands on the table, "let's talk about the mother's foster home as a reunification option."

This was something we didn't know: Farzana had agreed to take in Gaby. Jon straightened up in his seat and crossed his arms over his chest.

The supervisor pressed Farzana about her availability. The baby could never be left unattended by the foster parent, so how would it fit her work schedule? Farzana, it turned out, was a night-shift nurse, which explained the dark circles under her eyes and the drowsy look at the mid-morning meeting.

"My daughter, Habiba, can watch baby at night," Farzana said, looking sideways.

"But your daughter isn't certified," pointed out Jackie. "We can't allow that."

Sandra and two dependency investigators now all bore down on Farzana, emphasizing how much work she'd have to do: caring for Gaby around the clock, taking her to all her appointments and visits, all while making sure Jenna kept up with school, therapy, and other services she'd been ordered. They also hinted at an increased oversight from DCFS and the court over how well she'd do it all. Under the county's scrutiny, it wouldn't be so simple.

"I am change my mind," Farzana said tiredly, "about allow baby in my house." She paused and added, "It's okay with me if its mean Jenna have to move out."

With this new development, the five social work professionals now circled Jenna, pressing upon her their compromise proposal: she'd move into a foster home closer to Gaby, a home where Jenna could get the "wrap-around services" for the support she herself needed.

The DCFS intentions were now made clear. There was more than one way to decide what was best for Gaby. At the moment though, DCFS preferred not to disrupt Jenna's kids' safe placement in our home. They were focused instead on ensuring Jenna completed her own court-ordered services and stayed in school. If Jenna agreed with the plan, the judge would have to accept it.

Jenna pulled her sweatshirt hood over her head. Her lips were tight and colorless; her eyes, in contrast, were blazing.

The meeting facilitator produced the Child Safety Action Plan, drafted before we walked into the room, and all the "team members," Jenna included, signed it.

"Until a new home for Jenna is found," pronounced Sandra, ready to wrap up, "she can have one visit a week with the baby, somewhere halfway between your," she pointed at us, "and Farzana Hafeez's homes. Oh, and before we leave, you guys brought pictures of the baby?" she asked us.

"Yes," I said, the first and last word I uttered in the entire meeting. Jackie had asked for them.

I gave the envelope to Sandra, who leafed through them with a kindly smile and passed them on to Jenna. Jenna took one out of the stack, looked at it, and broke into a quiet sob.

The Breast Milk Dilemma

Offering us to take Jenna's children, social workers had told us very little about Jenna's own history except that she was a white teen and originally from the Midwest. How did she end up in foster care in California? Why was there no birth family to claim Marianna and Gaby once they were officially in foster care as well?

No information. All we were told was that at age 11 or 12, Jenna was placed in a large orphanage-type group home in eastern Los Angeles County.

Jenna, I noticed at the visits, could be loud and belligerent, quick to alienate anyone. But at times, she appeared depressed and withdrawn. Were these signs of some clinical condition or the product of the trauma of being in foster care? Both? I couldn't tell. Underneath it all, though, there seemed to be a normal, strong-willed teenager, a child who deserved a decent childhood.

Every time my worry about the children subsided, I felt deep sorrow for Jenna. Would she ever be able to stabilize and to heal?

What was becoming clear to me was that if Marianna and Gaby were to stay with us, Jenna's continued presence in their

lives wouldn't be to their benefit. More likely, it would be chaotic and confusing. Would she be an appropriate role model for
them growing up?

These questions, albeit purely hypothetical in July 2006, were
already weighing heavily on my mind.

§

On Saturday, per the "team decision," Jenna was having her first
visit with Gaby. Farzana and I had arranged a location accessible to both of us: Heritage Park in Santa Fe Springs, outside a
DCFS office.

In the parking lot, Jenna came up to me with a plastic supermarket bag.

"Here, I brought my breast milk for you to take home."

She caught me off guard. Staring at the bottle in the bag,
without an ice pack, I needed to make a decision quickly. Even
if the milk didn't spoil by the time we got home, how would it
work with Gaby's other feedings? She was used to the formula
every three hours around the clock. What if Gaby got used to
the milk but Jenna stopped visiting again? That was an enormous commitment for us to take on.

"I am sorry, Jenna, I can't take it. But you can give your breast
milk to the baby during the visit if you wish."

Jenna looked aside, said nothing.

I turned around to unstrap Marianna from her car seat and
brought her out of the car. Jenna didn't ask to see her. In fact,
she hadn't asked to see Marianna or in any way inquired about
her in two months. But when I had called Jenna's counselor to
arrange a visit for Gaby, I was told to bring Marianna as well.

"Hello, sexy!" Jenna smiled to Marianna and pulled her close
with her free hand; the other holding the bag with the breast
milk bottle.

Marianna pulled away. Jenna set the bag down on the sidewalk and with both arms tried to pull Marianna in the direction of a picnic table a few yards away.

Marianna screamed and struggled with her mother to the
point that she twisted herself out of Jenna's hands and plopped

down face first on the asphalt in the middle of the parking lot.

"She hit her lip?" Farzana, worried, asked Jenna.

Jenna didn't reply. She scooped up the crying Marianna and carried her to the table. I followed behind, carrying Gaby in the car seat.

At the picnic table, Jenna held Gaby in her arms almost the entire time, and frequently kissed and hugged her.

Marianna sat at the table's far end with Farzana and me, mostly in my lap.

"Marianna, come to Mommy," Jenna called out to her once.

"No!" Marianna replied with an angry frown.

"C'mon, come to Mommy. Mommy's waiting."

Marianna climbed out of my lap onto the concrete bench and walked from me to Jenna and back.

"I didn't interfere," I wrote later to Jackie, "since during the visit, Jenna is supposed to be responsible for her children's movements. But just in case, I extended my arms alongside the bench to catch Marianna, should she slip. Marianna fell twice between the table and the bench, right by her mother and too far for my reach. Marianna didn't appear hurt, but it made me concerned about her safety."

The second hour passed more peacefully. Jenna left Gaby with Farzana and me and took Marianna to look at the profusion of birds in the park's aviary.

Back at the table, Jenna gave Gaby the bottle while reading to Marianna from a couple of children's books that she'd brought. It looked peaceful, normal: a mother and her two little daughters spending time at the park. I felt conflicted. On one hand, this lovely vision of a birth parent reunited with her children was exactly what we worked so hard to support; on the other hand, what about the kids' other parents, other family, the one they were a part of day in and day out—our family, the maybe family?

I had to get up to go to the bathroom, and immediately Marianna jerked away from her mother to follow me.

"Come back! Come back here, now!" Jenna yelled at her, but to no avail—Marianna took off after me.

Jenna got up, and with Gaby on her hip, waddled after Marianna. She grabbed her by the shoulder right when she was about to enter the men's restroom.

They paced outside the men's restroom until they saw me come out.

Marianna then extended her arms, "Up! Da-da, up!"

I glanced at Jenna.

She nodded.

I picked up Marianna and carried her back to the picnic table, where she sat with me for the remainder of the visit. When it was time to go, though, Marianna absolutely refused to be led by her mother, jerking herself away and crying.

"You can take her back to the car," Jenna told me over her shoulder.

In my arms, Marianna's shrieks stopped as if switched off. I strapped Marianna back into her car seat while Jenna was doing the same with Gaby on the other side. Jenna did not come around to Marianna's side to kiss her or say goodbye.

De Facto

Going into public adoption, we were unfamiliar not just with diaper changing but also with the legal side of it all. We'd never actually had to deal with the court system, save for traffic tickets. We certainly never had to deal with the Children's Court.

In April 2006, after Marianna had been with us five months, we applied for the *de facto parent* status over Marianna, which would have allowed us to attend and participate in the court proceedings, and, if needed, contest them. Jenna would still have all her parental rights over Marianna, including the right to reunification.

We applied on our own, simply following the court website instructions. How grossly naïve. We were quickly—routinely, as we were told later—denied. It took Judge Hooke twenty-four hours to throw our little petition out. There was no hearing.

Learning from that mistake, we decided to go back with an attorney, and scheduled to meet him—Ron Griggs, a member of the Children's Bar Association—at the courthouse.

But first, the milieu. Edelman Children's Court, a cluster of buildings, rises like a fortress high atop a hill overlooking the intersection of two busy freeways. Its clean, geometric look stands in stark contrast to the overgrown, dried-up weeds surrounding it on the barren hillsides. Few people rounding the bottom of the hill below are aware of the thousands of children whose lives were being decided a hundred feet above their sunroofs. Mine was one of the few cars that would trickle off the freeway to course its way, like a lucky pinball, to the top of the hill.

Waiting for Mr. Griggs to come out of a courtroom, I was observing a busy, noisy scene around me. Young women in revealing shorts and skirts and tattooed young guys in baggy outfits, much fewer in number, sat idly. Grandparents in drab clothes with mouths clenched tight on concerned faces. And there were kids everywhere—some probably subjects of that day's hearings, others simply because there was no one left at home to watch them.

A curvy woman, white, not older than 25, sat down next to me and struck up a conversation.

"They won't let me see my baby."

"Oh wow, really?"

"Yeah."

She looked unassuming in her generic pink blouse, ivory khakis, and neat ponytail. She stared at me, searching for compassion.

"Your first one?"

"My Mom's got the other two, my boys. I'll get them back too, but first I need to get my baby."

"Is your baby with your mom too?"

"With my aunt. Oh, I love my baby *so much!*" she said emphatically, chest heaving, eyes squeezed to pins, as if about to cry. "But this judge, she just hates me. Gave me all these orders but wouldn't give me any more time. She's gotta be a lesbo. That bitch . . . I'd fuck her if that'd help me get my baby back, I don't care!"

The outburst didn't harmonize well with the conservative blouse and khakis.

"Why did they take away your baby?" I shouldn't have asked but, well, I got curious.

"I had to, um, go to a correctional facility, you know? I didn't do it, I swear. Anyways, I don't want to talk about it. And then I get out, and this fucking dyke still wouldn't let me have my daughter."

"When did you get out?"

"Like, nine months ago."

"So your baby must be what, two?"

"No, she's five."

"Five? That's interesting." But right then I spotted a tall, gray-haired man making his way toward me. "Sorry, hon, that's my attorney. Good luck to you."

§

Ron Griggs and I took a table in the cafeteria.

Looking rather detached, Griggs handed me his bio and a "Juvenile Dependency Court Reference" flyer from his firm and described his experience with de facto petitions.

"Who's the judge?" he asked.

"Candace Hooke."

"Tough. She favors reunification. And the counsel?"

"I don't know."

"I'll find out. I know them all. It's a small crowd, you know."

"You think we might be ready for Marianna's reunification review on July 11? It's just a couple of weeks away."

"I don't see why not. I'll help you with the declaration and make sure your petition gets heard."

I didn't particularly like him. Griggs came off as slick and self-absorbed. But he knew the players, which could help us.

I agreed to pay him $2,500 for the filing, the serving, and one court appearance.

Several weeks later, on July 11, I was back at the courthouse, this time with Jon. Griggs was up ahead, checking with the bailiff on the case schedule for the day.

The Children's Court was running at full steam with family groups filling up its spacious pastel hallways and wide benches. Parked by my leg was a rolling briefcase filled with files—should any question come up, any question whatsoever, we would have the answer. In it was also a copy of our 50-page declaration, documenting, with scores of photos and records, our relationship to Marianna as her sole caretakers during these last eight months. I put it all together over the Fourth of July weekend: drafting the text, scanning and editing photos, faxing and emailing it piece-by-piece to Griggs's assistant.

Jon changed two words in the declaration.

Griggs? Not a single one.

§

Around 10:30 a.m., Marianna's case came up, and the bailiff whisked us into the ante-chamber and, a few minutes later, into the courtroom. The place had the feeling of a dimly lit movie theater with the back rows sinking into the shadows while the judge, elevated like a referee above the rows, took the center stage.

Judge Hooke looked exactly the way I'd pictured her—a dry, middle-aged white woman with reading glasses perched at the end of a thin nose and graying hair cropped short on the temples. Jenna's attorney, Janine McCloud, was a Black woman with bouncy, shoulder-length curls, big-boned and cheerful; Bertha Moore, the County counsel—a middle-aged white woman in a wide-brimmed, artsy hat embroidered with flowers. Margaret McPherson, the children's attorney, whom we saw for the first time, was also white, looking clean-cut in an executive pant-suit.

With her back towards us, McCloud fired immediately, "Your Honor, on behalf of Marianna's mother, I'd like to request that you deny this motion. Eight months is not enough to be considered a parent."

I looked up at Griggs.

He was silent.

McPherson took over. She praised our care eloquently. In her conclusion, she pointed out that we'd been parenting Marianna longer than her mother had.

Moore said she concurred with McPherson's statement, adding nothing else.

Judge Hooke spoke from the bench, "While the court acknowledges the fabulous care these gentlemen," a nod to us, "have provided to Marianna, I don't think the time has been long enough to claim a parental status. Otherwise, we should consider anyone who spent several months with a child a parent. I also think that this would interfere with the reunification process."

Griggs objected, "The de facto parent status my clients are asking for is part of concurrent planning, independent of reunification."

Not replying to Griggs, Hooke ruled, "This request is denied."

Instantly, McCloud piped up, "I'd like to ask to have these gentlemen excused from the courtroom."

"Sustained," said Hooke.

"Okay," said Griggs, "we're leaving."

Why did Hooke even agree to hear our motion? She could've simply thrown this one out too, just like the one in April. Did she do it out of respect for Griggs? Out of curiosity to meet us, the gay couple raising the little girl and now her baby sister? Whatever her reason, our deposition, with all its photos, testimonies, expense statements, wasn't even discussed. The whole exercise took less than three minutes. It would've taken longer to lose $2,500 at a craps table in Vegas.

§

Outside the courtroom doors, Jon and I stood looking at each other, stunned by the swiftness and finality of our defeat. A total fiasco. Even Griggs looked surprised.

Moore stepped out into the hallway.

"Hang in there," she told us. "You're good parents, we all know that. This judge has just denied a similar request from grandparents in my other case. Grandparents, you hear? What she's doing is ridiculous. It's bizarre."

I wanted to believe Ms. Flower Hat, but did she genuinely mean it, or was she simply helping out her client, DCFS, to smooth out a wrinkle that might disturb a secure placement? Why should I trust her? Trust, I realized, was not a given in those pastel hallways; it had to be earned.

Griggs asked us if we wanted to appeal.

We said that yes, we did.

We followed him downstairs to the clerk's office and filed the paperwork.

§

The days after the court appearance were physically hard. So much of my energy had gone into preparing for that hearing. I felt empty, deflated, unfocused. I couldn't face calling Mom and Dad, the distance of one and the pity of the other. Instead, I gave a brief report to Natalie and Babushka and asked them to relay it to my parents.

"It was an insulting, expensive mistake," Jon kept repeating. "Dismissed like we're nothing to these kids."

Jon was still harboring the hope that Jenna, seeing we were so committed to Marianna as to hire an attorney, would let go of her.

"Jenna's young; she'll disappear again. Wouldn't it make a lot more sense for her to ask us for an open adoption? We'd keep her daughter safe and she'd still have access to her."

Wishful thinking, I thought, *except it will never happen.* While Jenna had bounced from home to home, her children had remained her sole tangible possessions; she really had nothing else. The fact that she couldn't parent Marianna, that she had to put her in foster care, didn't matter. *I've raised my daughter since she was a baby.* Claiming Marianna was Jenna's attempt to right her wrong. Losing her would be admitting it and also setting the stage for her losing Gaby. She had nothing to gain from letting Marianna go. We were in it for the long haul.

Part 2
Underground Families

Lane and Jon, San Francisco, 1997
© Lane Igoudin, 1997

Pathways to Parenthood

My earliest knowledge about gay parenting comes from, of all places, *Newsweek*. Back in 1996, working a student job at the Stanford University PR office, I picked up a glossy issue from a stack of magazines that came in, intrigued by the cover blurb, "Gay Families Come Out."

Those were different times for gay people in America. While the decades of criminal persecution had largely ended, followed by rising visibility and growing acceptance, full equality was still years away. Just two months before the article's publication, President Clinton signed into law the Defense of Marriage Act (DOMA), prohibiting federal recognition of same-sex unions.

The *Newsweek*'s five-page feature, complete with a star interview (Melissa Etheridge and her partner), and a normalizing, the-kids-are-alright, first-person narrative of a daughter of a gay mom, gave the readers the lay of the land.

In 1996, only 13 states allowed lesbian women and gay men to adopt. California, my home state, along with Ohio and some New England states, was colored the "highly tolerant" green on the map accompanying the article.

"Even then," the writers noted, "usually only one partner is the parent of record—leaving the other in legal limbo. Courts allowed adoptions by a second parent in some of those states, although the law is still in flux."

"Flux" characterized the state of being a gay parent. In some states, one could still lose a child, even one's own biological child, because of being a homosexual(v). To protect their children and families, many gay parents had to stay in the closet. But some began to confront their kids' schools and other public institutions to demand acceptance.

The *Newsweek* article sparked hope in me; there *was* a way for a gay man to have children, and luckily, I was living in a green state.

I saved the clipping and started a file, but I wasn't ready. As a single grad student living in San Francisco, I never saw myself as anyone's husband. Relationships would come and go without affecting me deeply, but what I saw, like a prophecy within, was an image of a single father with two kids. Entering the adoption process years later was simply following my inner path. I knew I would never be fulfilled if I didn't have kids.

Gay men with children were still rare—a novelty, fitting poorly into the sexual politics of the time, when refusal to procreate remained a pillar of homosexual identity, an unambiguous divider between the oppressor and the oppressed. "Be gay. Don't breed," read a popular magnet sold in the city's gay neighborhoods. Parenting wasn't for us. Persecuted, marginalized, defamed, disempowered, and discriminated against, we were at least freed from the toils of raising children. Would gay parenting be the ultimate betrayal of our special destiny, or the ultimate proof of our emancipation? The community's attitude was ambivalent.

§

One year later in 1997, Jonathan and I met in San Francisco and fell in love. Our dating was breathtakingly romantic, and our relationship grew ever more passionate with every week and month.

From the very start, Jon made it clear that becoming a dad wasn't on his agenda.

"With nine siblings and 25 nieces and nephews," he told me, "I don't particularly feel like I need to have my own children."

His lack of interest in parenthood couldn't dampen my curiosity. Two years passed, and Jon was transferring within his corporate insurance firm from San Francisco to Long Beach to live with me. In between searching for our future nest, I dropped by a Maybe Baby meeting in West Hollywood for prospective LGBT parents. Adoption options, support groups, helpful attorneys—in Los Angeles, the process seemed less politicized, more manageable. I scribbled down as much information as I could, along with the phone number of a representative from the PopLuck Club, LA's gay dad organization.

The following month, Jon moved down the coast. After two years of weekend commutes, we were finally living together and in true bliss. Outside our spacious apartment on Ocean Boulevard in Long Beach, the city lights never dimmed, nor did the palm trees ever stop swaying gently by the sandy beach across the street. Neither of us having ever lived with a partnerw. It was time for us to really get to know each other, to scale down personal demands, to divide the household minutiae, to interweave our cultures—my borscht and his upside-down pineapple cake, my Shabbat dinners and his Christmas tree.

Soon we bought our first home: a Mission Craftsman bungalow, a short walk from the beach. We fit perfectly with the neighborhood: a preppy gay couple, nights out at art openings, shows, clubs, globe-trotting from Prague to Venice to Machu Picchu.

We were fortunate; life was busy, but not hard. During the day, I was managing communications projects at a private hospital, and in the evening, in our bougainvillea-covered bungalow, I would escape into writing the novels that I would try, disastrously, to get published. Nonetheless, my by-line started to pop up in local magazines under a stream of music and theater reviews of new productions around Los Angeles and out of town—an opera in San Diego, a Cirque du Soleil show in Las Vegas, or an all-weekend gay dance party in Palm Springs. My background was in music, but at that point, my true interests had coalesced around language: using it to make a living, writing about what interested me, possibly teaching it(vi).

Good times didn't dim my vision of becoming a father. I joined an online gay adoption listserv, entering a pipeline of stories, crises, questions, and tips. California was still a "highly tolerant" state compared to those places where people like me had to hide their partners during home study inspections.

A gay dad got profiled in a local magazine. I highlighted his story throughout: his step-by-step foster-to-adopt path, his desire to have a set of siblings so that the kids would always have a blood relative no matter what happened. The resource list that followed the article was helpful too.

Now, in my early thirties, armed with information, I felt ready to pursue parenthood. But "I" wouldn't be enough, it had to be "we."

§

Several months after 9/11, I got laid off. The hospital's new CEO cut forty-five positions, including mine. The 2001–2002 recession was now in full swing. My savings plummeted. I needed a job, fast, to dig myself out of the hole, to keep providing my half of our lifestyle.

Seven miserable months followed. A job for which I was a finalist fell through. Then another one. Then another.

Staring at the computer all day long, searching desperately for a job, brought on a persistent neck pain that kept me up at night. I was getting depressed, cranky. Jon was withdrawing into himself.

On my birthday, which fell close to our fifth anniversary, Jon cooked dinner. It was a very nice dinner—halibut, exceptional rice, exceptional salad. He gave me his present: the hushed get-down flow of Maxwell and Erykah Badu, the soundtrack of our first dates back in San Francisco, was pouring softly from the speakers.

After the dinner and dessert, we sat down in the living room, and I thought this would be a good time.

"Jon," I said, smiling, "I've given it a lot of thought over the last several months. I'm out of work at the moment, but I'll find a job, you know that. Meanwhile, I'd like to start the adoption process. It will take months, if not years, so why not start early, start now? What do you think?"

"Hmm," he looked at me, "I don't think this is the right time. We've been having problems. I can't say I'm always happy in this relationship."

I felt like I'd fallen off a cliff.

The arguing started. A litany of complaints came pouring out of Jon. I'd noticed his coldness, but never guessed the reason. There was more than one, apparently. We'd been drifting apart. Some things I'd said, or the way I said them, hurt him. Now we were hurting each other.

Tears rushed to my eyes. I was choking.

"Jon, dear, why is this happening to us? Let's say our relationship is this big whole," I made a wide circle with my arms, "and our problems," I drew a small circle inside, "they're in there, and I expect them to be there because no relationship is perfect. Am I missing something?"

"To me," he said, "our problems are as important as our relationship itself."

What could I say? It felt like the beautiful world we'd built was collapsing before my eyes, piece by piece.

I went upstairs to the office and just sat there, astonished at what just happened. An hour ago, I spoke of adopting a child. Now we seemed to be through. In less than ten minutes, our happy union was shattered.

§

I had to keep moving. Being unemployed and soon-to-be single forced me to take a fresh look at my life. I kept looking for a job but thanks to the layoff, I now had time to take a writing course at a local community college. What I found there was an unexpected sense of joy. Writing aside, I noticed how much I looked forward to these evening classes, to being with adults of many backgrounds and ages, adults who'd make the classroom walls vibrate with their life experience, enthusiasm, and humor.

Could this be the place to combine my love of writing with teaching English, my primary language? Was I not the perfect person to pass on such knowledge—an English learner myself, an immigrant who'd lived on both sides of the language barrier?

Following my hunch, I asked to observe some ESL classes. There I saw adult learners who braved long workdays and family obligations to master college-level English. This, I realized, was who, what, and where I wanted to teach.

I spent the rest of my involuntary break filling out grad school applications for the second time in my life. Our relationship was collapsing, Jon was leaving, and my unemployment benefits were running out—life as I knew it was coming apart. Yet I held onto the hope for a change, for something meaningful, turning over a new leaf, starting a new chapter. Maybe no marriage, no kids for now, but at least a new career.

Late in the fall of 2002, I got admitted into the graduate program in linguistics with the ESL teaching option at CSU Long Beach. At the same time, I received a job offer from Cal Poly Pomona, a sister state university in the east end of the county, for the public affairs position in its business school.

"I'll take it," I told Jon, "but only as my last communications job. If it doesn't work out, I'll just have to take out loans until I graduate and start teaching."

"If that's what you want," he said distantly.

At least he was no longer talking about moving out. We were discussing plans for our future. Inching back toward harmony would take us a few more months.

After New Year's, I traded my longish hair for a buzz cut, put on a suit, and went back to work. Three weeks later, my grad school classes started. A new chapter indeed.

I was now splitting my days between two campuses: an administrator on one, a student on another. One night, in the middle of a three-hour lecture, my mind suddenly went blank from fatigue. Recovering, I quickly reattached to the topic—children's language development—its focus so peaceful, a refuge from my daily grind. What would it be like, I wondered, to actually witness the miracle of a child effortlessly, unconsciously acquiring human language? Would I ever have a chance?

After the class, crossing the empty, misty parking lot, the night air damp and heavy with jasmine and peach blossom, aromas of the coming spring, I felt dead tired yet content. Content and hopeful.

The Turning Point

A year after my job crisis, our lives were fantastically different. My university job was going well and so was night school.

Things were going well between us, too. Jon's anniversary card said it all.

Dear Lane,

I know we have had some very difficult times over the last year. But look what happened. We made it through! Thanks for allowing me the time to work through my issues, thoughts, and fears, and to address my needs and feelings. I really appreciate your patience and kindness. I think we have both grown in many good ways over these six years. I know that love is still in our house and in our hearts. Yes, I do love you very much and always will. Thank you for giving me six years that no one else would or could. Happy anniversary, honey!

Love always,

Jon

"Still thinking about adoption?" Jon asked me one January afternoon.

"Why, yes. Often." I was surprised but glad to hear him ask. "In fact, I want it so much that I don't mind putting off my career change if we could start the process. How do you feel about it?"

"Well, I might be interested," he said. "But keep your job. We'll need your benefits, mine are a joke. And I'm not getting any younger."

"Let me show you something," I said to him a couple of nights later.

I pulled up an Internet adoption site featuring "waiting kids" and showed Jon. Their bright, fresh faces were framed with accolades like "adorable, playful, a wonderful singing voice, a smile to brighten your heart."

A soft-hearted man, Jon got flustered.

"Wow, I didn't know. Poor kids . . . and so many of them! But the bathroom? Wouldn't they need their own?"

"Bathroom? We might need a different house! This bungalow is just too small, and the neighborhood, while great for us, isn't all that kid-friendly." I replied.

"If we decide to do it," Jon said pensively, still staring at the screen, "we could look at a different house. Let me do some research."

This was encouraging.

The turning point came at The PopLuck Club meeting. A homemade cake in hand, we walked into the rec room of a West Hollywood park. Immediately our voices were drowned in the din from dozens of toddlers and teens chasing each other; parents—men only!—talking, gesticulating, and feeding smaller kids with bottles in their laps and strollers.

This rambunctious club had been running since 1998 when a small group of guys started meeting regularly so their kids could make new friends while their dads (and prospective dads) could discuss the issues—parenting, emotional, legal—that they faced. A potluck meal became the centerpiece, hence the name.

Sadly, two of the PopLuck co-founders, Daniel Brandhorst and Ronald Gamboa, and their adopted three-year-old son David, died aboard United Flight 175 when it crashed into the second tower of the World Trade Center on 9/11. But the club, while preserving their memory, continued to grow and expand. By the time we arrived at our first meeting, PopLuck was probably the largest gay father's club in the world, numbering hundreds of member families and hosting meetings all over Los Angeles and Orange Counties.

Seeing other gay dads with kids and hearing their stories showed Jon that it was all possible. Most of the guys looked downright suburban and professional, not like the chiseled and tanned Adonises one might expect to find in the heart of WeHo.

Josh, a tall, brawny cop with the county Sheriff's Department, volunteered to mentor us. He'd adopted a sibling set of three Hispanic boys, whom he was raising alone.

"It's the most amazing and fulfilling thing you'll ever do, but you've got to know your risks and keep an open mind. The county takes the kids out of their homes because of abuse or neglect, but ultimately it wants them to go back to their parents. This *family reunification* is central to the process, and your job is to support it."

Josh's tone was encouraging, but also cautionary.

"Support it? But what we want is to raise our own family, not just be some else's helpers," I said naively.

"That's why it's so tricky," Josh replied. "Like when I was still fostering my boys, they got attached to me early on, started calling me daddy, and I fell in love with them instantly. To them, I was their parent, their around-the-clock dad but to the court I wasn't. The court expected me to raise them as my own children, but also to be ready to give them up at any moment. It breaks your heart. You can bypass all of it if you just go after the kids freed for adoption—those whose parental rights, a social worker would tell you, have been *terminated*. But there are so few of them, and they tend to be older because of how long these reunifications take."

"Sounds like a lot to navigate," Jon said.

"Oh yeah. That's why you need a gay-friendly foster-to-adopt agency which will make sure everything goes smoothly. They provide these services to DCFS because there are just way too many kids in the system for the county to handle. Try Our Bright Futures, they're great. I used them—so have a few other dads you see here. Trust me—having an additional advocate on your side is really helpful, especially if you're new."

Noticing the signs of worry written plainly across our faces, Josh added, "Don't let it all put you off. There's a kid for you out there. I know it."

§

Crystal chandeliers and white-glove servers greeted Jon and me at a sumptuous banquet orientation for prospective foster parents hosted by DCFS at the Wilshire Grand hotel in downtown Los Angeles. This pulling out all the stops was hardly surprising: with 30,000 children in its care, over one third of all foster children in California and a sizeable portion of the 517,000 foster kids in the US in 2004,[7] DCFS was simply desperate for more certified parents and homes.

In this straight, mostly middle-aged crowd of about a hundred people, we, the only male couple, didn't feel unwelcome. Times had been changing in our "highly tolerant state." The heartwarming photos in the DCFS's slick new brochure now included a gay couple with a boy, along with the inclusion of "an unmarried couple" among those "who can become a foster, adoptive, or resource parent," and advertised a commitment to "respect diversity and welcome anyone interested in providing a safe and loving home to apply." Those coded signs of acceptance didn't pass us by.

We were now quickly absorbing a lot of new information: mandatory parenting classes, CPR trainings, "care reimbursement rate" schedules by age and medical condition, visits required by social workers and court representatives, and so on. It was a lot to take in, but also practical, relevant, as if the information itself were shaping our dream into reality.

In conversations after the orientation, Jon and I no longer said, "if we adopt" but "when." A timeline emerged: orientations in the spring, home study over the summer, and foster placements beginning in the fall. We were going to risk taking in the kids whose rights weren't terminated because we wanted to raise younger kids, even if we wouldn't get to keep them.

At that time, it sounded perfectly rational. We would face the true emotional costs of our choice later.

§

What children would we wish to raise? This was the question Jon and I were struggling with, poring over the county's Child Desired Worksheet.

It started with the prospective child's age and number. Fairly quickly, we agreed on a "sibling set of two" (so they'd always have each other), ages "zero to five." In other words, two kids—two very small siblings.

"Now, gender," I said. "Any thoughts?"

"I think girls—they would have an easier time with two dads," said Jon. "There'd be no masculinity questions, nor stigmas. One less thing to worry about."

"I agree," I replied. But I didn't just agree with Jon, I *loved* his choice. Raising a girl was familiar to me; I'd helped to raise my younger sister Natalie, and we remained close throughout our adult lives.

So, we marked "two females" and moved on.

"Would you be willing to provide care for a child of a different race or ethnic group? If 'yes,' how would he/she be accepted in the neighborhood, in the school, by relatives and friends? How would you help the child maintain connections with his/her own culture?"

Tough question, but one too common to many families today. Cultural heritage can be priceless in giving an adopted child a sense of roots. It may also become a source of contention. Whose culture do we honor by continuing? Conversely, whose do we not?

How, for instance, would I feel not bringing up my child

Jewish, erasing the 4,000 years of my history and traditions? Would such "cultural sensitivity" align me with the Jew-haters of the world who would love to wipe out my heritage? How would Jon feel raising a child without honoring his African American heritage?

In the end, we marked all ethnicities, with a preference for "Mixed Race."

The next eight and a half pages of the worksheet took several nights. Score upon score of potentially debilitating conditions had to be debated and marked as "acceptable," "unacceptable," or "willing to consider."

We were now in the familiar, quintessentially American milieu—the marketplace—walking the aisles: emotional problems this way, physical handicaps and mental disabilities up against the back wall, stopping at each item, evaluating the options.

How about "Biological parents are mother and son; father and daughter"?

Not acceptable. The familial relationships were too close, which would lead to genetic complications, we reasoned.

"Biological parents are stepparent and stepchild"?

"Acceptable" for lack of genetic risk.

"One parent is unknown," including "unknown because of rape"—acceptable.

Then came a list of health issues: multiple sclerosis, diabetes, parent's mental illness, fetal alcohol syndrome, heart murmur, club foot, blind in one or both eyes, crossed eyes, harelip, etc. Our voices would rise and fall, testing the limits of what we could handle, looking for the compromise.

The drug section was relatively easier. Educated by a county pamphlet[8], we marked all options in "child tested positive for" drug list, including heroin and crack cocaine, as "willing to consider." Cocaine babies, we'd learned, fare better than those born to alcoholics, and heroin reportedly washes out of the baby's body easily.

We were also "willing to consider" a wide gamut of emotional and behavior problems like "stealing," "lying," "biting," "kicking," "fidgeting," "uses profane language," "talks back," "bossy," "manipulates to get own way, [or] to divide parents," hoping we wouldn't get all these traits within the same pair of children.

In this process, I noticed we were engineering the child we hoped to parent. Our union, based on love, companionship, shared interests, property, and sex, was not different from heterosexual unions with one exception: procreation. Surrogacy and adoption, the primary means of reproduction for gay couples then and now, are entirely sexless, eliminating from the process the non-committal, blinding, and irrational ways of sexual desire. Divorced from sex, homosexual procreation is by default intentional, focused solely on the child's and family's future. Our conception doesn't stem from impassioned lovemaking. The child is always conceived in the mind.

In this post-modern blueprint for family-making, it was as if we, as adoptive parents, were designing our future children. We could, up to a point, pre-screen them. We could say yes or we could say no.

§

Our last weeks in the bungalow would come soon. That summer of 2004, Jon found us a new home—an old house near a decent public school and big enough to accommodate the kids.

I was jotting down the comments of Our Bright Futures's home inspector, trailing him through our new house. "Kitchen knives—move into the container above the fridge . . . hammer, nails, pliers, poisons—to the garage . . . medicines—in the lockbox above the oven . . . plugs in the outlets everywhere in the house . . ."

Fingerprints, LiveScan criminal background check, vehicle inspection, First Aid, CPR certification documents were already in our file. Beds, toys, books, and car seats were being hauled in from the stores.

There were a few documents to fill out. On the "Facility Sketch," a rough plan of our house. We circled the two rooms reserved for the children—a bedroom we painted green and the adjacent playroom. Before submitting the plan to the county, I drew some daisies all around the "facility's" yard to indicate flowers—a queer touch.

§

"Have you considered a surrogate?" a well-meaning friend asked me bluntly when hearing that we were starting the foster-to-adopt process. "It's expensive, but you two can afford it. Just take out a second mortgage on your home."

"It's not that simple."

"Isn't it? You know how dreadful the foster system is? The drug babies, the judges, the cases that never end? And here you can have *your own* kid—yours, no one can ever contest it, no headaches—*your kid*. You're younger than Jon, you probably have better sperm, put it to work."

"Glad you care about my fine sperm . . . but frankly, I don't care if the child looks like me. It might even be for the better that they don't. I've got lupus on one side of the family, cancer and heart disease a-plenty on the other. Too much in-breeding in those cloistered, Eastern European *shtetls*."

"Well, then adopt from another country. I heard Guatemala's still open."

"We could. But what's the point of bringing children from Guatemala when there are thousands of kids who need a home right here in LA, probably five minutes away from our house? Aren't we all responsible for these children too?"

"What do you mean?"

"Jon and I want to give a home to a child or, hopefully, children from this very community. We want to be *their* dads. Charity starts at home."

"Well, good for you, but you're just making things more difficult for yourself."

Noted, the criticism didn't make a dent. It had to be LA children, born of its sunbaked, gas-soaked soil; one, two, three of, sadly, so, so many. We could step in, help them, help their families, and help their communities.

It was those convictions that put us on this path, that would bring two children into our home, and that would eventually lead us to the windowless "team decision" room with Jenna, Farzana, and four social workers.

The Search

Among several options available to us in our search for a foster-to-adopt match, one took us outdoors.

The sun was beaming with growing ferocity, the milky marine layer all but burned off. A beeline of airplanes lining up to land at LAX was hovering over us.

Down here, in the dry hills of Kenneth Hahn Recreation Area in the very heart of LA, the air was warm and heady with the scent of the eucalyptus leaves crushed underfoot.

Kids, tots to teens, were busying themselves with arts and crafts as social workers stood guard, looking on, as other adults were circling the tables casting long looks at the kids, straining to observe as many details as possible, conversing in hushed tones among themselves.

This was an "adoption fair"—a quarterly event to which the Los Angeles County Family Services brought out adoptable kids, mostly harder-to-place sibling sets.

There was talk of lunch, which would double as an opportunity to examine the kids' food preferences and table manners.

There was talk of a clown.

This being our third fair, social workers greeted us by our first names. Jon and I felt valued, like a hot commodity—a double-income-no-kids (yet) gay couple with a large house and an approved home study.

"Myles and Jaevonne are such great athletes," they'd praise a sibling group, "and look at Taisha and her sisters, they've got such good chemistry. Aren't they just adorable?"

Sure they were. Is a child's natural beauty the most decisive factor in being considered, I wondered, looking at them?

"The moment I saw him," confided a friend who'd found her nine-year-old browsing the photos of Russian orphans, "I knew he was the one."

For "the one," the blond, clear-faced boy, she'd traveled half the world, and braved Russian bureaucracy. She was yet to discover his true age, his smaller build because of malnutrition, and a very mean temper—a product of years of abuse at the orphanage. All that aside, he indeed looked adorable.

Beauty, however, isn't the only factor in adoptive selection, I realized. Age matters too. At these fairs, I could read signs of resignation on the faces of older kids who knew the game, and their dwindling chances of winning it. It was in that sideways glance they gave you when your eye glided over them toward the younger kids.

And yet some learned they had to take charge. Life wasn't just going to hand them a permanent family on a plate.

A girl, probably nine or ten, with a prematurely sharp, unsmiling expression, intercepted us as we were getting up from a crafts table.

"Look! You like it?" She jerked up a plastic bead bracelet to my face.

"Oh, it's lovely," I replied cheerfully. "You like making them?"

"Yeah, I like making things, many things . . ." Her face relaxed a notch. "I can make you a rainbow loom bracelet too. And a paper plane."

I couldn't quite place her—chestnut skin, raven hair cropped in a bob, yet her face looked oddly European.

"I'm Tania, I'm nine," she informed us briskly. "Let's go meet my brothers, c'mon."

She grabbed Jon's hand, and we followed her through the dusty playground to meet two toddlers of a similar heritage, probably a mix of Black and Latino.

"Adrian, Mario," Tania hollered, not letting go of Jon's hand, "come say hello!"

Adrian and Mario obliged. They clearly looked up to her, the big sister.

"See, they're nice, very nice, not fussy, never ever," she informed us. "And we're good in school."

"Excuse me." Jon gently extricated himself from her grip and walked off, disappearing behind a row of swings.

"Listen, Tania," I said, "we're really glad we met you and your brothers, but my partner, he isn't feeling all that great . . . we'll catch you later, okay?"

She nodded but didn't move, her two younger brothers standing sheepishly by her side.

I found Jon sobbing by the park fence.

"This is too much, Lane. I can't do it! Can we leave now?"

I was moved too, but I wasn't about to lose it. We were all there for a purpose. All these kids brought out by the county wanted a family just as much as we did.

But if this wasn't brutal, I don't know what is.

§

Adoption fairs were just one way of searching for adoptable foster kids. Most leads would come from Suzanne Cohen, either from the monthly placement lists she'd receive from the county, or based on the phone calls or emails sent directly to her by county social workers.

Fully certified, we were now in the pipeline. The telephone would ring any day of the week. Wrong matches most of the time—two boys, three boys, too high risk of being sent back to their family or too medically fragile for us to handle. We had to stick to our goals and criteria; we knew our limits.

I saved some notes from those calls, scribbled hurriedly on odd stationery:

"Liam, bi-racial, two years old, prenatally exposed to crack but fine now." One child, and a boy— not for us.

"Jolene, Black, 6, no siblings, doing well in school, reunification ended, sexually molested, right arm broken." Would our all-male household be appropriate for her? Doubtful.

"Roseanne and Elijah, 21 months and 8 months, healthy, on-target. Detained because of domestic violence. Dad shoved mom, mom fell on TV, TV fell on Elijah (at six months). FR (family reunification) not terminated, no known relatives. Mom marginally complying with court orders. Dad not complying. Dad: burglary, theft, resisting arrest, prison. Kids probably in the same foster home." Risky: mom is trying to comply. Still, we expressed interest but by then the kids dropped off the list.

In the summer of 2005, Suzanne's calls inexplicably slowed down to a trickle. Sometimes the phone wouldn't ring for weeks.

Time to get more proactive, we decided. Contrary to common sense, the information about the foster children in LA was not centralized. Some kids appeared on the county lists, others in photo albums kept by the state-contracted regional agencies that assist children with disabilities, others called in by the social workers who personally knew an agency staffer or certified parents searching for children.

But where there is a mess, there is opportunity, I learned over and over in this process. *Those photo albums, what's in them?* I wondered.

We drove to a regional state agency in Torrance to take a peek.

The albums were indeed thick, bulging with headshots of adoptable kids, mostly sibling sets, many older kids. Many photos, judging by clothes and haircuts, seemed from ages ago. Were these kids still in the system?

One set caught our attention: Delano, two; Genie, three; and Orlando, four. Three beautiful mixed-race kids: two dark like their Latina mother, and one blond like his father.

Something about them spoke to us, maybe because of Jon's similar multi-racial background. We agreed to a so-called *match*, i.e., to meet these kids for a potential foster-to-adopt placement but asked Jane, the social worker, to find out more.

Over the weekend, we went for a walk by the ocean, excited

by the possibility. The spring afternoon sun rippled gold flakes on the bay as we followed the beach path, passing straight couples, some pushing strollers. This could be us, soon.

"The kids look great, in good health," Jon said. "And they've been living together in the same foster home the entire time."

"It's all very encouraging, Jon, but are you sure we can handle three?"

Jon heard me, but the siblings were just much too cute.

"We'll manage."

"We'll need at least one bigger car, two spare bedrooms instead of one. Gosh, we'll need more of everything . . ." I was growing uneasy. "And what's more important, it's just the two of us, Jon, we've got no one to help us. One of us would have to quit our job. How're we going to pay the mortgage? Jon, dear, we're talking about three kids!"

"Single women do it all the time," he said. But I could tell from his face growing sad that it was becoming clear to him too: we couldn't go from zero to three overnight in our circumstances.

On Monday, with a heavy heart, I rang the social worker to withdraw our request.

"That sibling set of three—Orlando, Genie, and Delano—we saw on Friday—"

"Wait, I did get some more information for you. That picture is two years old; all kids are still in the system but the mother has four kids now and is pregnant with the fifth. Last Friday, while you were here in my office, she had a visit with her youngest, the baby, and ran off with him. The county has issued a search warrant for her and the child. You still interested?"

In September 2005, one year after we got certified, we received a call—not from Suzanne but from the agency's foster care director. An infant was left abandoned in one of their Our Bright Futures' foster homes, ready to be transitioned towards adoption. Her name was Marianna.

Part 3
A Pink-Striped Ladybug

Lane and Jon with Marianna, January 2006
© Lane Igoudin, 2006

Mija (Darling)

"One girl, turning one . . . strictly foster . . . needs to be moved . . . mother: young, white teen; father: adult Hispanic . . . likable, chubby, cute," read my notes about baby Marianna.

For us, searching for a very young, adoptable child, especially a girl, this was a very good prospective match. Marianna was apparently an only child with no birth family to claim her. The path to the termination of the absent parents' rights seemed quick and inevitable.

We agreed to meet the infant at the agency. As more information emerged, I noted my thoughts in my diary:

"Marianna's mother has been missing from her group home for six weeks. The baby girl is healthy and in a stable foster home. The mother was in love with dad. Nobody knows where he is. Even if he knows about Marianna, claiming paternity would mean admitting a statutory rape of a fourteen-year-old. There are no other known relatives."

"The downside: Marianna isn't yet a ward of the court. Should we expect a long legal process ahead of us? What if the dad or his family emerge?"

These were all red flags, but I had no way of knowing that

they would indeed turn a quick and inevitable adoption into a multi-year ordeal with no end in sight.

§

Marianna was lovable. Dressed in a pleated, pink-striped dress, she looked like a knee-high ladybug with huge, light-brown eyes on a smooth, wide face framed by cropped hair of a similar chestnut hue. The agency receptionist unkindly called her a "chunker" but to me, chunky babies are healthy babies. To me, Marianna looked solid, and that was great.

The little girl was crawling fast around a carpeted playroom, jetting between a plastic kitchen display, a toy box, and a basket filled with colorful bouncy balls. Clearly, she was a very determined child, especially when she'd pull herself up to the top of the toy box, her legs wobbly but her hands clasping its edge firmly.

Marianna acted neither clingy nor shy. She wouldn't ask to be picked up, nor would she mind if we did. Her face carried a singular expression best described as a concerned frown, with her eyebrows pulled in a tight triangle over the bridge of her nose, wrinkling her forehead.

Jon was quickly drawn to Marianna, playing with her, joking blithely with the receptionist and Vernon Brezins, the agency's social worker assigned to us, an elderly, tall, bearded man in a buttoned-up shirt, jeans, and cowboy boots.

I'd expected to connect instantly as well, but I didn't. Marianna was a truly cute baby, but all I felt at our first meeting was curiosity mixed with a great deal of worry. This child needs a home. But were we the right parents for her? Was she the right child for us? How can you tell?

The half-hour visit felt short, so we asked for a second one. Here we heard Marianna produce her first word, pointing at a giant, red-faced doll in a denim outfit, "*Em-mo*."

Marianna craved mobility. There was so much to get to, to experience: the kitchen set, the colorful balls, the curious stuffed dolls (which probably included us too), and the six-foot walking, talking Elmos.

Suddenly, we heard Marianna laugh. Something about seeing a rubber ball rolling across the floor set her off. Her laugh rang deeply, melodiously; she wasn't holding it back, instead reacting fully to the ridiculousness of what she was seeing.

"I thought you were tickling her," said Vernon, coming into the room to check on us.

When it was time to go, Marianna cried. Having to leave the playroom upset her. I noted that even when crying, her voice was not as shrill as some other kids'—loud, certainly, but pleasant to the ear.

All my life I'd wanted to be dad. Marianna could finally fulfill my dream but the gravity of the decision we had to make was weighing me down.

"How do you know she's the one?" I asked Jon on our way back.

"She's cute, healthy, no family in the picture, why not?"

"But she's the only child. We want two, we've been asking for two—"

"It's just going to be her then."

I didn't like Jon's reply. But then, one child was still infinitely better than none. We could work on the second one later.

§

The next time we met Marianna was at her foster home, a modest house in Highland Park, near downtown LA, where many stuccoed Craftsman cottages, painted in wild, tropical colors, crammed its hills. This *barrio* was bursting with life: crowded buses, families walking the sidewalks, hands full of supermarket bags, the chimes of the *paletero* (ice cream vendor) carts, orange and lapis-lazuli taquerias, brash signs of auto shops and evangelical churches competing for the eye's attention, and overgrown gardens and stubborn palm trees spilling over the chain-link fences.

Over the years, I'd grown to know and love Highland Park with its organic, haphazard beauty, the pulsating energy of LA's Latinx heartbeat. I'd come here for the art and the Chicano artists like Roberto Gutierrez, Frank Romero, and Patssi Valdez, whose vibrant, gritty vision of their hometown reflected my own. I'd save up my money to buy their works from Avenue 50 Gallery, just a few blocks from Marianna's home, and later directly from the artists themselves, who, by then, had become our friends.

Señora Teresa, an elderly lady in thick-rimmed glasses and short, graying hair parted on the side, ran her small foster home with her daughter. She'd take no more than four babies at a time, and only as an emergency. Children would pass through her house without staying long—some back to their birth families, others on to foster placements.

Señora Teresa's other foster kid, a two-year-old Black girl named Maisha, attached herself to Marianna like a sister. She'd kiss and bear-hug Marianna and try to protect her from us, the intruders, by slapping Jon on the head.

The two girls competed for Señora Teresa's attention. If Maisha got the prized spot in the old lady's lap, Marianna would start crying until her caretaker would put Maisha down and pick her up instead.

Stern but friendly, Señora Teresa spoke very little English. Pushing the limits of my Spanish, I took notes about Marianna's routines: what she eats, plays, watches on TV, when she "*hace pipí o caca*," and when she goes to bed. The specificity of my questions seemed to win Señora Teresa's approval. It made it clear that we were serious.

On the wide porch, where Señora Teresa, Jon, and I stood talking, Marianna was slamming her red plastic walker with gusto into patio chairs.

"*Es fuerte esta niña y muy intelligente, muy intelligente* (this girl is strong and smart, very smart)," Señora Teresa would stress, wincing with every new crash.

"Marianna," I called.

No response.

I tried again, "Marianna?"

She babbled something in response but wouldn't turn her head.

"*Mija?*" called Señora Teresa.

Marianna turned and looked up at her, eyebrows pinched.

This old woman, I realized, week after week, month after month, was all she had in terms of a family, all she could count on for her physical and emotional care. The child didn't respond to her name because for months, save for an occasional visit from Jackie Willis, her social worker, no one came to see her.

§

In the next few weeks, we visited Marianna twice a week. We'd bring her treats and take her out to the playground nearby. She'd usually start with a whimper while getting into the car but once at the park—the clunking chain of the playground swing; boys hitting the soccer ball on the grassy lawn nearby; noisy trucks rolling down the street; the heavy, orange wheel in the playground tower, screeching as she'd turn it—everything fascinated her.

Marianna invented a game where she'd squeak, wait for us to squeak back, and then she'd squeak again, laughing hard, eyes all but disappearing into her big cheeks, and the game would continue.

To my eyes, with every visit, Marianna looked more and more adorable. I noticed a slight wave in her thick, chestnut hair, dimples in a lovely, round face, a high forehead, and a small round nose above a tiny mouth with her first teeth—two on top and four on the bottom. Her light-brown eyes, their corners elongated, looked huge, as if taking up half her face. Those eyes looked out upon the world with openness and a hungry curiosity.

It felt strange, audaciously novel. Not just that the sight of two guys with a baby was uncommon in 2005 but simply the sight of the two of us, a Black man and a white man together, stood out in an exclusively Hispanic neighborhood. Some Latina grandmothers stared discreetly at the oddity of the two of us with a *güera* (light-skinned) baby but getting used to the stares, I was learning, is a rite of passage for an adoptive parent.

Coming Home

Marianna was born the previous September at Holy Names, a large Catholic group home, which was an orphanage in all but name, for young mothers like Jenna and their children. In April 2005, Jenna voluntarily agreed to place Marianna in foster care for six months with the obligation to visit her regularly (ix). Her continuous contact would preserve her natural rights and allow her to take Marianna back before or at the end of this temporary foster placement.

Jenna's visits, rare as they were, stopped in early August. After that, as Señora Teresa's daughter noted in her visit log: "Marianna's mother no came to visit her daughter." Jenna had disappeared.

With the placement term ending while "*the child has not been reclaimed*," to quote California Welfare & Institutions Code (x), the DCFS was going to petition the Children's Court to formally detain the abandoned infant. The court would then place her in long-term foster care, and, given Jenna's absence, she would be fast-tracked for adoption.

We signed the placement documents to become Marianna's long-term foster parents.

§

During those weeks, between that work, teaching, school, visits, and home, Marianna was on my mind a lot. She felt like a new special friend, one I was slowly getting to know. I began to look forward to seeing her, sketching the vision of us as a *family*. What would it be like—Jon, me, and a one-year-old?

Yet there was always a fear gnawing in the back of my mind. Her becoming part of our family seemed easy and painless, yet if someone from her birth family stepped forward, we might just foster her for a while, and then see her go back to her birth family. A lot of what-ifs, a lot of uncertainty.

§

We were getting deeper into our family-building process, but our regular lives didn't slow down. Jon's work after his promotion seemed to have intensified with more client meetings. My PR job was always hectic. Besides, a career change was finally just around the corner as I was only one semester away from earning my Master's degree. Our lives went into overdrive in November as Marianna's move into our home was drawing near.

Diapers, baby clothes, bedding, shampoo, bathtub duckies—check.

Food processor, baby bottles with clear blue nipples, bibs—check.

The house itself had to be readied as well. We did more security walk-throughs. Do the gates on the stairs work properly? Do the crib's rails lock in the upright position?

My university bosses signed my leave papers, the paid leave guaranteed by the CSU union contract, and once we arranged Marianna's move-in date with Our Bright Futures, I notified my colleagues.

§

On Saturday, November 5, 2005, we brought Marianna to our house for an all-day visit. In the green bedroom, which was soon to be hers, Marianna took instantly to the crib, jumping up and down in it, laughing, throwing all the toys over the rails. Periodically, she would latch on to the rails with her gums and rub them sideways—teething, I guessed.

My sister, Natalie, stopped by, and Marianna treated her the same way she did when she'd first met us: navigating around Natalie like she was a couch.

Even though we never left the house, Marianna tired herself out enough to fall asleep on our way back to Highland Park. We wished we didn't have to take her back, but we had to. It's just a week, we consoled ourselves. She'd be moving in next Saturday.

§

Marianna's transfer took place at dusk. We stood waiting by Jon's car when, before handing her over, Señora Teresa kissed Marianna several times, firmly, as if bestowing a benediction.

Jon took Marianna from the old lady's arms. Señora Teresa turned to me then and, with tears welling up in her coffee-brown eyes, gave me a long hug.

I kissed her on the cheek, feeling my tears coming on too, "*Gracias, muchas, muchas gracias por todo!* (Thank you, many, many thanks for everything!)"

Jon strapped Marianna into the car seat, and soon the old lady was waving goodbye from the top of the hilly street, her silhouette growing smaller and melting into the evening darkness. Marianna cried a bit, but eventually turned her attention to a new toy we gave her—a handheld gadget that whistled nursery rhymes.

Marianna had no choice. With no one coming to claim her, she had to be moved from Señora Teresa's emergency placement. We were doing the right thing by offering her a permanent home—it was both law and common sense. And yet, I felt like a thief stealing a child from a home where she'd known happiness, taking her away from Señora Teresa, to whom she got attached as closely as a baby would to a parent, an adult. That day, the attachment bond was ripped for the second time in her brief life. How long would it take to heal? Would it ever?

By the time we arrived home, it had gotten dark. Jon took Marianna to the playroom while I set about fixing dinner for the *three* of us.

Marianna ate her mashed rice, chicken, and carrots contently, except that she shook her head—approvingly or not, I couldn't tell—every time she'd have to taste the carrots.

Our friend Fiona, a social worker, called in the middle of the meal. I filled her in on the details.

"Are you happy?" she asked, expecting the answer in the positive.

"More like tired," I replied. "Frazzled. Surreal."

"Oh, it will come," she said brightly. "Make sure to rest well. You'll be very busy from now on."

After dinner, we faced our first challenge. What were we supposed to do about brushing her teeth? Was she too young to use the baby brush we'd bought? Toothpaste or no toothpaste? In the end, we just put off the brushing until morning.

Our next challenge was using the diapers we had bought for the first time. While putting the first one on, Jon pulled the Velcro tag so hard it broke off. Marianna watched him suspiciously. To distract her, while Jon was trying the second diaper, I started clapping her feet up above her head, which made her laugh.

At my request, Señora Teresa had given us all of Marianna's possessions: her crib sheet and blanket, clothes, shoes, bibs, and baby bottles packed neatly into two shopping bags. Señora Teresa refused the money I'd offered but I slipped a fifty into the pocket of her housedress while she was passing Marianna over to Jon.

Around eight, we put the little girl into her crib, lined with her old sheet and blanket. I'd asked for them to keep the smell and feel of her old home for as long as possible. We warmed up the bottle, seven ounces, forty seconds in the microwave, just as Señora Teresa had instructed us, and Marianna drank the milk lying down. She wasn't sleepy—the new house was causing too much excitement. An hour later, she was sound asleep, lying face down with her behind sticking up like a pyramid, sucking loudly on the pacifier.

Marianna's Mother

Vernon Brezins, our agency social worker, arranged our first visit at a park in Diamond Bar. Located on the eastern edge of Los Angeles County, the park was a good forty miles from our home in Long Beach and at least the same distance from Jenna's foster group home in the opposite direction in Riverside County.

"*Es muy joven, su madre, muy, muy joven* (She's young, her mother, very, very young)," Señora Teresa had said.

I couldn't picture her then. But now I saw her—*joven* indeed. A plump white teen of average height, Jenna had an attractive face, pale and wide like Marianna's, a short straight nose, a small rounded mouth over a prominent chin, and light blue eyes tinged with gray, sunk deep into the cheekbones, guarded.

"Here she is," I whispered to Marianna, who was holding on to my index fingers. "Your Mommy. Remember Mommy?"

Jenna came over, smiling broadly to her daughter, picked up Marianna and hugged her tightly to her chest.

"You've grown, huh? So much bigger now. Look at your tummy . . . you remember me? You do, don't you?"

Marianna didn't respond. She looked at her mother blankly but didn't fuss or fidget in her arms.

"Hey, look," Jenna spun around to her friends trickling out of the group home van. "Look, it's my daughter. Cute, isn't she?" She lifted Marianna. "I'd been taking such good care of her until they took her away . . . oh, wait, wait, Mama brought you something special . . ."

Passing Marianna to one of the girlfriends, Jenna shuffled back in her flip-flops to the van. Her friend gave me a brief glance, asking for permission. I nodded my head and retreated to a picnic table between the parking lot and the playground.

On her return, Jenna took Marianna back from her friend and, balancing her on her hip, headed leisurely to my table.

"You mind?" I caught a touch of a sweet, country droll in those extended, ascending vowels.

"Sure, have a seat."

Slowly hooking one leg, then another, over the bench, Jenna planted herself on the other side of the table and sat Marianna down on her knee. She opened her hand, which contained a cup of yogurt, and then looked at me. "You have a spoon?"

I remembered a pack of takeout plastic utensils in the glove compartment.

"Actually, I do, in the car." I got up.

She wrinkled her nose in a cutesy way. "Would you have some napkins too?"

Jenna fed Marianna in short spoonfuls, holding the child back after each one to wipe her mouth with a napkin.

Marianna got fussy. She loved the yogurt, but with her healthy appetite, she liked to eat quickly and uninterrupted.

When the yogurt cup was emptied, Jenna held it for a few seconds in her hand, uncertain.

"Over there," I bent my head in the direction of a concrete trashcan at the other end of the table.

"Uh-huh." With a quick smile, she tossed the cup.

Marianna, meanwhile, began to grumble.

"What's wrong, baby?" Jenna looked at her with concern.

"She's probably wet," I said. "It's been a while since we left home."

"You've got diapers?"

"Yep." I reached under the table and pulled a diaper and a pack of wipes out of my bag, handing them over. When I realized that Jenna had nothing to put Marianna on, I reached down again and pulled out a baby blanket I'd thrown in just in case.

"Mommy's gonna take care of you," Jenna purred to Marianna, as she spread the blanket on the slab table. Marianna didn't protest being changed, but she kept her eyes on me. "See, baby, that's Mommy care."

The dirty diaper rolled up, Jenna held it up in her hand. I pointed with my eyes back to the trashcan near the table. She threw it in.

Jenna let Marianna lie on her back on the table and tickled her tummy. Then she took off the one-year-old's socks and, putting Marianna's toes in her mouth, started sucking on them. The child finally started to warm up, laughing.

Jenna picked Marianna off the table and balanced her on her knee. Tossing her head lightly to the side, Jenna opened her face and neck to the sun, and turned her attention to me, "What's your name?"

She asked the question, eyeing me playfully, her hand sweeping the mane of her curly brown hair over one shoulder, tilting up her bosom. Clearly, she knew she was pretty with her shapely curves, unruly big hair, and fresh, adolescent face. Jenna seemed to be striking out to assert her power over me, much like a woman in her twenties would, except she was barely sixteen and I was, on so many levels, the wrong target. This whole dynamic was making me feel quite uncomfortable, but I kept my tone neutral, as if oblivious to it.

"I'm Lane, Marianna's foster dad. And you're Jenna, Jenna Sewell, I believe?"

"Yeah. How do you know my name?"

"It's in the court papers."

"Well, I'm glad you remembered it." She gave a little giggle. "Then you know she's coming to live with me?"

"Oh?" I raised an eyebrow. "I didn't know that."

"Uh-huh . . ." Jenna glanced at the child in her lap. "Does she talk?"

"Marianna? Yeah, she does," I replied.

"Does she say Mama? She was talking when I saw her last."

I couldn't tell Jenna that her daughter did not say "Mama."

"She's got a few words," I said, "like Elmo." Seeing Jenna now raise her eyebrows, I shrugged. "Don't be surprised, she loves Elmo."

"Elmo? You like Elmo?" Jenna called out to Marianna.

"Em-mo!" said Marianna firmly, the first word out of her mouth since the start of the visit.

Jenna turned back to me. "Are you single? I wouldn't want my baby to be alone in a home with a man."

"You don't need to worry," I replied calmly. "She is in a very safe home."

I had to go to the bathroom. Instantly, Marianna got up, too, and tried to follow me, pulling her mother along. She couldn't walk yet so Jenna had to hold her by the hands as she made unsteady, yet determined, steps. The child was clearly getting worried. I turned to her and assured her with signs I'd be right back.

The visit ended soon after with Jenna hugging and kissing Marianna plenty. The van left.

§

We can make this work, I thought, driving back.

If Jenna gets her act together, then the county will find a group home for both her and Marianna, maybe even the same Catholic group home they'd lived in originally, Holy Names. Otherwise, Marianna will be staying with us. Jenna will be going to school, possibly taking some vocational program, working part-time, but she'll stay involved with Marianna while we're raising her. Marianna never had a father, but she has a mother, and that was something we'll never be able to replace. And Jenna is the only one claiming her, without any other family. We can work something out.

An open adoption then? Visits, phone calls, dinners at our house?

The details of my vision were fuzzy, but it was a promising vision.

§

Why did Jenna come back? From what we learned from Vernon, the details emerging slowly, she simply had nowhere else to go.

After running away from a group home in Los Angeles, she lived with one guy, then another. Social services filed a missing person's report with the police. Whether she found herself alone, or had to leave someone, in the end, she simply walked into a local police department and told them she was sixteen, a dependent of the court, and that she needed a home.

The police, after checking the records, set the social service machinery in motion—intake, interviews, assessments, drug and STD tests, and the resulting placement in a local group home. Back in foster care, Jenna asked to see her daughter.

Once word of Jenna's return reached the Children's Court in LA, Judge Candace Hooke, who was presiding over her case, ordered the county to provide drug and substance abuse counseling, parenting classes, as well as mental health services for Jenna. Marianna was to stay in her emergency foster placement with Señora Teresa until the court could decide what to do with both the mother and the daughter. But by the time the judge's order trickled down the caretaking chain over the course of about two weeks—children's attorneys, social services, the foster agency—Marianna had already moved in with us. Had we waited just a few days more, we might not have gotten her.

§

I didn't learn about Jenna's new pregnancy until her second visit. Sitting herself down again at that same cement-slab picnic table, Jenna told me matter-of-factly that she was on her third month, and that "the home the county is looking for isn't just for me and Marianna, but for me and both my babies."

I was too stunned to react.

Just as impassively, Jenna added, "They told me that my new baby is going to have Down Syndrome."

She gave no further details.

"Does the baby have the same daddy as Marianna?"

"No."

"So how come you're not with him?" I knew I shouldn't have asked, but I couldn't help myself.

"He's nice, he really is, sometimes. But I had to leave him because of . . ." she pursed her lips to one side, "what do you call it . . . domestic violence?"

§

Jenna's revelation changed our future in an instant. Still adjusting to the around-the-clock caretaking of a fourteen-month-old, we were now faced with a possibility of a second child coming into our home. The county would want to keep the siblings together, which bode well for us since we wanted two children. If we, however, refused the newborn, the court would likely take Marianna away from us for the same reason. On the other hand, if Jenna completed all the court-ordered reunification services, she would take them both.

But this second baby, Down Syndrome? We'd marked 'no' on the county's Child Desired Worksheet because we knew even then that we weren't prepared to deal with it. And now, with Marianna alone being a handful, could we really commit ourselves to fostering a medically fragile child alongside Marianna? This would be a very tough call.

Six Months

After Marianna moved in with us, for five days—*five days*—no one from the agency or the county called to check on her. But when a week later, on the request from the DCFS, the court formally detained Marianna, a rush of activity ensued. Now everyone had to see the child, who was finally a ward of the court, and report to the court on her well-being. Detention made her visible.

Reviewing reports from Jackie and the attorneys, Judge Hooke found it unsafe to return Marianna to Jenna, and thus *disposed*[11] of her at the next court hearing by keeping Marianna in foster care, but also by giving Jenna an opportunity to reunify.

State law is quite specific about the timeframe for family reunification services: "For a child who, on the date of initial removal from the physical custody of his or her parent or guardian, was under 3 years of age, court-ordered services shall be provided for a period of 6 months from the dispositional hearing…, but no longer than 12 months from the date the child entered foster care."[12]

The brevity of a six-month reunification window made sense; in the life of an infant, every day counts. Reporting to the agency on Marianna's progress, for instance, I noted all these new behaviors in just one week:

- November 18: Asked to be led around by extending her index fingers to us.
- November 20: Used the sound *uh* for "up" to show she wanted to go up the stairs.
- November 20: Ran across the playpen, grabbing hold of the opposite rail before falling.
- November 23: Figured out how to turn on the TV by pressing its red 'Power' button.
- November 24: Climbed up the carpeted stairs. Only up, not down, but completely on her own.

In offering family reunification services, however, the court ignored the seven months Marianna had *already* spent in foster care. That placement had been voluntary, but this one wasn't, so the clock restarted as if Jenna had been there all along and Marianna had just been removed from her at fourteen months.

I couldn't help noticing that this decision came at a considerable cost. While the returning mother was given time and services to get it together, we were being paid to raise her child; judges, lawyers, bailiffs, court clerks were running the legal side of the process; child welfare professionals in social services were carrying out, monitoring, and reporting on the court order compliance, and so on. Was this typical?

I went online to learn more about the system. In its previous fiscal year, 2003–2004, DCFS, with its 6,200 employees, and a $1.5 billion budget,[13] oversaw 38,839 children, a quarter still lived with their birth parents as part of "family maintenance services," but the rest were placed out of home, some with relatives, most in foster homes. 7,854 children were, like Marianna, undergoing reunification.[14]

Of the remaining kids in the system, 17,500 were ineligible for, or past the point of, reunification and considered to be in a "permanent foster placement." One would think that these kids would be fast-tracked to adoption, but they weren't. In sharp contrast with the 32 percent of foster children nationwide, and 34 percent in California, only 13 percent of the Los Angeles County's foster kids would exit foster care into adoption within two years of placement in 2004—a dismally low number, but actually a third higher than the year before.

§

Jenna missed the next visit. I drove to the park, sat at the same picnic table, called her group home and our agency six times, and fifty minutes later left with the agency's blessing.

Here's something I learned in just two visits with Jenna: she was protected by two sets of legal rights. As a birthmother, she was given the opportunity to reunite with her daughter if she completed the ABCs ordered by the court—parenting classes, rehab, and counseling—she would be presumed ready to assume her parental responsibilities over Marianna.

But as a foster child herself, Jenna had to be assisted in her reunification efforts by DCFS and her own foster parents. "My staff," as she called them—as in "you can arrange the next visit with my staff"—had to schedule and deliver her to all her appointments. If she didn't get along with her foster family and had to be moved, DCFS would have to restart all these efforts from zero.

How can the same person be viewed as a potentially competent, responsible parent and simultaneously as a dependent under the care of adults who support all her actions? This contradiction was at the heart of the situation we were all in.

§

"They're still looking for a place where I can be with my babies. It's just that there is no opening yet. But they keep looking," Jenna confided at the beginning of the next visit that actually happened.

"And will they help you if your baby has Down syndrome?" I asked.

"No, no Downs," the doctor said. My baby's going to be alright."
I exhaled, "Well, good for you!" And for us.

Jenna brought some Graham crackers and a cup of applesauce to this visit, though no spoon. I had no spoons either. Marianna ate the crackers.

Jenna asked me if I'd brought any toys.

"Sorry, Jenna. This is supposed to be your time with your child. You decide what you want to do and bring what you need."

Jenna didn't like what I said. She tightened her lips, spun her head sharply, as if excluding me from her surroundings, grabbed Marianna, and carried her to a swing nearby.

A few minutes later, I noticed Marianna pooped, first by Marianna's exerted facial expression, and then by the smell. I pointed it out to Jenna who kept bouncing her on the swing. Luckily, our visit bag was fully stuffed with the diapers and wipes. Marianna let Jenna change her with no fuss.

§

A DCFS dependency investigator, whose job was to provide an independent assessment to the court, called me later in the week.

"I'm preparing a report for the court about Jenna and Marianna's interaction. It seems that the daughter's distant geographic placement is negatively affecting her family reunification," he said in a slightly accusatory tone. "I need to see her right away; the hearing is next week."

Marianna was developing a serious cold; still, we had to comply. A visit to the park was promptly arranged.

After driving forty miles in traffic, and with her cold now in full swing—runny nose, watery eyes, congested chest—Marianna was not in a good mood. Seeing Jenna at the park, she cried and clearly wanted to leave. The mother-daughter reunion the dependency investigator was witnessing wasn't a happy one.

At the court hearing five days later, Judge Hooke ordered the mother, not the child, to be moved closer. The visits, however, were to take place now twice a week and be monitored by the foster agency staff.

Signed "Lane & Jon + Marianna"

Monday, November 21, 2005 9:07 A.M.

Dear Friends,

We are happy to share with you some wonderful news. Marianna, a curious, determined, and an absolutely adorable one-year-old, has recently joined our family. We brought her home after visiting her in her prior foster home for two months. She seems to be adjusting well. We've taken her in with the intention to adopt, though we won't know if it happens for a few more months. Those of you familiar with the foster-to-adopt process know its joys and perils. At this point, we are still emerging from the placement crisis mode (hence the delay with letting you know). Things are settling down, and we are finding ourselves a bit nervous and very happy.

Lane & Jon + Marianna

We finally went public with this email sent out to our friends and relatives, as well as to the entire PopLuck mailing list. Our plans, known previously to only our closest circle, took many by surprise. Congratulations and *mazel tovs* flooded my in-box.

Jon's insurance company—in the conservative Orange County—threw an all-out baby shower in Marianna's honor. At the restaurant in a suburban mall, the cause of the celebration sat proudly in a high chair, surrounded by bright pink gift bags with toys, clothes, and baby foot-shaped *IT'S A GIRL!* balloons.

Becoming comfortable in the presence of others was probably the biggest change in Marianna since moving in. We took her everywhere: supermarkets and stores, lunches with friends, the beach, and a hair salon where she had her first haircut. At a Christmas play at a friend's church, sitting in my lap in a cream-colored outfit decorated with lace and bows, Marianna looked completely engrossed in the show. Her eyes focused on the stage and she clapped her hands in time with the songs. Being out and about, she was loosening up, growing friendlier.

Or so we thought. Inga and Roger invited us to Tommy's first birthday. There at the party, Marianna spotted an appealing toy, the truck the birthday boy was playing with. She crawled over, punched Tommy in the face, and, oblivious to his crying, ripped the toy out of his hands.

Shocked and embarrassed, we apologized profusely to Inga. Clearly, a long road lay ahead of us in improving Marianna's social skills.

Not all went smoothly at home either. After a few initial weeks of calm, now used to her new home, Marianna started to test the limits, spitting out food on the kitchen table and fighting the diaper changes.

Marianna was growing developmentally as well. In November, she began to take a couple of steps at a time, especially between objects close by, like the couch and the coffee table, or holding to the walls. We encouraged her with cheer and applause. Soon, Marianna graduated to short distances, like to Tommy's house next door, up to ten steps at a time. Sometimes, she'd fall on her butt, her fall cushioned by the diaper, and be amused by it, apparently considering walking some kind of trick.

Her vocabulary began to expand: to the initial "*Em-mo*," she added "*wah*" for "water," "*gee*" for "bib," "*nyam-nyam*" for food, rising to the emphatic "*NYAM!*" if she really liked it. She started to differentiate between "*ta-ti*" (me) and "*tah-ta*" (Jon).

A week is a month, and a month is a year in the life of a small child, I learned. How lucky we were to witness each misstep, and each milestone.

§

My two-month leave of absence was coming to an end. Fun as it was to be home with Marianna, I longed to go back to work, away from the never-ending domestic labor. There would hardly be any break during the day between cooking, feeding, cleaning, changing diapers, running the washer and dryer, outings in the stroller, reading storybooks, and visits, visits, visits. Nine visits alone to see the mother and several more for the foster agency worker, the court investigator, and the doctor. A simple visit to the doctor would take four hours. A visit with Jenna would take at least the same amount of time, considering how long it took to prep Marianna and pack the diaper bag, drive, and then unpack.

Those days stay with me as a blur of domestic routines. Few activities seem to fall under the "What Matters" category, those that were interesting, entertaining to remember. In retrospect, I know that everything matters. Every feeding, every bath, every diaper change.

Scraping off Cheerios glued to Marianna's cereal bowl while she was building blocks in the playpen—matters.

Sprinkling sugar together on the strawberries to help them release juice—matters.

Diligently wiping the sand out of Marianna's derriere after a trip to the beach—matters.

Watching *Teletubbies* daily at 11:00 a.m. on PBS, Marianna cackling with delight at the baby-faced sun rising at the start of each episode, clapping her hands with the music, laughing at the squeaking and farting noises the 'Tubbies would make—all that matters too.

A Friend in the Courtroom

The more I was getting attached to Marianna, the more the visits began to bother me. At first, I was reluctant to report on Jenna's shortcomings—after all, she was just a teen. But if she wanted to prove to the court that she was fit to parent Marianna, the court would need to know the truth. Otherwise, it wouldn't be safe for Marianna to go to her.

Starting with the Christmas visit, I began to report exactly what I saw.

That day, Jenna arrived from a new group home, one close to the park, accompanied by the home supervisor, Ms. Anita, and another teen.

"The visit went fine," ran my report to the agency, "except for the fact that Jenna let her friend play with and walk Marianna, and at some point, Marianna was up first in Ms. Anita's and then the other girl's arms with Jenna standing by."

When the situation repeated itself at the next visit, Vernon noticed it too and told Jenna gently, stooping grandfatherly over her, "This is your time to be with your baby, Jenna."

At the same visit, I noted that "Jenna lets Marianna crawl up the playground ladder to open platforms without being sufficiently close to prevent her from falling out. Sometimes, the mother is on the wrong side of the structure, or on the same platform, but not close enough, or standing away from the structure."

Visits or not, how could I make sure the one-year-old wouldn't get hurt?

§

"You need more allies in the courtroom, Lane. Someone who can speak for what's best for the child," recommended our friend Corri Planck, a foster-to-adopt parent with more experience with the system.

It made sense. After the New Year, I made my first overtures to Marianna's court-appointed attorney, Margaret McPherson. I called her twice asking to discuss Marianna's progress in her three months with us. My calls were not returned.

"Keep trying," suggested Corri, "but remember, you're walking a fine line here. On one hand, you want to make friends to speak up for Marianna, but on the other, if you push too hard, you can be seen as trying to influence the court."

Margaret McPherson still wouldn't respond. Then how about a letter, I thought, updating her on Marianna's life, her physical and psychological development? The reply won't be necessary, but if faxed, it will have to be read.

I put it all in, from describing Marianna's playroom which houses her "toys, Legos, miniature kitchen set, and shelves with children's books and videos" to the change we'd seen in the "quality of Marianna's interaction with other people," to how being aware of her lack of social skills, we were making sure "to expose Marianna to outside life," and so on.

The fax went out on February 20.

Within a couple of weeks, we received a visit from Carl P. Jackson, McPherson's representative.

"Now, is this the child Marianna?" He pointed to the little girl hugging my leg, looking up at him warily.

"Yep."

He inspected her closely. "She's a good eater, looks good, healthy. You feed her well."

I nodded.

The rest of his visit was a chat about Marianna's life growing up with us and our plans for her. Carl was impressed with our neighborhood and our home. He particularly admired the collection of African American art displayed on the walls, Jon's lifelong passion.

"Must've cost a pretty penny," he quipped.

"Not necessarily," I replied. "Jon has a good eye. He can pick out a museum piece at a Salvation Army store. He has, in fact."

"Has he?" Carl replied, squinting his eyes at the artists' signatures.

An exchange of friendly phone calls with Margaret McPherson followed. Our side's goal was to assure her of complete openness to her oversight and of our commitment to Marianna while McPherson's was to confirm that she'd read the fax and the visit report, and that she was pleased to know Marianna was doing well in our home. This was the opening of an important relationship.

Keys to Our Future

At the agency's foster parent training in February, we again saw Señora Teresa.

"*Cómo ha crecido, la niña! Se ve bien!* (How much she's grown, the little girl! She looks good!)" she exclaimed.

Marianna showed no recognition, no smile, simply no sign of interest. When Señora Teresa reached out to pick her up, she waddled away to Jon.

I couldn't understand Marianna's reaction, or more exactly, her lack of it. It had only been three months since Marianna left her home. Could Marianna have forgotten her so quickly?

The seminar was starting. Señora Teresa, her daughter, Jon, and I took our seats together to listen to a speaker talk, coincidentally, about early childhood trauma.

"Studies show that many neglected and abused children respond to the trauma by emotionally numbing themselves, and are in danger of growing up unable to feel the suffering of others," explained the presenter. "They shut down; they split off from traumatic experiences when they are traumatized. It's a survival technique."

Could it be, I wondered, looking at Marianna playing with

crayons in my lap, that her loss of Señora Teresa, her caretaker, a second major loss in her short life so far, caused Marianna so much pain that she had to forget her, to lock up this wounding memory? That this was her way of coping? Will she forget us just as easily, if she were to return to Jenna? Will she block us out of her memory as another experience of loss and betrayal of trust?

I returned to work at Cal Poly on a three-day work schedule, so as to keep two days working from home open for Marianna's visits and appointments. My new schedule got approved, but with a 20 percent pay cut. For those days when I had to go to campus, we decided to enroll Marianna in Playtime Learning, a neighborhood preschool, consisting of a hive of cottages and playgrounds tucked away under century-old oaks and sycamores.

§

January, February, March. How neatly dates fit, one following another. You look back at the records, and everything falls into a logically unfolding timeline. Yet very little seemed logical or predictable at the time.

After the New Year, Jenna's requests for visits suddenly stopped. Why? No one would tell us.

I remembered that at her last visit, Jenna told me she was due around March 30. Then she told Vernon she was due in May. May or March? She was in her seventh month. Had she gone into labor early? Where was she?

I made a call to Jackie Willis, Marianna's social worker. In three months of Marianna's living with us, we had yet to meet her in person.

The reply came, as usual, via voicemail at home. Not a word about the visits, but there was some clarification on the due date.

"I know Jenna's been telling different things to different people. She's not in labor. She's due in late May. By the way, are you willing to take the baby?"

By the way.

We were ready for Jackie's question. We'd already decided back in November when we first heard about Jenna's pregnancy, even knowing that the child might have special needs.

"We will gladly take Marianna's sibling as well," Jackie's voicemail was recording our response. "Keep us in the loop. Any idea if it's a boy or a girl? We need to plan the color scheme."

It appeared that we were going to have a second child after all, just as we had originally planned: a sibling set of two, ages zero to five. Late May at least gave us some breathing room. I could continue to work, finish the first ESL courses I started to teach in Orange County, complete my thesis, graduate, and carry on with Marianna's visits and the rest.

That, of course, is if Jenna didn't deliver early. The keys to our future as a family lay in her belly.

§

On February 27, Jackie Willis finally came for a visit. Jon opened the door to an impeccably well-dressed, statuesque black woman in her mid-30s.

"Oh!" she exclaimed upon seeing Marianna sitting high in my arms. "Don't you look healthy, little girl. You've grown quite a bit since I last saw you."

Five months, to be exact.

"What a beautiful home," Jackie remarked, craning her neck at the architectural details of the house, the art on the walls. "How long have you been here?"

"About two years. We used to have a smaller place near the beach, but it wouldn't have been big enough for the kids."

"And this is her bedroom? Sure is big . . . and she has a play-room . . . mm-hm, girl, you just hit the jackpot," Jackie quipped with approval, glancing at Marianna. "Big enough for two girls, or four. Sure you don't want to take a few more? I know you can afford it, and look at all this space . . ." She raised her eyebrows in a mock challenge.

"That's all we can handle," I declined, smiling politely. "It's just the two of us, you know. Otherwise, we would consider it."

Back in the living room, Marianna showed Jackie what she'd been learning, pointing out her "*no-oh*" (nose), "*tee*" (teeth), eyes, lips, and ears. I added that Marianna's other new words included "hi," "no," and the hilarious "*hh-hh-hh*" ("hot-hot-hot"). At a year and a half, her speech development was fully on target, following closely the language acquisition stages I was studying in grad school, theory unfolding into reality.

Jackie took thorough notes and acted friendly, even if professionally detached. Marianna's secure placement apparently sent her case toward the bottom of her client list.

"Pee-pee," interjected Marianna.

"You sure?"

She nodded.

Good timing, I thought, time to demonstrate our crowning achievement. Proudly I walked her to the bathroom, but . . .

"Uh-oh," Marianna said, peering into the diaper. She'd already gone.

"We've been teaching Marianna to say 'pee-pee' if she's ready to go." I told Jackie while changing Marianna's diaper. "Sometimes, it's after the fact, like now. To her, it's just a game, but it's beginning to fall into place, so to speak."

At Jackie's and our request, a psychologist from Harbor Regional, the state's center for disabled children, came in to assess Marianna. Her report showed some developmental delays in motor skills and cognition.

"Are you ready to raise a child who won't be going to college?" asked Fiona, a friend and a social worker familiar with these reports.

She meant well, but I panicked at the thought. I'd earned a doctorate from Stanford and was finishing my second grad school in the middle of the process. What does it mean not to go to college?

But then I'd look at Marianna and see with my own eyes, as a parent, as a teacher, how quickly she'd grasp drawing with chalk, or playing hoops with Tommy. How intently she was following the preschool teacher's instructions to share, to wait for her turn. How instantly she'd react to Cookie Monster and Big Bird's skits and jokes on TV, laughing at them, repeating their words to herself. There was nothing wrong with her. In the right environment, she'll catch up, she'll blossom.

The Collective Parent

After a five-week absence, Jenna requested a visit. I took the call in New York, at the National Business School PR Conference. I said yes, expecting to be back in LA on Sunday, the day before the visit.

That night in New York, my friend Marc, an art expert with the Wildenstein Institute, took me to the Whitney Biennial—a wild, cacophonous, contemporary art show. In one room, we came upon the paintings and sculptures of Reena Spaulings. I admired the richness of her ideas, the wide diversity of her artistic expression . . . except, I learned, she didn't exist. Reena Spaulings, the sign explained, was a fictional artist, whose many works on display were produced by a collective of real painters and sculptors.

I burst out laughing. That's us in California! All of us—Jenna, Jackie, Judge Hooke, Vernon, Jon, and I—have been Reena Spaulings parents to Marianna: each of us pitching in, but no one having all the rights and responsibilities. Only, Marianna is not an artifice. Marianna is real. This process is ultimately about finding suitable permanent parents or continuing with this makeshift, unstable parenting collective for only God knows how long.

While in New York, I went to a *Democracy Now!* benefit at a club on the Bowery. Bands played. Amy Goodman spoke to a crowded room. The Iraq War was dragging into its third year with no end in sight. But what I remember the most is chatting with Larisa, a successful young violinist, Russian-Jewish like me, not about the war, but about Marianna, our life with her.

"Wow, you two are the real new millennium!" Larisa said. "I didn't even know it was legal for gays to adopt."

"It is in some places, but not everywhere."

With the Bush administration, carried into the White House by a swell of religious neo-conservatism, our families were under attack. On my flight to New York, I read an article in *USA Today* about a bill introduced in the Ohio legislature that would bar all adoptions and foster care by gays and lesbians. "It is among efforts in at least sixteen states," the story said, "to put into law the view that children should be cared for only by a mother and a father or by heterosexual singles." The accompanying statistics, showing that only 50,000 foster children, i.e., one out of ten, found permanent homes each year, underscored the viciousness of this new gay panic. The right-wingers would rather have these kids rot in the foster system than give them a home with committed adults like Jonathan and me.

§

From Manhattan to Montebello. Our new meeting place, the Whittier Narrows Park, was again a geographical compromise. With Jenna moved into a group home in the San Gabriel Valley, the three vehicles would arrive at the Montebello location twice a week: her group home van from the east, my old Suzuki with Marianna from the south, and Vernon's shiny sedan from the west to observe. For me, this was an improvement: a fifty-five-mile round-trip versus an eighty-mile one.

Marianna sat nestled in my arms in a red Elmo sweater and fleece pants, snug as a fluffy chicken. Jenna was running late. I didn't know what to expect; we'd had a few weeks of uneasy, visit-free quiet, and Jenna was, after all, seven months pregnant.

Twenty minutes after the scheduled visit time, her van pulled up. Jenna emerged, her belly and the rest of her body grown considerably bigger. When she put out her arms to pick up Marianna, Marianna burst out crying. I gently pushed her over in Jenna's direction. I had to. Marianna kept crying, thrashing violently in Jenna's arms, reaching out toward me.

I turned away, my heart beating hard to the point of choking. Jenna sat down at a picnic table fifty feet away and stayed there for a while, feeding Marianna chunks of pineapple. Vernon found another bench nearby. I stayed in the car.

After about twenty minutes, Jenna rose and walked Marianna back to the parking lot, telling Vernon and me that she had to leave. She looked tired. There was a hint of relief in her goodbye.

§

At the next visit at the Narrows, on an overcast day in March, Jenna was again late. Marianna was buzzing around the playground in her new pink suede shoes, a pair of jeans, and a pink and green paisley shirt.

I finally spotted Jenna, dressed in a black T-shirt with *ROCKSTAR* emblazoned in glitter across the front, sweat pants, and flip-flops, walking slowly—not from the parking lot, but from the bus stop far out on the main road.

Jenna positioned herself at the bottom of a slanted kiddie slide, lying down in it at a forty-five-degree angle. The bottom of her pregnant belly was popping out from beneath her shirt. I didn't blame Jenna; her weight had to be taking a toll on her back.

She put Marianna between the humps of her breasts and her belly and began rocking her, which made Marianna laugh. I was observing them from a respectful distance, sitting under a tree with a stack of papers in my lap, too far to hear what Jenna was saying to Marianna, but for once, it looked like the two of them were having fun.

§

In that spring of 2006, besides working in my public affairs position, I already started teaching the first three ESL classes.

My career transition from the former to the latter depended on graduating—my third job. I simply had to graduate. To do so, I was stealing away every extra minute between taking Marianna to the visits, working, and teaching classes to work on my master's thesis. Overall, pieces were falling into place astoundingly well—the new degree, classes, and contracts for the fall—but I slept very little that spring.

Jon, supportive as ever, took care of Marianna the four nights a week when I taught and never complained. He was telling me to quit my job, but I knew we needed the money, so I chose to stay for as long as possible, which would primarily depend on how well we could manage Marianna and her expected baby sister.

Working so feverishly hard helped keep my mind off the drama surrounding Marianna. Jenna's reunification review was coming up. One night, Jon said we should think about returning Marianna to the county if Jenna got the extension.

"We could use the time to try our luck with other kids, lower-risk. I don't want to be 45 and starting all over with another child," he said.

This hurt me deeply. Just when I was going out of my mind about Marianna's future and the arrival of a newborn, I had to face a threat on the home front—that my partner would consider such pre-emptive surrender. Did he not love her as much as I did?

I couldn't sleep for a couple of nights after that. I didn't want to be close to him.

A few days later, I told him we had to talk; we couldn't go on like this.

Pointing at Marianna lost in *Teletubbies* in the living room, I told him firmly, "I am not sending her back. If the court takes her away from us, I will have to accept that. But we're not returning this child of our own volition. Should her mother get an extension, we'll just have to ride it out."

"Fine," he replied.

This conversation jerked me back to my own childhood. I was five when my parents divorced. After the acrimonious parting of the ways, my mother, who got full custody, denied my father's requests for visitations. My father was willing, albeit reluctantly so, to go along with her wishes. It was Babushka, my grandmother, who refused to accept it.

"This is your son!" she screamed at my dad. "You can't just give him up. You've got to fight for him!"

And fight she did—for him and for me, pushing my parents to talk, calling meetings. Through mediation, the custody agreement was modified to allow my father weekly visits, which would continue for the next thirteen years. He didn't lose me, nor did I lose him. To this day, he is my closest friend in the family.

I couldn't give up Marianna. This was not a decision based on reason or calculation. After eight months, I'd grown too attached to her to send her back just because of an uncertain future. I couldn't hurt her.

Walking with Pride

The anti-gay onslaught was ramping up. On May 18, 2006, the US Senate's Judiciary Committee approved the draft of the Federal Marriage Amendment (FMA) to the US Constitution which stipulated that "neither this Constitution, nor the constitution of any State, shall be construed to require that marriage or the legal incidents thereof be conferred upon any union other than the union of a man and a woman."

To rally support for the amendment, the right wing was recycling the save-the-children rhetoric first used by Anita BJackt in the 1970s. With so many politicians and media juxtaposing predatory gays with innocent children, gay families—previously safer in the shadows—hesitantly, but unavoidably, began to pop up in the news. The day after the FMA passed the Senate Judiciary Committee, a federal district court struck down Oklahoma's two-year-old Adoption Invalidation Law, which denied recognition of an adoption from another state by more than one individual of the same sex. Children adopted by gay parents would no longer be legal orphans in Oklahoma.

It wasn't just politics. American culture remained ambiguous reconciling the notions of being gay and being a parent.

This was simply too new. Children and procreation, after all, had been the domain of the heterosexuals for millennia, and here we were tearing down this age-old norm, offering an alternative. A change in society's attitudes, a change so profound, couldn't happen overnight. You didn't have to be homophobic to be, at the very least, surprised that two men would parent a baby. But did it mean you had to deny an opportunity of fulfillment to another person just because the very thought of it was new or odd to you?

These thoughts were swirling around my head as I was pushing Marianna's stroller down the middle of Ocean Boulevard, past the thousands of Long Beach Pride spectators, past the windows of our love nest apartment where Jon and I had first moved in together seven years earlier, where I had been dreaming of being a father one day.

Our local PopLuck contingent, a dozen gay fathers with their kids, got a lot of cheers. We looked good, and we knew it. Handsome, happy, confident, and with healthy children to show—the younger ones like Marianna in the strollers and wagons and the teens and tweens weaving among us on their scooters and skateboards.

Ahead of us was a colorful Latinx float. Our hometown mayor-elect followed us in a convertible. Behind him, a gro up of leathermen was bringing up the rear.

"Be nice to straight people!" the MC urged our rambunctious contingent as we passed by. "They can't help being heterosexual, they're born that way!"

Fending off the rainbow balloons tied to the handles of Marianna's stroller, I was waving to the crowds filling up the sidewalks and balconies along our parade route. Most of the spectators were not gay. Some brought their own offspring to watch the Pride. "Go, daddies!" some shouted, clinking beers.

I was waving to them with pride and joy, and yet I couldn't help wondering, *What do they see in us, these straight folks? What are they applauding? An oddity, sweetly weird and amusing? Rebels fighting their second-class citizen status? Or messengers of the next gay generation, of the fully accepted and equal tomorrow?*

Wherever we were—a black man, a white man, and a pale-faced Hispanic girl—our presence alone would make a statement that gay men *can* be fathers, without hiding or denying who they are. Some people would cheer us on, but others would look at us with suspicion, fury, or contempt.

As parents, we are the same, gay or otherwise. There is little camp or glamour in a gay dad's daily routines. Like straight moms or dads, we'd make healthy lunches for Marianna to take to Playtime Learning, shop at Target for the up-sized clothes, and get half the town on the phone to find the best cure for her pink-eye.

We *were* different in other ways. Few straight parents would report their latest family news as upcoming court dates, minute orders, or drama from the birth family visits—the norm in our parade group where most of the kids were "from the system," their social worker and attorney's numbers programmed into their dads' cell phones.

The more others see us, the more they're willing to accept us, I realized. That, not the applause, was what made me so pleased with our little contingent showing up in the parade. We'll have to keep on being visible until our visibility is so normal, it will become invisible.

Deceived

Jenna got moved again. She was now living with a Pakistani family, her fourth home in the seven months I had known her. Her new foster mother, Farzana, a traditional Muslim woman who kept her head covered and never looked me directly in the eye, had somehow grown to like me, and confided at one visit that Jackie had asked her to purchase a bassinet, blankets, diapers, and an infant car seat.

"Just don't open them," Jackie told her. "Keep the receipts and then return them after Jenna's delivery. We don't want her to run away nine months pregnant."

With a tired, wry smile on her face, Farzana added in her strong but comprehensible accent, "Jenna keep asking me unwrap baby furniture, but I tell her it's bad luck in my culture. Not until baby is born."

Poor Jenna, I thought. This was going to devastate her.

Jackie confirmed Farzana's revelation when she came for the home visit in May.

"Of course, I don't tell her everything. I can't trust her. If she knows we're going to detain her baby, she'll hit the road again. Let her focus on having a good birth, a safe birth. Her and her baby's safety are my primary concern."

As May 2006 was drawing to a close, our lives were syncing up to the imminent birth of Marianna's sister. Just like Farzana, across the county, we too were getting prepared, saving the receipts for the baby bottles, clothes, and diapers.

A grand bassinet, a loaner from our friends George and Jorge, was installed in the guestroom. It was a frilly thing with built-in lights for night-time feeding, cooing noises—the works. With Marianna in our lap, we spent the evenings watching the DCFS DVD with the instructions for how to take care of a newborn, which would be a new experience for us.

Everything being ready to receive our second child, we were waiting with excitement and trepidation for The Call—for Gaby.

Part 4
In the System

Babushka with Gaby, August 2006
© Lane Igoudin, 2006

Contradicting Liabilities

Gaby's birth in June 2006 and her subsequent legal detention and disposition created her own court case. But what happened to Marianna's?

After our removal from the courtroom at the July 11 hearing, during which we requested the de facto parent status over Marianna, her six-month reunification review with Jenna got postponed.

I heard it, actually, from Griggs, who ran into McPherson at the courthouse cafeteria.

"So no decision was made, one way or another?" I asked.

"Apparently, one of the parties contested the evidence presented in court, and a new, contested evidentiary hearing on FR has been scheduled for a month from now. My guess is the birthmother's attorney contested the county's request for the termination of family reunification."

I couldn't understand half of his legal jargon, but it sounded mildly reassuring. The case was continuing. We didn't achieve the de facto parent status we'd asked for, but at the end of the day, of every day, Marianna was still with us. As was Gaby. And I felt thankful just for that.

And there was something else. Not all was lost, I felt, when we got thrown out of the courtroom. Once I'd been inside of it, its walls no longer seemed so utterly impenetrable. Our de facto petition upset the shaky equilibrium in the case, highlighting both options for Marianna and Gaby's future: to be raised by two committed, loving adults who'd guarantee them a safe and stable upbringing or by a teen mom with a chain of foster homes behind her and equally bleak prospects ahead. The judge and the attorneys could no longer pretend the children had no one else to claim them after hundreds of pages with photographs of us feeding, walking, bathing, reading to, and playing with Marianna passed through their hands. We left the room, but our presence, plan B, would stay on as the parties continued to battle.

§

Some interesting news came from Habiba, Farzana's daughter, who, although not certified, nonetheless drove Jenna to the two-hour Saturday visits in Heritage Park. Her mother was working the weekends.

"Jenna told me that if she doesn't do what the judge ordered her to do, she's going to lose her older child, Marianna."

"What did the judge order?" I asked, keeping an eye on Jenna tickling Gaby's toes at a picnic table a few yards away.

"I don't know. Last week, my mother asked the social worker to move her out of our house, but they are begging her to let Jenna stay until they find another home." Habiba paused and added vaguely, "My mom made the call after Jenna did something . . . that involved the police."

She didn't elaborate.

§

Jackie Willis shared with me that at the next hearing, in August, Judge Hooke would review, and likely extend, Jenna's reunification services with Marianna for another six months. Jackie was giving credit for this new development benefitting Jenna to Janine McCloud, Jenna's attorney.

. While playing skillfully on the county's double responsibilities towards Jenna—for her care, and also for assisting her in reunifying with her children—Janine was questioning if the DCFS supported Jenna enough in her capacity as Marianna's mom in assisting with counseling, visit transportation, and so on.

"Anything new concerning the baby?" I asked, clenching inside.

"Well, as part of the June 22 court order, we're supposed to search for a new foster home—to place both Jenna and the baby together under the same roof."

"Yes, I remember. Are you looking?"

"Oh yes, I *am* looking. I've called a number of homes. The list I've prepared for the court is quite long. None of them will take a teen mom and a baby." Jackie paused. "That's not surprising; I know those homes."

Hold on a second. I turned the "I know those homes" phrase over in my head. Did Jackie mean that she'd only made calls to the homes she already knew wouldn't take both the mother and the baby? Was this a new DCFS strategy to sabotage the order to relinquish Gaby to Jenna?

"But I did find a new home for Jenna herself. Closer to her children and you guys. It'll sure make the judge happy. She's moving this weekend."

As the week progressed, however, Jenna disappeared from Farzana's home. Jackie issued a missing person's report and a search warrant. I couldn't imagine what might have moved Jenna to do something so reckless with her kids' court hearing just three weeks away.

Several days later, Jenna returned.

"She was spending time with some guy thinking she wouldn't have to go back," Jackie told me vaguely. "In any case, she's back, and like I told you, moving to a new home—close to you."

§

At home, whether because of testing limits with her nanny Gloria, tense visits with Jenna, or simply by being an almost two-year-old, Marianna's tantrums escalated. Her first response to just about anything we'd offer was an emphatic "no," but then she'd change her mind and get upset if she didn't get it.

"Would you like some watermelon, Marianna?"

"No!"

I put the watermelon away.

"Melon! Melon!" she'd yell, and start pounding on the table.

"Stop hitting the table and say 'please'," I'd say calmly.

"No!"

"Okay, then you don't want the melon. Go play."

Seeing the attitude wasn't getting her anywhere, Marianna would quiet down and eventually say "please" as if recalling how to behave properly.

With the visits now moved back to weekdays, our weekends opened up for fun things we could all do together. The first Saturday in August, we took the kids to a large powwow in Hawaiian Gardens. As the drums were beating and a procession of California tribes—Cahuilla, Maidu, Pima, Shoshone, and Tongva—was circling a grassy meadow, Gaby slept soundly, but Marianna was captivated.

"Wal-kin', wal-kin'," she was pointing at the dancers in colorful regalia.

The following weekend, George and Jorge invited us to their block party. The street was closed off to traffic. Tents were set up in front of modest homes, in which families—Black, Filipino, Latino, Samoan, white—congregated in lawn chairs while the communal potluck was being set in the middle of the street: fried chicken, lumpia, sticky rice cakes, enchiladas, hot dogs, and rows of sodas. The DJ mix in the background leaned heavily on classic West Coast rap, Tupac, Snoop, and Coolio.

While Marianna, Jack—George and Jorge's son, and other kids were jumping and belly flopping in a red and blue bouncer inflated in front of George and Jorge's house, Gaby curled up in her favorite spot: on Jon's chest, her ear over his heart.

A Father Regained

After a two-week hiatus, the visits with Jenna restarted at yet another location, a foster agency this time. Two hours before the visit, Jackie caught me in the middle of a class. She reminded me of the visits' new location, and:

"Before I forget, the baby's father is coming too. His name is Tony Girona, let me give you his cell number. Tony wants to see the baby, and his aunt said she's interested in helping him. So yep, the baby now has the father. Strictly speaking, we treat Tony as an alleged father until we get his DNA results, but the court's dependency investigator gave him an okay to start coming to the visits."

She hung up. It took me a few seconds to gather my bearings. Gaby's father? Aunt? Visits? When the classroom came back into focus, I saw the worried faces of my students trying to understand why I stood frozen in the middle of a sentence.

§

That memorable meeting took place in front of Vernon, me, and Maya, the host agency's social worker. Later I logged in the details:

Jenna spent most of her visit time with Gaby or standing around talking. She tried to breastfeed Gaby under a baby towel.
Tony enjoyed seeing Gaby and holding her.
He also played with Marianna, drawing pictures for her with crayons, and so on. Jenna interacted minimally with her. She asked Marianna for a hug and a kiss, to which the child replied "No". Marianna enjoyed the agency's toys, which she liked so much she didn't want to leave. I intervened only once when Marianna, unsupervised, picked up a small plastic object off the floor and put it in her mouth. I told her to take it out, which she did.

What I left out was how my heart dropped when I saw Tony for the first time. Even though Gaby was barely two months old, the resemblance was unmistakable; I needed no DNA test to see that.

Tony was attractive, I noted as someone who appreciates the beauty of men. Slim, tanned, and well-proportioned, he was likely Latino and something else—maybe Black, Moroccan, or Sephardic—with his curly dark hair, low hairline, and obsidian eyes that resembled Gaby's.

Tony clearly lacked child-rearing skills. When Gaby began to cry in his arms, he looked confused, lost, and immediately asked Jenna for help. Yet he seemed intelligent and confident, simply more mature, being nine years older than her. He *could* learn to take care of the baby, to become a proper parent.

How normal he looked in comparison with Jenna, who was prancing about agitated.

"C'mon, Tony! Let's take a picture of you, me, and my girls, my princess number one," she pointed at Marianna playing solo on the floor eight feet away, "and my princess number two," the finger stretched toward Gaby crying in Tony's arms.

"Oh, hey," she asked me, "can you take a picture of our family?"

I was ready to oblige, but Marianna disrupted Jenna's plan. When Jenna picked her up to seat her in her lap, Marianna screamed and had to be let down. The group photo didn't happen.

Jenna and Tony left their joint visit together hand in hand. Someone crossing the agency's parking lot on this sultry

August afternoon might have taken them for a young couple out on a date. The girl looked pretty, giggling and clinging to him. The guy stood erect with a touch of bravado. I heard some talk about going to the movies later. Then Jenna got into her foster home car, and Tony swaggered off to the bus stop.

§

I don't believe that finding love is a matter of destiny, your *bashert*, your pre-destined loved one. No one is meant for anyone. A man or a woman selects a mating partner from an array of lovers limited by a particular time and place. From what I was told, one year earlier, Jenna and Tony had met at a bus stop.

With Marianna in Señora Teresa's care, Jenna continued to live at Holy Names with the expectation that she'd bring Marianna back there at the end of her temporary foster placement. But Jenna became rude, oppositional, and finally the sisters had enough. The county had to pick her up from Holy Names and move her to a regular group home. There she had less supervision. Older, confident, and tough, Tony offered a winning ticket out of the system. What was there to lose?

Jenna seized the chance. She said yes to the guy at the bus stop and moved into his home—a converted garage of a sprawling stucco compound on a barrio street lined with sporadic trees, spiked fences, and rusty cars. That street would become familiar to me in the months to come. The house wasn't his, but clean enough, and his family, though not particularly liking Jenna, accepted her.

Is this where Gaby was conceived? I'll never know. What I do know is that Jenna was 15 at that time—Gaby's neonatology report dated the beginning of gestation at two weeks prior to Jenna's 16th birthday.

I am also aware of Section 261.5 (d) of California Penal Code, which defines such conception a criminal act: "Any person 21 years of age or older who engages in an act of unlawful sexual intercourse with a minor who is under 16 years of age is guilty of either a misdemeanor or a felony, and shall be punished by imprisonment in a county jail not exceeding one year, or by imprisonment in the state prison for two, three, or four years."

Assuming the 25-year-old Tony was Gaby's biological father, wouldn't the pending DNA test results warrant a prison sentence?

Babushka, Abuelita, Grandma

That August of 2006, three languages were being spoken in our house.

"*Ay, mamá, ¿que pasó, que pasó? ¿Que pasó-o?* (What happened?)" cooed Gloria, our nanny, while stretching a fresh diaper under Gaby and fastening it on the sides.

Gaby turned her head to the side and, scrunching up her face, sneezed twice.

"A-ha! Ouchies! Ouchies! *Estas mojada, niñita.* (You're wet, baby girl.)"

"*Mamas.*" In her normal voice, Gloria warned Marianna, who, crawling clumsily over the bed to the stuffed Nemo, barely missed Gaby's eye with her foot. "*Ten cuidado, mija, o lastimarás a tu hermanita con tus pies.* (Be careful, darling, or you'll hurt your baby sister with your feet.)"

Marianna ignored Gloria, and, reaching Nemo, tossed it across the bed.

"You don't want Nemo, no? Don't like your little fishy?" I asked.

"Fshh . . . fshh . . ." replied Marianna and shook her head.

"*Dile 'ho-la Abuelita,' mamas*," suggested Gloria, finishing

Gaby's diaper and handing her over to Babushka, my grandmother. "*Dile, Marianita, ver, dile 'ho-laaa' a tu papá, 'ho-laaa,'* (Say 'hello, Grandma, hello, Papa.)"

"*Ho-laaa,*" I echoed. "*Dime 'hola,' mija; Mariani-ta, ay, que bo-ni-ta,* (Say hello, Marianna; oh, how pretty you are)."

Marianna smiled at my lame attempt at rhyming in Spanish, but refused to *hablar conmigo* (talk to me).

Babushka, in her Cleopatra wig, dangling pearl earrings and loose, leopard-print silk robe, swept up Gaby into her embrace and carried her to the kitchen.

"*Kuklyonochek . . . kuklyonochek, skazhi 'agu, agu' a-gu, a-guu . . .* (Baby doll, baby doll, say ga-ga)."

Gaby didn't mind Babushka's cooing, though she wasn't rushing to join. Her eyes were fixed on Babushka's while her mittened hands were waving randomly like semaphores.

How tightly my grandmother held her great-granddaughter, Gaby's body small like a bunny's, with knees pulled up. How unlike the photo of my mother holding me as an infant—á la Raphael's *Sistine's Madonna*—at arm's length from her body, presenting me to the camera and giving me away.

"*Na-ash rebyonok, khoro-oshii rebyonok,* (Our child, good child), he-he," Grandma cackled. Since arriving from the Bay Area the night before, she'd taken to calling Gaby, this sleepy-eyed child with curly raven locks who looked nothing like her, "*nash rebyonok.*" At 84, over my objections, she came wanting to help.

Marianna stumbled into the kitchen.

"*Oy, smotri, Marianna prishla!* (Oh, look, Marianna's here!)" Grandma exclaimed. "*Idi syuda . . .* come to me," she self-translated in her thickly accented English.

Marianna came—to me. She grabbed my knee and observed the shimmering leopard mountain of my grandmother from a safe distance.

Later the same morning on the deck behind our house, Grandma, stooped, yet with her wig and earrings intact, was bouncing a beach ball back and forth with Marianna. They were both laughing, shouting at each other. Soon, though,

Grandma's palpitations rose. With her pacemaker unable to keep up with a boisterous toddler, she grabbed her chest and had to sit down to rest.

At the lunch table, Grandma—wigless now, her gray hair cropped close—and ever the retired psychiatrist with half a century of experience, was observing Marianna.

"Look, Sasha," she said, using my Russian nickname, "*Mariannochka* uses her left hand to pick up the spoon. Is she a lefty?"

"Probably."

"She's taking after me, then . . . yep, she holds her spoon very well, good grip."

Marianna scooped up the soggy noodle from the bowl, picked it off the spoon delicately with her fingers, and delivered it into her mouth.

§

After lunch, I heard Grandma in the backyard, chanting "*Mari-an-noch-ka! Mari-an-noch-ka!*" and clapping her hands. I picked up my video camera and went out onto the deck.

Clad in a lemon-colored bathing suit, Marianna was belly laughing and beating the water in her baby pool to the sound of Babushka's claps.

"Let's see the source of this *gevalt* (noise)," I said, panning the camera towards Babushka.

"Why me?" she said. "Here," she pointed at Gaby asleep on a baby blanket on the patio couch. "Film the baby; film your sleeping *kotik* (kitten). She's so loveable . . . or maybe yourself. Are *you* ever in your home movies? C'mon, get in, get in there."

"Fine," I said, handing the camera to Grandma. "All you have to do is—"

"Think I need your help to push the button? Go, go." She waved me off.

I stepped into Marianna's pool.

Watching the video all these years later, I see just how awful I looked. The drama over Marianna and Gaby had brought me down to about a hundred and forty pounds, a good thirty pounds below my normal weight. My collar bones, shoulders, and elbows jutted out like wire hangers on a six-foot frame; my eyes were gaunt, cheeks sunken. Yet in my skeletal shape, I was smiling and laughing as Marianna and I were splashing up the pool water onto each other.

"Her Majesty, Love"

"Please don't speak Russian in front of them. *Ya proshu tebya* (I'm begging you)."

"Okay."

"No, Babushka, you have to promise me. I don't want them to know anything about us."

"Okay, Sasha, okay! I promise. Why are you so tense?"

We were crossing the parking lot to the foster agency in the hot, chalk-white August sun. I was carrying Gaby in her car seat; behind me, leaning on her cane, Grandma was leading Marianna with her free hand.

Jenna, Tony, and Maya were already there. I set down the car seat. Grandma nodded to them and let go of Marianna's hand.

§

Later on, back at the house, I was frying the onions and carrots on the stove for the dinner borscht. Babushka was peeling the beets, swearing under her breath every time the peeler ran sideways. Grandpa Isaac used to say, "*Tomochka* (Tammy), why do you have to swear like a sailor? You shouldn't, it's unbecoming of you. You're an intellectual!" And she'd always promise,

"I won't do it again, Izya," and inevitably let out another juicy profanity when the situation called for it.

"So what do you think?" I couldn't help asking the question.

Grandma moved on to the pile of potatoes.

"He is perfect for her, this Tony."

"What do you mean?"

"Your Jenna might have many problems, but she's not stupid when it comes to her future. Once they emancipate her at 18, where's she going to go? And here's a guy with a job and a home. Plus, she's got nothing, so the state will support her and her babies. And between his job and her benefits, she might get to stay home with the babies, be a housewife. Not a bad plan."

So simple, so obvious, and so demoralizing.

"I didn't think of it," I said, not letting my feelings show. "It sure explains a lot."

§

We arrived for the pickup just as Jenna and Tony were leaving the agency, Jenna carrying the car seat with Gaby; Maya, a center worker, followed behind with Marianna.

Tony and Maya were chatting behind the trunk of my car, and Jenna, bent over the back seat, was strapping in Gaby's car seat, when Marianna suddenly refused to get into the car.

"C'mon, Marianna, it's time to go home, c'mon sweetie . . ." I pleaded with her.

"Uh-uh," she said resolutely, and swerved her head to underline her point.

"*Mariannochka*, we shall play ball together when we go home," Grandma suggested in English from the passenger seat.

Marianna leaned away from the car and looked stubbornly at the ground. I was trying to get her in, gently but firmly. Marianna was refusing, wiggling out of my hands. What on earth had gotten into her?

"*Tebe nuzhno yey* . . ." Grandma piped up with an untimely, "You should."

"Shut the fuck up!" The words escaped my mouth before I could stop them. Had I not asked her not to speak Russian in front of them?

Tony and Maya's conversation outside ceased. The two of them and Jenna were watching me. Jenna would make a fuss. I was going to pay for this.

Marianna got in the car.

§

At home, talking about the visit somehow turned into a rehash of the details of both children's cases.

"Did you tell the kids' attorney that . . . ?" asked Grandma.

"Of course I did."

"But how about . . ."

"We've gone over this too."

"Then how can they . . . ?"

"Simply because the law says so."

"You must've overlooked something."

"Are you telling me this is *my* fault?" I snapped again. "That there's something I can do that I haven't done? That I'm not doing enough? That I don't know what the hell I'm doing? Did you come all this way to criticize me?"

"Poor boy, you are a cluster of nerves!"

I apologized. I meant none of it. Quite the opposite; I was so happy to see her, ill and aged, flying in just to spend time with us. There was no reason to get her involved. What could she do, anyway?

The ensuing silence cooled the tension.

The phone rang.

"Lane," Suzanne was calling from the agency, "Jenna just called, upset. She said you were rude and frustrated at the visit. That you yelled at Marianna."

I explained to her what happened, though not without some degree of resentment. Who were they in this process—a helper, or yet another layer of oversight? Why didn't she and her agency—our supposed advocates, the agency cashing fat county checks for these children every month—monitor the visit to make sure it went smoothly?

§

Grandma and I put the kids down for a nap and sat down to go over the draft of her article advocating for gay marriage. Citing scientific research, historical examples, and her own fifty-year psychiatric practice in Moscow, this full-page spread in the Bay Area's Russian weekly was sure to rattle a deeply homophobic community. Undeterred and unwaveringly supportive of our family, Grandma was not afraid to speak her mind, even if it would cost her friendships. Her article concluded with "People's homosexual or heterosexual marriage choices depend on HER MAJESTY, LOVE [sic], which includes an infinite and very subtle variety of personal relationships."

Babushka's *chutzpah* aroused my admiration. Not for the first time—three years prior, at age 81, she'd hired a tutor to teach her to use a computer and Microsoft Word. Then she had high-speed Internet installed in her senior home apartment. Now she was editing her newspaper articles on the computer and emailing back and forth with her editors.

My sister, stopping by after work, popped her head into the door. We went down to the kitchen, where I'd already set everything up. With Jon, Natalie, Grandma, and the two kids perched in high chairs, our precious little world, our sacred circle, was complete. Natalie lit the candles, and we recited the Shabbat blessings. The chicken and the garnet-colored borscht turned out delicious, paired perfectly with dry Riesling. I was finally relaxing.

After dinner, Natalie and Grandma sang Russian songs, competing jokingly over who remembered the lyrics better. Marianna clapped along.

§

At the airport, we had a full hour before her departure.

"You amaze me, both of you, how you two grown-up, manly guys, are taking care of these babies," Grandma said with a perceptive smile. "It's not just the diaper changes, but all these tiny little details, like you're trying to anticipate every need. I don't know if I ever watched your papa as much when he was little. Still, look at him, he turned out just fine."

She fell silent and looked out into space, squinting her left eye. It seemed she had something to get off her chest.

"Anti-depressants," she finally said. "That's what you need, Sasha. Something to steady your mood."

Good advice, actually. I hadn't yet thought of meds.

"Have you heard of Paxil? I can have it shipped from Russia, you know. Won't cost you a thing. We can talk about the dosage."

"Let me think about it," I said to her, "but thanks."

I knew just then how much I was going to miss her and that there was no telling if we'd ever see each other again.

"I love you, Babushka." I smiled, and we hugged our goodbyes.

One Child at a Time

Jenna was absent at the August 14 hearing. This wasn't exactly her fault. Jackie had overlooked arranging Jenna's transportation. At the last minute, Jackie made a dash across the county to drive her to court in person, but it was too late. Judge Hooke postponed the case review until mid-September, effectively extending Jenna's reunification with Marianna by another month.

Meanwhile, we decided to abandon the appeal of our de facto petition denial. Consulting with the lawyers, I discovered that to appeal in this system, you had to be either really destitute or really wealthy—that is, either eligible for free counsel, or ready to foot the bill starting at $60,000, which we didn't have.

"Take out a second mortgage on your house," advised Griggs.

More important though was the timing. By the time the appellate court decision would come down—7-9 months later—Marianna's return to or permanent removal from Jenna would have been decided. What good would the de facto status over Marianna do us then?

§

Lying awake, my body contouring to Jon's body, my arm resting along the ledge of his long, muscular thigh, I was staring at the Pacific night outside. It was as dim and quiet as it could possibly get in our never-stopping, never-dark metropolis.

I was thinking of another quiet, but unsettling scene earlier that day.

I had come out on the deck. Marianna, straddling Jon's stomach, was brushing Jon's tight jet curls with her pale hand, pretending to be putting something on his head; her eyes, slightly slanted, looking into his, brown and almond-shaped.

"Daddy okay?" she asked.

"Okay."

She patted his hair.

"All gone," she said.

"What is all gone, Marianna?" asked Jon, putting aside the Sunday newspaper.

"All gone," she answered simply.

"You know what it is?" I asked Jon.

"No idea," he responded.

Marianna turned her head and looked at me, baring an incomplete row of teeth. "Pa-pa. Hello Pa-ppy, hello Pa-ppy."

"Hello."

"Hi Pa-ppy . . ." She frowned. "Baby cah-een."

That was true, or almost true; Gaby, sprawled on the blanket next to me, was cooing, replicating our sounds, or possibly calling for attention.

Having a baby sister was teaching Marianna empathy, thawing her inside. She'd bring us a bib or a diaper when Gaby needed it or pick up a finished formula bottle and thump to the sink to throw it in. Getting out of the car, Marianna would first ask, "Baby tita, baby tita?" How could I ensure they'd stay together? I felt I owed it to Marianna, even more so than to us.

A clear realization formed in my mind: I'll have to work through this process one child at a time. I can't allow myself to be torn between the uncertainty of Jenna's claim to Marianna,

Jenna's claim to Gaby, and now a competing claim from Gaby's father. I will never succeed running in all directions at once. To survive this process, I'll have to focus on the outcome for one child at a time. Right now, it has to be Marianna. Her situation is much more pressing; the resolution of her reunification more immediate. I will do all I can for Gaby but worry about her future later.

§

Gloria, the kids' daytime nanny, quit because of worsening diabetes. I spent the entire week searching for a daycare center within a drivable range. Few, I discovered, took in children under one. But we lucked out: Playtime Learning, Marianna's daycare earlier in the year, had two spots open.

A note about the economics of it all. Jason, my friend in Montreal, quoted the weekly rate at their son's "fabulous" Jewish Community Center daycare center at $35 per week. "Cost isn't such an issue," he wrote, "since this is part of the provincial daycare program. Seven dollars a day includes all meals, activities, everything, and it runs from eight to five."

That's nice. Ours was $200 per child, per week—considered reasonable for LA in 2006—and we had two children. Our foster payments did not come anywhere close to match that.

We had to choose between a nanny and a daycare because we couldn't afford both. We settled on a daycare, mainly because of Marianna. She clearly needed other kids to play with and improve her social skills.

Working full time and with no family to help us, we really had no choice. Yet the first morning back at Playtime Learning, I felt ashamed leaving Gaby there. How would she do there without us, handled by strangers? Were we letting her down? Jon felt even worse; he cried picking her up.

Our fears were unfounded. The Playtime Learning staff couldn't have been more warm or experienced. They picked up babies and hugged them to their bosoms. They also kept them on a strict schedule and gave us daily log sheets, recording each feeding and diaper change.

Gaby took easily to the infant room and was soon enjoying her new social experience. Perched in high chairs around the dining table, on the floor mats, or in adjacent cribs, babies chirped and gesticulated to one another.

Marianna was blossoming back among the kids. Tired after a day filled with games and activities, she'd come home hungry and ready to turn in early.

§

I left Cal Poly right before the start of the fall semester. My resignation email sent to faculty and staff across campus explained that I would be restarting my academic career, leaving the world of PR and communications behind to teach college-level English as a Second Language and linguistics. A flood of congratulatory emails followed, validating the change.

That fall, I was teaching twenty units of community college ESL courses—English basics at Coastline Community College, grammar at Cypress College, and advanced writing and reading at Long Beach City College—more than the teaching load of a full-time professor. Two more colleges offered me classes, but I had to decline. Three mornings and four nights was enough.

This schedule allowed me the flexibility necessary to fit in court-ordered visits with Jenna and Tony, which could only take place when the social workers and Jenna's group home staff were available—that is Monday through Thursday, 9-4. Meanwhile, it was Jon's income—that of a vice president of a large insurance brokerage—that kept our family budget afloat, making it possible to live in a relatively safe, urban neighborhood and afford a well-run, though by no means luxurious, Playtime Learning daycare.

But teaching English as a Second Language wasn't just a new job, I felt I could finally do something meaningful not only at home with the kids, but at work as well. I could help immigrants like myself succeed in this vastly rewarding society, advocate for them, see the seeds of my own immigrant experience flower into their successes.

"I am loving it!" I wrote back to Jason, an English professor himself. "I feel like I can breathe again, doing what I love."

Second Birthday

The Santa Ana Zoo was broiling hot. Setting up the birthday tables in a shaded picnic grove were about thirty of us—a rainbow coalition of families including straight, gay, and single-parented, with kids of many descents and backgrounds.

Waiting to board the toddler train, Marianna—in a pink and white striped sleeveless dress, her pageboy clipped by Natalie into two pigtails—was trying to climb the fence separating the old-fashioned train platform from the tracks.

"Just wait a couple of minutes, sweetie."

"Choo-choo." She waved at the brightly colored cars departing before her eyes. "Bye, bye . . ."

Natalie handed Gaby, who was writhing in her arms, over to Jon. "She's getting fussy. Don't know what's wrong with her."

Ninety-five degrees Fahrenheit and the din was my guess.

Gaby calmed down in the comfort of Jon's chest. From there, she'd pop up like a chick in the nest for a quick look around and then duck back.

The train car was just right for toddlers, but my knees rose like mountain peaks above the side walls. Gaby looked content curled up in Jon's arms as his hand lightly held up her head.

"She's going for a ride," said Jon, and his voice modulated up from the husky baritone. "Here we go on a choo-choo … going on a choo-choo … I brought her hat," Jon added in a regular voice, his hand smoothing out the sweaty locks on the back of her head.

"Yeah, yeah, choo-choo …" Marianna picked up from Jon in her bright voice. "Choo-choo go bye-bye."

"Choo-choo go bye-bye," "Daddy okay," "Baby crying." This was the beginning of sentence-making, of syntax, I noted, as she sat next to me, swaying breathlessly left and right, taking in the pigs, goats, and rabbits as the train chug-chug-chugged past their huts.

"Marianna's birthday went off very well," I wrote afterwards to Marsha Madison, a good friend at Cal Poly, remembering the toddler train, elephant rides, lunch, cake, balloons, and gifts. "No matter what happens, we're glad she had a decent birthday party."

§

At Marianna's case hearing, the case review got postponed again. I couldn't find out why. No one would tell me. The week after the hearing, though, Jenna got moved again. I recalled the summer court order, "Placed to be closer to the children,"—not so much anymore, with Jenna about 40 miles away from our house. This new group home, her 6th since the previous fall, was essentially a lock-down orphanage, and it wasn't unfamiliar to her: she'd reportedly entered the foster system there five years earlier, at age 12.

The orphanage didn't allow visits for the first 30 days, giving all of us a reprieve.

Meanwhile, Jackie informed us that Tony's DNA test confirmed his paternity.

"We're planning on transferring Gaby to her father as soon as the disposition decision comes down," she said.

"And when is that?" I asked, holding my breath.

"At the next hearing, October 26, the same day as her sister's."

"Are you telling me the court wants to separate them?"

"They are not full sisters, Lane." Jackie phrased it patiently, as if explaining it to a stubborn child. "To the court, the father's right as the birth parent supersedes Marianna's claim to her half-sibling."

Like a claim to a car.

As if Marianna hadn't been abandoned before.

As if her "baby tita" wasn't growing up in front of her eyes.

Was the court concerned about what this would do to her?

And we, the "substitute care providers," were nowhere in this equation. The baby would be removed from us, the devastated sister left with us. Or maybe not.

I didn't recount this conversation to Jon. As much as it hurt me, it would've broken his heart even more.

It wasn't only Jon I had to prepare for the sad news, I realized, but our friends and relatives as well, those who stood by us and helped us when they could. I had to get them ready for the prospect of us losing a child, the tragic finale.

§

After our first visits the previous fall, Jenna and I almost never spoke directly to each other. She kept her distance, and I respected it. Our communication took place through her driver, Vernon, or any other adult intermediary present.

At the last visit before the court, I broke that rule. Arriving at the agency, I let Marianna run ahead with Maya to the playroom. Handing over the car seat with Gaby to Jenna, I casually let it drop what I knew:

"Not sure if you know this, Jenna. The test results proved that Tony really *is* your baby's father. From what I understand, the county now wants the baby to go to him."

That's all I said. Jenna made no reply, but I saw it in her eyes, which for once were looking straight into mine. She'd heard me.

Notice of Withdrawal

In the month I hadn't seen him, Tony had undergone a make-over: shaved head, baggy white T-shirt and charcoal shorts, high socks. In his neighborhood, it could've been gang attire or simply a standard outfit for a young man.

He was taking the car seat with Gaby out of my car when a woman around 50, with a light-brown complexion and curly hair, ran out front, yelling, "She's here! She's here!"

Tony, beaming with pride, turned to show her the child. "So what do you think, Mom?"

"Oh my God, she's so cute! Isn't she beautiful?"

Another woman, tall, attractive, not much older than Tony, luscious curves accentuated by tight clothes, came up to the car as well. She said hello to me, and took a sideways look at the child.

"That's my aunt Sandra," he said.

With the car seat in his arm, Tony bolted up the steps of the large stucco house to, I assumed, his grandmother, who hadn't left her chair on the porch. The old woman looked down at Gaby, said something I couldn't hear, and reached down into the car seat to pick up the child.

"Thank you so much for taking care of our baby!" Tony's mother enthusiastically embraced me. "Such a cutie! And you guys have been feeding her so well."

I was stunned and plain flattered by this rush of praise. I was used to Jenna and Tony taking Gaby's clean clothes and healthy appearance for granted. Tony's mother, seeing me for the first time, genuinely appreciated our raising her grandbaby. That was a first.

I left with mixed feelings. Tony's relatives were by no means wealthy, but they seemed normal. Tony was inexperienced but eager to be a parent, and with these three women surrounding him, he could take care of Gaby.

"At least there's a family, a safety net—his relatives, his house, his job—to support her," I told Jon at home. "We've been her only parents, her only real family so far, but she'll develop new attachments. It will come to her, 'the call of the blood,' as Babushka would say. This is a very different scenario than sending her to Jenna."

I was trying to be pragmatic in the face of the coming defeat. If the court decided to take Gaby away from us, whenever it would come to pass, I just hoped they would move on quickly so we could move on too.

"You'll go through a period of grief if you lose her, and then you'll be back here looking for the next one," Suzanne commented matter-of-factly, hearing of Gaby's developments. Right, no biggie.

§

"Hey, are you Lane?" A boyish-looking young woman in baggy khaki shorts greeted me in Tony's driveway at the next visit.

"Yes."

"Viv." She gave me a robust handshake while Tony picked up Gaby and kissed the child on the forehead.

Tony smiled at me, pressing his cheek against Gaby's. "We're buds. We used to hang out a lot, we go way back." There was a change in his tone—friendly, sweet even, not just transactionally polite.

"Tony's been telling me you and your husband are taking care of his baby," said Viv, pulling out a cigarette.

I could see through it. Tony sent his lesbian friend, ostensibly a member of my tribe, to charm me. We could all be friends, we could be *buds*. He probably expected me to stay on and chat with Viv while he was spending time with Gaby.

He was laying it on a bit too thick. Someone clearly told him to be nice to me—I could make trouble. I didn't trust him.

"Well, great to meet you, Viv." I turned to get back in the car. "Tony, enjoy your visit. I'll be back when you're done."

§

And so it had to come to this.

"Let it be known that on this 24th day of October, 2006, I, Lane Igoudin, give Playtime Learning Children Center and Preschool two weeks' notice of withdrawal of my daughter Gabriella from the program. My child's last day will be November 4, 2006."

The "Notice of Withdrawal" ended with "Thank you, and best wishes towards your child's future!"—a topical mismatch between the sender and the recipient of the form.

We were losing Gaby. Jackie had called to confirm that, as she'd told me earlier, Judge Hooke was going to order the release of the child to Tony at the upcoming hearing in two days.

"Start getting ready, Lane, notify her daycare," she said. "Things are going to start moving quickly now."

"But is she moving into a safe place? We know so little about him. What's his history? And who is going to take care of Gaby once she moves in? Doesn't he work? His relatives don't seem all that excited about taking her in."

"I know he's not perfect, but he *is* her father. And trust me, Tony's family is behind him all the way. They've got his back."

"I'm trying to beat the rush hour," Jackie had said when she delivered the baby to us five months earlier. This was the aftermath and the end.

As if this wasn't enough, Jackie added, "But you'll get to keep Marianna."

"I'm sorry?" I thought I'd misheard.

"We asked Tony if he would take both girls, but he said no."

I was so shocked that for once, I fell speechless.

To move Marianna—to Tony? Who was he to her? To rip her away from us, from our family, from our home in which she found love and stability after all she'd been through in her short life?

Jackie had no time for my silence. Dozens of other cases on her desk demanded attention.

"I'll check in with you after the court," she promised before hanging up.

§

Trying to absorb the news, I recalled a story Babushka had told me. When her baby daughter, her only child besides my father, died at six months of dysentery, her first thought was not of sorrow. Grandma wondered how to break the news to my grandfather, how to handle it in a way that wouldn't estrange him, that would—in the aftermath of her death—keep their relationship intact, their family together.

I, too, had to protect Jon as much as possible. I didn't see how he could function—get up in the morning, go to work, take care of Marianna, of himself—waiting for the baby growing up like a flower blooming on his chest to be taken away.

The daycare withdrawal form will remain a secret for now, I decided. *I'll tell him nothing until we get the official court order.*

I handed the notice to Estela, the Playtime Learning director. She already knew why Gaby was leaving.

Estela didn't ask me if I was okay. She didn't convey empty wishes like "Let's hope, things will work out for your little Gaby," to bring our uncomfortable transaction to a smooth end. She just looked at me like she understood what I was going through, and that was enough.

I recognized that look—an eagle-like stare from under dark brows on a chiseled, mestiza face—the hardened, unyielding look of a woman who'd seen much in her life.

I stared back. No, it wasn't over. I wasn't giving up.

Premature Reunification

What was at stake? Everything.

We knew firsthand about the potential dangers of these so-called "premature reunifications"—when children are returned, or in Gaby's case, placed for the first time, with the biological parents who are often incapable of providing a safe home. Look at what happened to Sarah Chavez, a two-year-old whom our friends Corri Planck and Dianne Hardy-Garcia were fostering to adopt.

First, the police found a dead baby girl in the toilet at the home of Sarah's mother. When they checked on Sarah, the older daughter living with her maternal aunt and uncle nearby, the DCFS worker noted "unexplained injuries"—black eyes, cuts on the nose, scratches all over her face.

Sarah was removed from her relatives and placed with Corri and Dianne, where this boisterous, curious two-year-old thrived. DCFS noted Sarah's improvements in potty-training and speech, and her general contentment in the loving home of these two women, whose lives now fully centered on hers.

According to the report in *InLA Magazine*, the Children's Court judge—a proponent of family reunification, just like

Judge Hooke—had his mind set on sending Sarah back to her mother, while Sarah's court-appointed attorney barely took part in the court proceedings.

The judge ignored the worries of the DCFS social worker over Sarah's safety. Saying she was "tired of excuses for why this child hasn't been released," the judge liberalized visitations for Sarah's mother. Shortly after, despite the objections from DCFS, the judge ordered the release of Sarah back to her relatives.

The break-up was sudden. After about four months with Sarah, the stunned Corri and Dianne were given one hour to pack up the child they thought they'd be able to adopt.

"Sarah was devastated," and was shoving the clothes her parents were putting into a duffle bag back into her dresser, they told the reporter. "We had to . . . try to explain to a two-year-old what was about to happen, even though it was incomprehensible to us."

After Sarah's return to her aunt and uncle, Sarah's mother stopped visiting her. DCFS replaced the social worker who'd removed Sarah from her relatives with another one, who checked the apartment and found it to be "clean, safe, sanitary, and in good repair."

In early October 2005, the time when Jon and I were taking Marianna out to the playground near Señora Teresa's home, Sarah was brought to an emergency room nearby with a broken arm and other suspicious injuries. When the hospital staff suggested tests, Sarah's aunt took her home "with Sarah's arm in a splint but otherwise untreated," the magazine wrote. The hospital didn't alert the police or DCFS.

By the next morning, Sarah was dead. The preliminary autopsy report showed that the two-year-died of a blunt force trauma to her abdomen and "suffered multiple injuries before her death." Sarah's upper arm was disconnected from the rest of her arm, a finger broken, lungs bruised, and even her liver perforated. The subsequent DCFS report to the court stated that "Sarah had been physically abused on an ongoing basis and possibly sexually abused."

Two pounds of marijuana were found in the apartment, an illegal substance back then which, according to Sarah's aunt, they needed to make a living.

"Sarah was let down time after time by the social service, legal, and medical systems that should have protected her," Corri wrote in an email delivering the chilling news. "The numerous ways she was failed are maddening and sickening . . . . We think you will understand our profound grief and rage at her senseless and preventable death."

Back then, Sarah's story distressed me and aroused my empathy for our friends. But now that I'd given the notice at childcare and we were about to send Gaby into the great and dangerous unknown, I knew in my bones how Corri and Dianne must have felt the day Sarah's attorney came to take her away. I'd learned the difference between the graceful, surface grief you feel for someone else's loss and the searing, all-consuming rage of a parent about to lose their child.

§

Sarah's story would have been swept under the rug like so many other breakdowns of the system had it not been for Corri and Dianne, longtime activists, who managed to get Sarah's story out to the media and eventually force the Los Angeles County Board of Supervisors to launch a public investigation of the case.

And yet a month after Sarah's death, "the partly decomposed body of an infant boy, Mikeal Wahhab, was found on the bed of an empty room in a cheap Monterey Park motel," reported the *Los Angeles Times*. "He died of a head injury."

The same article put the number of children who died from abuse or neglect under the DCFS watch in just one year at 32. Those included a two-year-old girl who died of starvation, another two-year-old killed by a stranger with whom his mother left him, and a 6-month-old baby suffocated by a sock his mother shoved in his mouth.

Was Gaby going to be next? How much did we really know about her birthfather and his family? Would we hear about her on the evening news, see her broken limbs poking through the worn-out public safety net? Going from our home—to that?

Tony's Troubles

At the October 26 hearing, Gaby's case swerved 180 degrees. As I learned from Jackie, DCFS finally did something it was supposed to have done a long time ago: it filed a so-called "sex with minor" petition against Tony. Because of the filing, or in conjunction with that, the judge was deferring sending Gaby to Tony.

I hurried to Playtime Learning to retract the withdrawal notice and only then told Jon about it. He first got angry, just as I'd expected, but later relaxed, realizing that the disaster had been avoided, at least for the time being.

Marianna's case was also reviewed and . . . postponed again.

"I was so hoping that this hearing would be Marianna's last," said Jackie. "My report provided plenty of evidence that Jenna cannot reunify, and that it's futile to expect it in the future."

DCFS also assigned us an adoption social worker, Yun Hee Park, to facilitate the concurrent process—a good sign, albeit still very hypothetical.

Jackie added, "I also mentioned to the judge Jenna's verbal wish to allow adoption."

That I knew. Tony—Tony, of all people!—told me at his last visit, "Hey Lane, you know that Jenna is putting Marianna up for adoption? She'll be yours." He gave me a complicitous look.

Jon, at home, was just as optimistic, saying we were nearing the end, which made me feel like an old-world Jew, which I suppose I am. Nothing is ever simple or final; there's always plenty to worry about.

In court, Jenna changed her mind about letting us adopt Marianna. And Judge Hooke ignored Jackie's report on Jenna's reunification and reiterated her order that DCFS make sure Jenna continued to get two visits per week with *both* children.

"The judge, at least," Jackie said, "dropped the charge that we didn't provide Jenna with 'reasonable reunification services.' That charge led the July hearing into the August and September trial. Jenna can't claim that we didn't help her anymore. God knows, we've done so much for her. We've gone," she sighed, "above and beyond."

Thus, the hearing expected to end family reunification for Marianna and release the baby to her father accomplished neither.

Is there a glimmer of hope that the kids will stay with us? I wondered. Or just another continuation of the permanent impermanence?

§

"'She was 19. That's what she said!' Tony told the judge," Jackie told me, chuckling, after the first sex with minor hearing, "but she didn't seem too sympathetic. Even if Tony can talk his way out of the last year's situation, he clearly sought relations with Jenna two months ago when they had joint visits with the baby. Didn't he see her being brought in by her foster family? *Foster* family, Tony? Someone needs to do the math."

And now, Jackie continued, Tony wanted to marry Jenna. "'Are you serious?' I asked him, and he said, 'Yes, ma'am, she is the mother of my child.'"

How abruptly things change in Children's Court. The week before, we had been expecting Gaby to be going to her father. A week later, we wondered if he'd be going to prison. "*Der mentsch tracht, un' Gott lacht* (Man plans, and God laughs)," I recalled a Yiddish proverb.

"Your Jenna is facing a dilemma," commented my wise Babushka when I relayed the conversation to her later.

"*My* Jenna?"

"Yeah, *your* Jenna. Like it or not, she's part of your family now. She's given you your children. In any case, she'll have to make a choice—testify against him or withdraw the charges and save her potential provider from prison. Didn't I tell you she was going to dangle this child in front of him, so they could be together once she turned 18?"

"Don't say it, Grandma. You make it sound like it might happen."

"Of course it might! But only if she can get her act together. Otherwise, he is going to prison, and she'll be alone again."

§

Judge Hooke ordered DCFS to split up Tony and Jenna's visitation schedule so as to avoid the overlap allowing for interpersonal contact. In the meantime, she was going to re-view the sex with minor matter and decide if it merited the DA's review.

The separation of visits affected us too. Gaby now had three visits per week—two with Jenna and one at Tony's home. With his work, he no longer had time, he complained to the court, to take the bus to Maya's agency. I was now required to deliver Gaby to his doorstep, with his aunt as the newly designated visit monitor.

Tony's troubles were deepening beyond the rape charge itself. The court ordered Jackie to take a written statement from Jenna about the alleged abuse she'd suffered from him during those runaway months in 2005.

The court also ordered Jackie to investigate the number of people living in Tony's home and his Aunt Sandra's plans for childcare. That aunt again—why the aunt, why not Tony himself, his mother, or his grandmother Donna, whom I'd seen now a few times on the porch of the house—her house, as I would gather?

§

I was pulling into the driveway of Tony's home for his first visit after the court when I saw him approach the car—alone.

"Where's Sandra, your aunt?"

"In the bathroom," he said testily.

"And your mom or grandma?"

"Not here, obviously!"

"I see."

I handed the car seat with Gaby over. Tony picked it up and took it inside.

I drove off a few blocks and called Jackie, who, miraculously, answered.

"Hi Jackie, I'm here at the visit. Brought the baby, but there is no sign of his aunt Sandra, who is supposed to monitor the visit. He might be alone with the baby."

The pause was pregnant with meaning. Despite the judge's order, Sandra had only been present at one of the seven visits so far, the very first one. Jackie knew that.

"All right, just to make sure. Go back and check if she's just running late."

I did as she said, keeping the phone on.

The driveway was empty.

"Nope, not here."

"Where's the baby?"

"In the house."

"Hold on, don't hang up. Let me call this aunt."

I waited.

"Lane, you still there? I got Sandra on the phone; she's out shopping at the Del Amo Mall. It'll take her at least a half hour to get home. So, tell Tony that the visit is canceled and you're taking the baby home."

"You tell him, Jackie. I don't want to be caught in between."

"Okay, put him on, but I only have a few minutes."

With the phone in my hand, I walked cautiously up the stairs to the front door and waved to Tony. He stepped out. I handed him my phone.

Waiting, I repositioned myself behind my car. I could see Tony clearly through the screen door with the light inside, a soap opera on TV, Gaby down in the car seat by the couch, unstrapped. Tony was pacing back and forth, talking agitatedly into the cell phone, slicing the air with his free hand. Oh my Lord, he was crying! So volatile, swaggering one minute, then crying the next.

What is he going to do now? I wondered. *Pull a gun on me, the cause of his visit cancellation?* Call it overreacting, but between his criminal record, this high-crime neighborhood, and his increasingly erratic behavior, I was glad I had the car between us. *I'll have to wait here, with my car as a shield, and see what he does next, call the police if needs be. Wait, I can't—he's got my phone!*

"How did we end up here?" Jon had asked me at that memorable team decision meeting. Now I was asking myself exactly the same question.

And then, the epiphany. It's my idiotic Jewish progressivism that put me into this situation, delivered me straight to the crossroads of other people's messes. Heal the world, *tikkun*-freaking-*olam*! My beliefs have led me on a quest to give a home to parentless children. Had I cared less, or chosen surrogacy, I wouldn't be hiding now behind a car in the barrio.

Tony moved into the darker reaches of the house, where I couldn't see him anymore. I was still waiting. In a minute, he tensely brought out the car seat and my phone. He kissed Gaby, who had slept through all this, on the forehead. I said nothing; neither did he.

§

Apparently, Jackie Willis wasn't the only one interested in Sandra.

"How is Tony's aunt?" asked Margaret McPherson on the phone, in her controlled, crystalline voice.

"Sandra? Only met her once."

"Interesting…that's what I heard too…" She didn't elaborate. "I know you wanted to know what's happening with the kids' cases. Well, the judge continued them both to after the New Year.

With the baby, everything is now on hold because of the statutory rape petition. The petition, however, reset the clock on Tony's reunification period."

"I'm confused, Ms. McPherson. Tony is getting extra time to reunify?"

"That's right. His reunification cannot be reviewed until the rape charges against him are sustained or cleared, and who knows how long that will take. How can we plan Gabriella's future if her father's own is so uncertain? Clearly, he can't provide a home for her if he's in prison. So, his reunification has been restarted to . . ." the sound of shuffling papers, "to October 26."

That was a new six-month purgatory. At first glance, it seemed better than losing Gaby outright. But then I thought of her, five months old now, starting to babble and sit up with support, I felt a profound, overwhelming sadness wash over me. She was going to spend six more months with us and her sister, and then the loss would hurt us all even more deeply. And what would happen to her after that? Would she at least be safe?

"Now, Marianna . . ." McPherson went on. "At the last hearing, we were able to set the stage for a procedural compromise with Jenna's lawyer, making it easy for her to withdraw her request for the continuation of reunification with Marianna and not contest it. Let's see what happens."

That part of the conversation left me mildly optimistic about Marianna, yet up until that point, nothing had gone according to anyone's plan. If anything, the only constant was that plans would change.

The Wedding

"Why do you run around so much?" my mother asked from the living room couch, while watching CNN with her husband, Mark, and Inna, her cousin from the Midwest, in town for the wedding.

"We barely have time to get everyone ready, Mom. The wedding reception is in just a couple of hours—"

"Well, *I* am ready," she said, not taking her eyes off the flickering screen.

Staying at our house for several days, she had yet to lift a finger to help. I had literally been waiting on the three of them at each meal, running their errands, and driving them around on sightseeing trips. Gaby would be deposited in the playpen or someone's arms; Marianna relegated to the status of a free-roaming pet.

So yes indeed, I *was* dashing around the house with a large canvas tote, tossing in diapers, hair clips, a sweater, a camera, the card, the gift, and meanwhile checking on Gaby in the crib. Gloria, Gaby's former nanny and her babysitter that day, was still on her way. In the kitchen, Jon was ironing our white shirts and Marianna's dress. I still needed to get Marianna bathed, combed, and dressed, and then get myself ready.

There was a growing coldness between my mother and me. A comment she made the night before still stung. I asked her if she was comfortable in the guest room on the ground floor.

She responded, "You think it's so easy for me to stay here, knowing what's going on up above my head?"

Directly above her guest room was our bedroom.

I said nothing. Later I wondered if I was too gracious a host, or simply a coward.

We made it just in time to the Wayfarers' Chapel in Palos Verdes, an airy glass and wood sanctuary perched high above the Pacific. My sister dazzled in the dress she and I had picked out together: thin yet curvy, her face professionally made-up, hair up in a perfect French twist, and not a single strand out of place.

My soon-to-be brother-in-law, Devlon, looked dashing too in his well-fitted tux, tall, nervous, and happy. The sun was high and bright, reflected in the ocean's azure beyond the cliff—a splendid day.

"Your daughter is so beautiful!" gushed Devlon's mother as we were lining up in rows for the family photo in the rose garden. Marianna, in a burgundy velvet dress with puffed sleeves and a pearly chiffon skirt down to her white shoes, ran up to the front to stand by her aunt and uncle.

In the chapel, set in a redwood grove, glass walls running to the treetops, I led Natalie to the altar. Natalie's father, who divorced my mother a decade earlier, wasn't attending. To me, leading her down the aisle was a great, well-deserved honor. After all, I'd always been more like a second father to her than an older brother. So with intense happiness, I kissed Natalie on the forehead and gave her away to Devlon, who was gazing at her with true devotion.

We were late to the wedding reception. Somewhere along the way, Marianna peed copiously, and her diaper content overflowed into her leggings. The dress, miraculously, was still dry.

I rushed with her to the hall's old-fashioned men's restroom. There were no extra clothes in the bag, but luckily, I dug up a pair of Gaby's lacy white socks left over from a visit. Throwing my tie over the shoulder, I spread a large plastic bag, another great find, on the tiled floor, removed her diaper and tossed it along with the sopping onesie, undies, and leggings into the trashcan. I cleaned her sticky legs with baby wipes and stretched Gaby's socks over her feet. When we joined the party ten minutes later, Marianna looked perfect again.

My mother rose to deliver a toast to the newlyweds. In halting but grammatically impeccable English, she congratulated them on their union, which, to her, "symbolized the beginning of a great friendship between Russia and America, after the decades of the Cold War."

"*Smeshno* (ridiculous)!" Inna berated her back at the table. "Are you out of your mind? You should've said something nice about the newlyweds. Who the hell cares about 'Russia and America!'"

"What I said was appropriate for the occasion," my mother replied tersely. "You think *you* know better? With *your* education?"

"What you said was perfect," her husband Mark attempted to placate her.

It was no use. My mother and Inna broke into an argument, the loud exchange in a foreign tongue attracting the attention of the other tables. I considered intervening, but opted for another cosmo.

Devlon and Natalie, now husband and wife, were making the rounds among the tables, thanking the guests. My sister looked happy. To me, that was all that mattered.

Another Messy Christmas

Christmas markets were sprouting at busy intersections—bunches of emerald-green Douglas firs clustered beneath date palms. At home, we were wrapping presents for Gaby and Marianna, sliding them under Jon's own festive Christmas tree. We also dropped a hundred holiday cards in the mail.

Those 2006 cards were quite special. James Gooding, a British photographer (and Kylie Minogue's boyfriend) came to do a session at our home as part of his gay family series scheduled for the Paris Photo show at the Carrousel du Louvre. I was familiar with the Carrousel, an underground shopping and exhibition space near the museum, from my grad school days in Paris ten years earlier.

In Gooding's photo, Marianna in a red-and-yellow sleeveless dress is perched high up in Jon's arms. She is like a giant juicy strawberry, the golden light of sunset deepening the colors of her dress,

"Very lush, very Southern California," Jon said, reviewing the proof.

Gaby is absent from the shot. With all the uncertainty, we figured, why let her image hurt us all year long?

§

My first semester of full-time teaching was rolling to its end, bringing along a mass of work: writing and grading new exams, computing the course grades, and so on. I was eagerly awaiting the week of rest between Christmas and New Year's.

Fat chance. Holidays only meant more visits, more, and more visits! Responding to Tony's and Jenna's requests, Judge Hooke granted each birth parent an extra holiday visit with Gaby. This translated into five visits to accommodate during the holidays: hers December 24, his December 26, hers December 28, his December 30, and his again January 1.

"I'd rather work," I told Jon. "That way, my time and my mind will be occupied with something other than the court and the visits."

During the visit on Christmas Eve, our friend Kevin had invited us to the Christmas celebration put on by his UP (Understanding Principles for Better Living) Church. There, at the Bel Age hotel on Sunset Boulevard, the joyous atmosphere and the festive, multicultural audience, into which we immediately blended, reminded me strongly of Glide Memorial Church, which Jon and I had gone to in our San Francisco days. And just like Glide's Reverend Taylor, UP's founder, actress Della Reese, attired in royal red, exuded confidence at the pulpit, her booming voice backed by a full gospel band and choir.

I glanced at Jon; he was enjoying the upbeat service, clapping along with Marianna in his lap, grinning broadly. How happy I felt to have instantly said yes to the invitation. Jon would usually say that after his mother's strict Pentecostal upbringing, he didn't "do churches," but in the right setting, religion seemed to affirm who he was, where he came from.

The word had gotten out about a gay couple with two kids—still a novelty, even in this progressive congregation. A few people came over to greet us, to welcome us, and to ask questions.

Gaby slept through most of the service, first in her car seat, then on Jon's chest. When the music got too loud, she woke up whimpering, and I took her out to the lobby.

Wearing the same suits, Jon's charcoal grey, mine off-white, we traveled 30 miles east, from the opulent hotel to Heritage Park. Since our previous round of visits, summer had turned to winter, which meant occasional rain. The rose garden at the park's entrance—a common summertime wedding site—was pruned back and bloomless.

Jenna, beaming proudly, pulled out of the van a leaf-and-lawn trash bag with the Christmas gifts she'd assembled from the holiday donations to the orphanage.

I thanked her. She gave me a nod and hugged and kissed Gaby and Marianna.

Tony, to whom I took Gaby two days later, had no presents for her.

§

A new year promises a new beginning. Maybe that's why I felt a bit more hopeful, noting the random signs of change all around us.

George and Jorge finalized Jack's adoption from the LA County foster system, less than a year after his placement.

New Jersey legalized civil unions, following the lead of Vermont and Connecticut, while full same-sex marriage was surviving in Massachusetts.

Democrats had just swept the House and the Senate in the midterm elections. So much excitement was in the air; many expected the Iraq morass to end soon.

One other encouraging bit of news came from the Conservative movement of Judaism, the one I identified with. That December 2006, it approved the ordination of gay and lesbian rabbis and performing commitment ceremonies for same-sex couples. I welcomed the news, as it was finally putting my faith in sync with my identity.

And, as I learned from the Internet, the court of appeals had just overruled Judge Hooke in another parental case. The appellate panel threw out her ruling and remanded it to another judge with some choice words about Hooke's judgment.

I wondered if 2007 would be the year when the four of us will finally become a permanent, forever family—rather than a maybe family?

Roses and Courts

A few days after the New Year's ball dropped, I dropped our own big news into a mass email to friends and relatives.

On Tuesday, LA Children's Court ended Marianna's reunification with her birthmother. While this is by no means the end, it is a major breakthrough in our 16-month saga.

In foster care since seven months of age, Marianna is now almost 2.5. The incredibly lenient judge gave her mother chance after chance to reunify, extending the original six-month reunification period five times.

The mother's parental rights will not be terminated until May, as by law she has four months to appeal the decision. Our adoption proceedings can start only after that. In the meantime, we enjoy watching Marianna grow and change in so many ways. She is a superbright, talkative, beautiful toddler with a voracious appetite for life who has given us so much joy.

Congratulations poured in from friends and relatives around the country and as far as Australia, Israel, and Martinique.

Even my mother acknowledged the news on the phone with one terse sentence, "Well, good for you, if that's what you want."

Jon was in shock. But I, at some level, already knew it. I was just too afraid to believe.

Jenna gave it away at the visit two days after the court session. When she stepped out of the car, she acted just a tad more subdued than usual. My heart was beating hard right into Marianna's, who was sitting up in my arms. Jenna was just inches away. Mounting Gaby's car seat on the stroller, she wasn't looking at Marianna; she was averting her eyes. Why, I wondered?

When I returned to pick up the kids, Jenna muttered to her, "Look, Marianna. Daddy's here."

An odd choice of words, I noted. She'd never called me Marianna's "Daddy."

We walked back to the parking lot in silence, Marianna in the front, gripping my hand, Jenna pushing Gaby's stroller ten feet behind, her group home counselor bringing up the rear. The procession was leaving Heritage Park, past its quaint adobes, sentimental rose bushes, and the curved-back European benches, as dried up golden leaves, whipped up by chilly gusts, were showering down on us from the winter trees. I couldn't put my finger on it, but I felt a profound sense of change washing over us.

Roses—they were my second clue. An hour before Jackie's message came in, I was parking my car near the college. That day was even colder and windier than the one at Heritage Park; the sky was getting overcast, puddles of rainwater gathering in the parking lot.

The path to the steel-blue college building was lined with copious, blooming roses. Often, the larger ones had no scent. I made a wish: if the first rose smelled had an aroma, the court had turned in our favor.

I bent down to a grapefruit-sized pink-and-white rose and closed my eyes; a strong aroma hit my nostrils: apples, cinnamon, a touch of lemon. An aroma of hope.

Later in the classroom, when my mind drifted to the court-room twenty miles away, I'd think of the rose and hold on to that deliriously sweet smell.

This might have been irrational, but in those days, I often found myself crossing into the mystical dimension—prayer, meditative visions, Tarot readings. Denied real power over the events affecting our family, I searched, and I found, pieces of truth hidden in the world unseen. I learned to rely on intuition and transcendent signs, and hoped they'd guide me in the right direction. That wasn't new, of course. Jews, for one, empowered themselves with the Kabbalah, a mystical system of the universe, during the Middle Ages—the time they were most powerless, most vulnerable.

The court decision transformed the very vision of our family—like Dorothy and her friends in the Land of Oz—Jon, Marianna, and I, arms linked, had stepped into a new frame: same look, same clothes, yet the backdrop has changed, sorrowful violins replaced by jubilant horns. We were the same parents to Marianna as before, but now potentially legal, potentially forever. From that point on, it was going to be so much harder for anyone to wrestle her away from us.

This joyful vision only had three of us, for what was going to happen to Gaby even the cards wouldn't reveal.

Part 5

Home in the
Shadow of the Court

Gaby, Jon, Marianna, and Lane, August 2007
© Lane Igoudin, 2007

A Black-and-White Sunset

In the early spring of 2007, Jenna and I became allies.

"She's made a lot of progress in her therapy," Jackie explained. "She says she's letting go of both kids, not just Marianna, because she wants to keep them together."

More news came at Heritage Park.

"Starting with the next visit, I'll have a different driver, Morgan." Jenna told Vernon and me. "She is the counselor at the emancipation cottage. You know why?" At this, she threw up her hands and exclaimed, "Because I'm finally emancipating! I'm going to have my own freaking apartment, yeah! They're finally letting me go!"

"Congratulations!" I smiled. "Good for you."

"How soon are you moving out?" Vernon asked.

"Oh, it's not right away," Jenna replied. "First, I need to graduate."

So for now, Jenna was still going to be at the orphanage. And then what? Poor girl, she looked so hopeful, but what was waiting for her out there?

Margaret McPherson, who agreed to update me on the latest news from the court, said Gaby's case was still in limbo. Until the statutory rape issue got resolved, the court wouldn't touch Gaby's custody. That, she said, might take months.

Tony missed the January hearing—sick, according to his lawyer. At the March court date, Jenna testified about being locked up in Tony's home—something, I recalled, she'd told me at the beginning, at our second visit. DCFS, eager to send Gaby to Tony and close the case, wasn't all too pleased with her testimony going on record. In the end, Judge Hooke continued the trial through April.

But just so we wouldn't get our hopes up, McPherson ended her update with:

"Lane, I'd like to remind you that the court is in the middle of the trial, and regardless of the outcome, the father will still have the right to reunify with the baby. I want you to remember that."

Of course, I knew it. I didn't need to be reminded.

Gaby was now ten months old, but no one would reassure us of a positive outcome. Not a glimmer of hope cut this deep into the bowels of the system.

"Do what you can, and enjoy your time with her" was the best we'd get, and that came from our supportive Babushka. The boosterism we enjoyed at the beginning of our journey had gradually evaporated in the face of persistent, turbulent uncertainty.

§

Marianna's official termination of parental rights (TPR) was set for May 8, but Jenna continued to see Marianna as if their reunification were still underway.

"I find it sad," I wrote to McPherson, "that at the time when TPR is imminent, these visits seem to prolong and deepen the ambiguous connection between Marianna and her mother, and the resulting trauma."

I could see the trauma at play: Marianna would now act out after the visits, getting unruly and oppositional, refusing to be strapped into the car seat, screaming, and punching the back of my seat with her feet while I was driving.

Probably under pressure from McPherson, the judge reduced Marianna's visits to every other week, while still keeping Gaby's on the weekly schedule. But even on the days when Marianna saw her mother, Jenna kept her at the far end of the picnic table, interacting with her minimally, while cuddling her sister in her bosom. Marianna didn't want to be there, and would run to me the moment she saw me in the parking lot.

Why was Jenna so cold to her? It might have been her way of slowly letting go, or of readying herself for a permanent goodbye. Whatever the reason, the visits were distressing to Marianna, so why did they have to go on at all? Was I the only one who saw how fulfilling Jenna's wishes came at the expense of Marianna's long-term well-being?

Still I agreed because I felt I'd rather see it all end in a couple of months than fight over the visitation schedule. If this was an easier way for Jenna to let go, we just had to go along with it.

§

One Saturday night, the kids left with Natalie, Jon and I drove to Avenue 50 Studio, an art gallery in Highland Park, Marianna's old neighborhood. At the gallery show, we ran into Roberto Gutierrez, an artist we knew. I decided to buy his new painting: a sunset over Mount Washington, visible from the gallery, painted in black, white, and gray, denying LA its essential colors. It echoed my mood.

Afterwards, we stopped for a drink at Akbar, a gay bar nearby. We ordered cocktails, shot the breeze with the guys our age, mid-thirties to forties, friendly, wide-eyed and captivated by our kid-raising adventures.

The second drink spread the glow, melting the trouble. Relaxed now, I sensed the electric glances scanning my body in the dim atmosphere of the bar, returning an instant verdict, an unequivocal confirmation that I still looked good, that I was still wanted. I stretched my arms overhead—my body felt so comfortable, so tight. If I were single, I knew I wouldn't be leaving that bar alone. Look at all these opportunities, these handsome Eastside guys, oh my—all the fun I could still have.

I tried to step into the picture of this other Lane, the free, unencumbered, uninhibited Lane, and I went blank as if I'd suddenly lost my name or address.

Who would I be, I wondered, without caring for these two children?

Who would I be if I weren't a father?

Without these kids and Jon, who was I?

Meditating with my Zen group the following week, out of the cloud of anxiety and uncertainty hovering inside my head emerged a clear realization: my world revolved not around the kids, or their birth parents or social workers—no, at the center of it was Jon and me. That was the nucleus from which our family had sprouted. Without him in my life, and mine in his, there was nothing.

We've found each other.

We've built a home.

We've brought in the kids and shared our love, our strength and security with them.

We've done our best to care for and fight for them.

We'll make it through this rough patch, no matter the outcome, and still be together. But to get there, with the man I love, I'll have to do all I can to preserve our family.

The Poo Tales

Marianna was taking a bath after a messy playdate in Tommy's backyard.

"Tummy hurt," she complained, rubbing her belly.

"Why don't you sit on the potty? Maybe your tummy wants to go poo-poo." I suggested.

She loved doing it—sitting on the potty while watching potty training videos.

Marianna agreed, and I picked her out of the bath and positioned her, soap and water dripping on the floor, on the toilet.

She wasn't rushing.

"Una like choo-choo train. Choo-choo train," she illustrated, rotating her bent arms like train wheels, *Una*, of course, being her. "Tommy time out."

I sensed a connection between Tommy's train and his timeout.

"Did Tommy get time out because he didn't give you the choo-choo?"

"Tommy no give choo-choo Una. No-no-no."

"So Inga gave Tommy time-out?"

"Inga," Marianna made an angry face, "'Time-out! Tommy no give toys, Tommy—'", she paused and looked up at me joyfully, "Una pee-peed toilet! Una pee-peed toilet!"

"Good, good, but does your tummy still hurt?"

She nodded repeatedly, frowning, and opened her arms, wanting to get off the toilet.

I shook my head, and crouching on the step stool in front of her, cheered her on holding her hands. She started to go, which made her whimper, but once it was all done, she opened up her legs wide and, seeing the result, erupted, "Una poo-pooed toilet right there!"

I applauded, called Jon, who rushed in to join the celebration.

Marianna got up, ready to leave. I wiped her behind, and she ceremoniously flushed the contents. She was so happy, and so was I. A milestone passed.

There were other changes, too. One night, I was reading her a goodnight book illustrated with cutouts when she suddenly ripped out one of the cutout pictures.

"That wasn't good, Marianna. You don't want to destroy books," I said firmly, closing the book. "That's enough for tonight."

She usually stonewalled my negative remarks or shifted the blame for the wrongdoing to her baby doll. This time, however, her eyes swelled up with tears, face turned long, lips pouting. I was taken aback: suddenly she looked and acted like a real toddler.

I drew her to me. "Ooh, it's okay, honey! We'll glue it back together tomorrow."

§

Several weeks later, in San Diego, Jon was pulling a spacious moss-green double-stroller, like a royal carriage into a restaurant. Here we met several of my colleagues, who, like me, were in town for the ESL faculty conference. They all loved the girls. Mothers and grandmothers themselves, they prodded us with questions about the kids' routines and the court cases. Over dinner, my department chair discussed her insurance troubles with Jon. Like the baby shower at Jon's work, this too, I noted, was a step toward our family recognition, not only by close friends and family but also by co-workers.

The last day in San Diego, leaving Jon and Gaby at the hotel, I took Marianna to Legoland. There she gaped, wide-eyed at the boxy, pixilated characters, all Lego blocks, of course, popping up from the shadows during a cave ride.

The top of her pink-hued diaper sticking up from her jeans, Marianna jumped up and down with excitement at the sight of tiny plastic people walking the steep, hilly streets of San Francisco, a dear, dear city, where Jon and I had met, its Pier 39, Chinatown, the Lego-built gables of the "Victorian ladies" of Alamo Square, level with her, a two and a half-year-old.

Then came "Pappy I poo-poo!"

One men's bathroom after another, it was urinals and narrow stalls only, no place to change her. Apparently, in 2007, the idea that a *man* might have to change a child's diaper was yet to trickle down to theme parks. Finally, I spotted a sign for the *Model Mom Baby Care Center*, and marched right in. Bravely claiming one of the changing tables arranged in a semi-circle inside, I laid Marianna on it. Some women stared at me in wonder, as if I were about to breastfeed.

Inga described Jon as a nurturing mother, and me as the disciplinarian father. Natalie thought exactly the opposite. She said I was the protective, loving, worrying mother, much more than Jon with his stability, gravity, and a touch of distance.

But Jon would cry, and I wouldn't. I usually made decisions, but deferred to his opinion if he voiced it. Jon ran the laundry and cooked while I paid the bills and fixed things around the house, but then I also loved shopping for our girls' clothes and underwear, fretting that the patterns and colors would fit their looks and skin tone. How little those "mother" and "father" labels fit our roles in the relationship.

Partial Compliance

Was it April already? A whole month had swooshed right by. The March heatwave eased, followed by a week of heavy rain that turned LA into emerald tropics. Palm trees, jasmine, magnolias, and jacarandas were glistening in opulent, verdant green; the air was stiflingly humid.

Our friendly alliance with Jenna fell apart. Two months earlier, she was letting Gaby, along with Marianna, go up for adoption. At the April hearing, however, she notified the court she'd changed her mind and asked for Gaby's return.

At Gaby's April court hearing, Judge Hooke finally conducted the six-month family reunification review, and found Jenna and Tony to be in "partial compliance"—an ambiguous statement, both promising and frightful in its inconclusiveness. Gaby's birth parents seemed to be making progress, but not enough.

Siding with McPherson, who gave me the update, Hooke specifically rejected the DCFS opinion that Tony was ready to assume parental responsibilities. Tony hadn't visited his child in a month. He didn't even come to the hearing. Moreover, the judge apparently upheld at least some of Jenna's accusations against him because she ordered him drug rehab, drug testing, and training on domestic violence.

Whatever happened to the statutory rape, I wondered? Shouldn't the criminal proceedings be starting right about now? No word on that.

"Can I say something?" Jon said at dinnertime. This usually signaled a criticism or complaint coming. "Why do they keep continuing this case? Gaby is eleven months old. A newborn should be reunified in 6 months, or else—isn't that what the law says? How did six months turn into eleven, with no end in sight?"

"Ah, Jon, the law . . ." I shrugged, with that Old World Jewish weariness.

Jon, of course, had his own awareness of the unjust, unwritten laws, not only because his family fled the oppressive, bigoted South for California's Central Valley. In the years we'd been together, I learned much from him—the only Black employee in a large Orange County corporate insurance firm—about how grinding it is to always give 200 percent of your best to prove you are not the token hire; to overlook the surprised faces of the clients meeting him in person, who'd assumed his whiteness on the phone; to ignore the 'he-speaks-so-well' remarks.

Yet, maybe out of extreme caution, or sheer luck, Jon had never had to deal with the legal system; never had to battle it to set things right. For him, this was probably one of his biggest discoveries so far, a truly American discovery of the vast distance between law and reality.

"The intent of the law may be clear, but its application is quite subjective, and can be—shall I say, *stretched* through postponements, appeals, bargaining, information shared or withheld, and other forms of legal maneuvering. From what I've seen, Jon, there are some very real laws at play here, but not necessarily the ones in the books. One is that each party in the room has to protect its own interests first: DCFS doesn't want to be sued, the judge doesn't want her cases remanded, and so on.

Another is that relationships matter. No one is impartial. Personal biases, likes, and dislikes affect people's decision-making.

Those laws, strange to say, give us hope. Yes, Judge Hooke found Jenna and Tony to be in 'partial compliance'. But meanwhile, remember her mentioning our 'fabulous care' at that de facto hearing? She knows we've been good parents to these children. She knows that McPherson and the county favor us over their natural parents. *This* is our chance. We're not officially part of the case, but unofficially, we very much are. So don't lose your hope."

§

By early May, desert winds dried up the region and ignited a fire in Griffith Park near Los Angeles City College where I was teaching a writing course. Through our third-floor classroom windows, my students were nervously watching the tips of golden flames licking the tops of Hollywood Hills, threatening the Griffith Observatory and the LA Zoo. It was 97°F, windless, and the hot season was barely beginning.

Jackie left me a voicemail.

"Lane, I spoke with Tony. He can't visit his baby during the week. He's now working full-time, and with every visit, he misses a day of work. So we need to move his visits to the weekend. You could be his monitor, or if you don't want to, I can ask his aunt or another relative."

Trouble was heading our way. Having heard nothing from Tony for a while, we started to hope he'd go away for good. And now he was back, he wanted his visits, and he wanted our weekends. Tony's previous cancellations and reschedulings, upending our weekends, were still fresh in my mind.

I put my foot down and left Jackie a voicemail refusing to do weekend visits without an impartial, professional monitor. This was the judge's order, and they needed to follow it to the tee.

There was more, though. Vernon filled me in.

"Jackie called me last week," he said. "She knows weekend visits in the past were a disaster. But she still wants to do it . . . she actually said . . . well, uh, you might not like it . . ."

"Just tell me, Vernon."

"She said 'we want these visits on the weekends because we're moving toward placing Gaby with Tony, so we need to start to liberalize his visits, let him keep her for a half-day without a monitor, then a day, and later the whole weekend.' That's the full plan."

At least, I knew the full extent now. But this "direction" seemed so at odds with what I'd heard from McPherson. How could DCFS suddenly liberalize Tony's visits when he wasn't visiting? How could they move Gaby in with him now if her case was due for another review in August?

The pain of possibly losing the baby, weakened in the last couple of months, flared up; the inescapable, unquenchable kind of pain. I felt desperate.

"What can we do, Vernon? What can be done?"

"I don't know, Lane. Truly, I don't. I told Jackie it'll be horrible for the child if that's where they're heading. I asked her to *liberalize me* out of his visits."

§

The following week, I was in court for Marianna's termination of parental rights, the first hearing to which we, after almost two years into the process, had been officially invited. Going in though, I knew it would be a waste of time: Jackie missed the deadline for "service by publication," i.e., the publishing of court summons for a missing parent, Marianna's birth father in this case. They'd have to continue the case to another date.

In the courtroom's twilight, I saw Jenna whispering to her lawyer.

Judge Hooke greeted me from her elevated bench with a friendly wink.

"We're well aware what wonderful parents you've been to Marianna," she said. "She's so lucky to be with you and your life partner, after all the turmoil of the first year of her life, and to have you soon, hopefully, as her legal parents."

I nodded and smiled and mouthed "Thank you," though what came to my mind was a different rhyming expression. Still, Hooke's words left me feeling gratified.

Jenna's progress was reviewed first. Judge Hooke, nodding with content, read from the DCFS report that Jenna had been clean and sober, and enrolled in a cosmetology school.

Jenna, whom I saw from the back, asked to dismiss her case, which, I assumed, meant to allow her to emancipate early. Hooke thought it important to continue as, apparently, remaining the ward of the court was supposed to help her move into transitional housing. She didn't expect Jenna to emancipate for at least another four months—until September, when she'd turn 18. After that, I learned, she could still stay on at her facility until turning 21.

Marianna's case was brought up next. The judge reprimanded the county counsel for failing to publish the summons for Marianna's birth father in time. Volleys of abbreviated legalese flew between them.

Hooke then addressed me, explaining that the termination of parental rights would have to be postponed until July 10.

I know, I nodded. Nevertheless, maybe to please us, she put it in the court order that "the court finds Jonathan Clark and Lane . . ." she stumbled trying to pronounce my last name, and after a few unsuccessful tries I spelled it for the stenographer from the bench, "as *prospective adoptive parents* of Marianna."

"Do you have objections to the termination?" she asked Jenna.

Jenna did not respond. Janine McCloud, her counsel, tried to dodge the question with "she needs more time."

Judge Hooke pointedly repeated the question again and again until Jenna, through McCloud, stated, "No, Your Honor. I don't."

"Don't worry about the delay," Hooke then said to me, "I'll see you in July."

I stayed at the courthouse. I couldn't miss a chance to speak with Margaret McPherson in person. When I saw her exiting the courtroom an hour later, erect in a crisp pant suit, gait perfect, high heels click-clacking down the hallway, I got up from my seat and crossed her path.

"Ms. McPherson. Sorry to bother you."

"Oh," she squinted, "I'm sorry, Lane, that we had to postpone your foster daughter's termination. It's unfortunate."

"It's fine, I know. What I really need to talk to you about is her baby sister."

"Her baby sister?" She looked surprised.

"Yes, Gaby, it's urgent."

"What's new?" She asked.

"Her father, Tony Girona, hasn't visited in six weeks."

"I'm not surprised," she said with a little snort. "He didn't come to the last court hearing either. It all shows a lack of interest in parenting his child."

"Well, DCFS wants to move his visits to the weekend and have me, or one of his relatives, monitor them. How can I monitor them? Who would take my word against Tony's about what goes on at the visits? Everyone knows we want to adopt Gaby. And Tony's relatives? They're all on his side."

McPherson paused and phrased her reply in a calibrated manner. "I feel that the social worker is doing it because she doesn't want to put in any extra effort. That said, the court ordered the visits to be monitored by a DCFS-appointed monitor, and that can be anyone the social worker chooses to appoint."

I took a breath.

"Can we refuse having these visits on the weekend?"

"I have to caution you, Lane. Gabriella is under reunification with her birth parents. As foster parents, you are expected to comply with the court orders, and that includes providing the opportunities for the birth parents to visit their children. However, I think that the best would be for your agency worker, Dr. Vernon Brezins, to work out with Tony a suitable time for his visits, and monitor them. I know Dr. Brezins very well, I have a lot of respect for him. Let me have a word with the DCFS counsel. I can't prevent DCFS from appointing you or Tony's family member a monitor again, but should it happen, I'll walk-on it in court and question why."

"But what about this 'moving toward placing the child' with him?"

"Nothing will change until the August review. But as I told you before, Tony is her legal father; he may still get his child."

"Does anyone realize what all this would do to Gaby? And to Marianna—losing her sister?"

"Lane, as I've told you before, we're trying to put families back together, children and parents, even if the parents are sometimes less than ideal.

"You know as well as I do," she added in that sparkling voice of hers, "that even if Tony gets the child, a year or two down the line, she'll end up right back here in the system, after a drug bust, domestic violence, abuse, or something else. When she's back, we'll give you a call."

In my outrage, I dropped—for once—the mask of civility: "Drug bust, abuse, Ms. McPherson? She is NOT going there! Not from our house. Not out of our arms that raised her and into *that*!"

The image of Sarah Chavez rose before me, an ominous shadow. This was going to happen to Gaby and us too: the system gambling with children's lives by sending them to dubious, potentially dangerous homes with no more than a hope for stability, though with quite certain cost-saving benefits for itself. What is one life damaged or, God forbid, extinguished when you've got tens of thousands to manage?

McPherson gave me a detached look of someone used to people getting emotional in her presence. In her eyes, I saw files, not children. Files. To McPherson, these living, breathing children growing up in our home were the abstract sum total of the files she received and reviewed, reports written by other people about the children she'd never seen.

"I have to get back to court, Lane," she said. "Have a nice day."

Baby Visiting the Father

One thing that never ceased to shock me in our foster-adoption process is the extraordinary disparity between the standards set for the natural vs. adoptive parents, intending to raise the same children.

"Check the boxes that best describe the personal characteristics of your mother/primary caretaker when you were a child: worrier . . . perfectionist . . . domineering . . . isolated . . . happy . . . violent . . . substance abuser . . . outgoing . . . aggressive . . . temperamental . . . rigid . . . overly critical . . . self-centered . . . unforgiving . . ." plus thirty-four more. And then do the same for 'father/primary caretaker'.

"Check the boxes that best describe the way your parent(s)/ primary caretaker(s) disciplined during your childhood: lectured . . . spanked . . . made idle threats . . . physically punished (other than spanking) . . . shamed . . . grounded . . . removed privileges . . . withheld food . . . used physical restraints (e.g., tied to bed) . . ." plus twelve more.

This was back in October 2004 when we were filling out a requisite part of our home study—the AD-4324, "California Department of Social Services Adoption Questionnaire."

"Check the boxes that best describe your parents'/primary caretakers' attitudes about sexuality when you were a child: old-fashioned . . . believed sex was sinful . . . sexually repressed . . . sexually irresponsible . . ." plus thirteen more.

But then it wanted to know more. "Have you ever experienced sexual abuse or attack?" If 'yes,'" the county asks to "please describe."

And more still: "Check the boxes that best describe your early sexual experiences: limited . . . traumatic . . . awkward . . . exciting . . . regretful . . . frightening . . . confusing . . . shameful . . ." plus eight more.

What is the county's vested interest in knowing all this, I wondered? All prospective foster parents are fingerprinted and LiveScanned, their complete criminal records made part of the home study—shouldn't that be enough? Would having a perfectionist mother, a drug abuser dad, or feeling confused about an early sexual experience disqualify one from being a capable parent?

On the other hand, how many biological parents are subjected to questions like these? How many sexually assaulted women have their fallopian tubes tied, how many men beaten or bullied as children, or in other ways "experienced neglect or abuse as a child" are forced to undergo vasectomy—to prevent *them* from becoming parents?

Jenna and the birth fathers of her children certainly weren't.

§

One week after the court hearing, Vernon rang me. Jackie asked him to schedule visits during the week, but near Tony's work, so it wouldn't affect his work schedule.

"The first one is tomorrow," Vernon said.

I suggested late afternoon at a public park accessible by bus from Tony's work.

Vernon agreed.

Late in the evening, during class, I got another phone call from Vernon.

"Lane, you're not going to like this."

This was becoming a punchline.

"What is it now?"

"Tony whined to Jackie that he can't take time from work and has no car to drive. Jackie caved in. From now on, she wants you to bring the child directly to his work, during his lunchtime."

"To his work?"

"There's a little park around the corner."

I blew up. DCFS was sparing Tony the least effort. It wasn't the father visiting the baby, but the baby visiting the father—at the father's convenience. Jackie had worked out a brilliant solution.

"There is something else. Jackie told me that the department wants to liberalize Tony's visits right after the August review, let him keep Gaby over the weekend. They expect the judge to continue the case in August and release the child to him by December, which is the 18-month benchmark."

In other words, I thought, we had six more months with Gaby, and then she'd be gone.

I went back to class, tried to resume the explanation of comparative and superlative forms of adjectives, to reactivate the flow of thought, but failed.

I took a couple of breaths, looking straight at the glossy white wall, like I was taught at San Francisco Zen Center years earlier. My focus grew diffused, but my mind began to clear up. Finally, I heard myself talking. The machine was running again.

The next morning, I dressed Gaby in a pink polka dot onesie, matching pants, soft shoes, and a light pink shirt with embroidered collar, and drove her to a large windowless warehouse near the port. There I saw Tony come out of the building's front door and get into Vernon's car, and I followed them down the block to a postage stamp-size park.

In the two months I hadn't seen him, Tony had shaved his head, grown wider.

He came over to my car and exclaimed, "She got so big!"

Gaby let out a wail the moment she saw him.

Smiling broadly, Tony picked up her car seat and the diaper bag I'd packed. He closed the car door, and I swerved a hundred and eight degrees out of the parking lot.

An hour later, returning for the pickup, I saw Vernon standing with the car seat, and Gaby crying in it. To my left, I caught a glimpse of Tony walking away unhurriedly, crossing the parking lot in the warehouse's direction.

I took Gaby out of the car seat and put her on my chest, rubbing her back clockwise. Her heaving sighs subsided like a retreating tide, and eventually she calmed down.

Vernon said Gaby cried through most of the visit. Tony tried to get her to stop, showering her with kisses and patting her on the head, but nothing helped.

"Lay off her for now, Tony," said the wise old Vernon. "Give her some space. Let her get used to you. Think of her needs, not of yours."

Tony told Vernon he'd done everything Judge Hooke had ordered, got a full-time job and his own apartment. His baby, and Jackie knew that, was coming to live with him.

To Vernon's surprise, Tony kept asking about Jenna, how she was, if she was talking about him. Vernon, of course, told him nothing.

"Tony wants to see Gaby twice a week," said Vernon, looking down his beard at Gaby looking glum in my arms.

"What did you say?"

"Absolutely not. The baby doesn't know him. You can't rush through it."

"He's going to complain to Jackie."

"That he will," Vernon agreed.

In the evening, in our half-hour overlap, I recounted the day's events to Jon, omitting the "liberalization plan." Even without it, the news made his blood boil. Unfortunately, I had no time to calm him down. I had an evening class to teach.

"I cried after I put her to bed," Jon said from the couch when I returned later that night.

I came over and sat down next to him. "I'm so sorry, dear. I know how much Gaby means to you."

We talked, and though our moods didn't lift, at least, we knew that neither of us was alone in this. We had each other.

Charges Dropped

Suzanne read to me what she learned from Jackie. "The petition was sustained, but no findings were made for the court." The statutory rape charges against Tony had been dropped.

I gasped. Of all the crazy things that happened, this was the one I truly didn't expect. Judge Hooke, hardly a friend of Tony's, had forwarded the case to the criminal court, but the consensual sex between a 15 and a 25-year-old was apparently very low on the LA County District Attorney priority list.

I wished I could talk to Jenna, to find out where she was in all this. Since 1994, conceiving a child by rape in California, including a lewd act with a minor of 14-15, or a statutory rape if the mother is 16-17, was considered an 'aggravated circumstance', which may disqualify the father from reunification services.[22]

I pushed the agency to squeeze more details out of Jackie. There was nothing. Bertha Moore, the DCFS counsel, was apparently "disappointed because she'd really wanted to put Tony in prison." That was the only new thing Suzanne learned.

Tony's lunch-hour visits continued with the regularity of a sledgehammer. For Gaby's birthday, he was granted two hours.

Both his and Jenna's extended visits were dutifully incorporated into my schedule, filling up the slots among the spring semester finals in the five courses I was teaching. And so I drove, drove, and drove.

I asked Suzanne to talk again to Jackie, tell her about the visits, try to convince her to change the location. If Tony actually had to *do* something, the "liberalization" would have to be delayed, and we could win some more time with Gaby.

They talked. Jackie agreed that those visits showed no effort on the father's behalf, but refused to make any changes. The agency was equally comfortable with the visits: they fit Vernon's schedule.

Margaret McPherson washed her hands of the visits as well. Her only concern was their proper monitoring. Where and how they occurred, she said, was "of no consequence."

Bertha Moore, the Flower Hat lady, the one who had "really wanted to put Tony in prison," told Vernon that making it difficult for the father to get to the visits would be "punitive." With that, the county effectively shut me up. I had nowhere else to turn.

§

Amidst all of this came Gaby's first birthday. The celebration was subdued, the beginning of a long goodbye. We invited few people. My mother was in town with Mark on her way to a resort in Desert Hot Springs. Inga mixed berry mimosas. Natalie brought fruit salad and the birthday cake. Devlon was barbecuing on the deck.

We spent most of the time outside in the gazebo. Gaby, in a flowery dress, her black curls neatly trimmed, looked pretty as a china doll, as calm and sweet as usual. She played cautiously with my mother and others, but only as long as she resided in Jon's lap, "*dah*" as she called him. I didn't have a word yet.

This short "*dah*" for "Daddy" differed from her "*dai*" with its upward diphthong ascent, illustrated by the hand pointing at an object. Her "*dai*" came, most likely, from the Spanish "*dame*," which means "give me," which Gaby heard frequently at her daycare.

The night before Gaby's birthday, Mom and I took a long walk with a double-stroller to fetch the kids from the daycare. From there, we pushed the precious charges back home, not unlike her and me pushing a pram with Natalie down the tree-lined streets in another quiet neighborhood twenty years earlier and half the world away. This was my mother's third time seeing Gaby. She was friendly, if not overly warm, with her granddaughters, and I appreciated her being there.

At a get-together at Natalie's house the next day, for once it all seemed normal: parents (Mom and Mark) visiting their married adult children, staying with them, and spending time with their grandkids.

We didn't talk about Gaby's situation until their last day, over breakfast. Mark, my warm-hearted stepfather, instantly went fuming:

"How can they do that? Giving a child to a criminal, ah! These social workers are a bunch of fascists!"

Mom agreed, in her own way.

"Of course, it's not right, but in other families, people also sometimes lose custody of their children, of their *own* children."

I noticed the odd turn of the phrase, emphasizing Gaby wasn't our own. Still, Mom was saddened at some level; this was the best she could do.

§

My summer break started, leaving me with a lot more time to myself, and depression spread over me like a black cloud. I kept myself busy, catching up on the bills, developing my work website, and yet I felt detached from my projects, from the people around me, and, most often, numb. My numbness would continue even when I'd take the kids to the playground, where I'd sit withdrawn, staring vacantly at them playing.

I felt like I was watching an oncoming train wreck, a calamity I couldn't stop. I kept turning the whole thing around in my head, growing ever more dismayed.

Which way to go? How could I get us out of this mess?

Deep inside, I was growing resolved to see Gaby go away.

Strange how one can do that. We do adapt to anything, don't we? Even the prospect of losing a child you've raised since birth.

Gaby was a warm, cuddly child, but something about her was concerning. Next to her sister, she clearly seemed much less motivated. When Gaby wanted an object, say a plush toy, and couldn't reach it, her strategy was to sit back on her feet, rocking back and forth, look at the adult, then at the toy, then back at the adult. If the adult didn't bring her the object, she'd simply stick her thumb in her mouth and let go of her plan.

At 13 months, she could neither stand independently, nor even crawl. Sometimes, she'd make an attempt at bunny-crawling, propelling herself forward with her arms and elbows, pulling her bent legs along, but not using them.

Nor did she chew. Chewing is an instinct, and obviously, it wasn't kicking in. All she knew how to do was swallow food; a cracker or a Cheerio would make her choke. We were trying out lumpy Gerber, mashed bananas, cream of wheat—the first steps towards solid food. Nothing worked. Sometimes Gaby would swallow her food; other times, spit it all out whole, her jaws and tongue disengaged from the process.

At times, a strange, oblique stare came into Gaby's eyes, and combined with her puffed-up eyelids and small head, Jon said at those moments, she reminded him of a child on the autism spectrum we'd visited during our child search.

Both a child psychologist who evaluated Gaby in March, and now our family physician, Dr. Irvin Goldfarb, who saw her at a regular visit, said that she needed to be assessed by a regional developmental center to see if she required special services.

Dr. Goldfarb wrote a letter to Jackie, asking for exactly that. I faxed his letter to Jackie, along with a list of my own concerns. Jackie did not reply. Several days later, I forwarded a copy to Yun Hee. As Marianna's adoption worker, she had nothing to do with Gaby, but she walked my letter over to Jackie's desk and got her to initiate a referral to the regional center.

Jackie told Vernon that Tony kept demanding the weekend-long visits promised to him by the county, and that she was certifying Tony's grandmother Donna to monitor them.

Vernon shared this information with McPherson. For some reason, she got fired up hearing about the potential certification of Tony's grandmother.

"Call me if it indeed happens," she told Vernon, "and I'll walk-on[23] it in court in ten minutes."

McPherson asked Bertha Moore, the DCFS counsel, to confirm these liberalized visits, who "nearly jumped and said she would set Jackie straight."

What's going on within DCFS, I wondered? Are Jackie's and the Hat Lady's agendas out of sync?

McPherson sent a message to me via Vernon that she continued to oppose Tony's reunification with Gaby, and that I needed to lie low while she was parleying with DCFS.

§

It wasn't just the lack of toys or books at Tony's visits.

"I'm buying her a stroller, the best, the real deal," he said when I told him that Gaby had outgrown her infant carseat, and he'd need something to put her into next time he'd see her.

At the next visit, Tony came striding in from the factory— without a stroller. He had nothing to put Gaby in. When he took her out of my car, she instantly started screaming. Vernon audibly sighed.

On my return, Vernon mentioned something curious.

"I'll be staying with my aunt for a while," Tony told him.

What about his apartment?

It was gone "because it was in a bad neighborhood."

That was interesting. The county didn't care about the quality of neighborhoods, as long as the home itself was safe. In fact, most of DCFS business came from "bad neighborhoods."

My grandma saw right through it. "No money," she said in English upon hearing the news.

Where *did* his money go? He had no car, paid no rent.

The news elevated my mood somewhat. Seedlings of hope— false hope, possibly—were sprouting through the cracks in Tony's defenses.

§

Much is written about the function of the mother in the traditional family: the caretaker, the lighter of the hearth. An acquaintance, a high-powered Beverly Hills realtor and a father of four, once told me bluntly, "I hand over the care for the children to my wife. I earn us a good living, but she's in charge of the house. That's *her* job."

If a child is hungry or dirty, the mother is to be blamed. If the child looks healthy, is doing well in school, the mother gets the credit.

The father's role in the family is much less certain. In the traditionalist view, the father sets an example to his son, interacts closely with him in the 'manly' activities. But what is the father's place in his daughter's upbringing? An adoring spoiler of "Daddy's little girl"? A prototype of a man to marry: loving, dependable, yet not involved directly? It seems vacuous. The father—provider and protector—is in the background, but what does he actually *do* to raise her?

"He has brought no toys, no books, not even a blanket to put the child on during his visits," I alerted Jackie. Yet was it fair to expect Tony, a normal, in so many respects, adult heterosexual male to anticipate his baby girl's needs? Was it, instead, I who was acting abnormally, fussing about her food, clothes, or cleanliness?

A friend of mine, Harold, found out at his father's funeral that his father was, in fact, his stepfather. He was then, at 37, introduced to his biological dad. Harold nearly went crazy with adoration of this newly resurrected "real father." He severed relations with his mother, who had hidden the dubious nature of his birth: an extramarital shag. Harold now referred to his deceased stepfather by his last name—never mind that the man had raised Harold no differently than his natural children. Now Harold had a "real father" across the country he could fly to, "real siblings" he had never known, "real family" whose newly discovered biological similarities he could cherish, and whose last name he then legally adopted.

That bothered me. Isn't there a statute of limitations on not taking responsibility for your child, after which the child itself ceases to be your extension? Does a drop of sperm sliding off a man's penis make him a father? Is that all?

Somehow in Western society, *paternity* has come to equal *fatherhood*. And it held true throughout our process as well: having recognized Tony as Gaby's progenitor, social services would go to great lengths to forge those two concepts into one, bootstrapping Tony into the parent who could be reunited with his child.

A Handful of Cheerios

Our lives went on. We were moving forward with the planned kitchen remodel, drafting, shopping, and interviewing potential contractors. I was also busy replanting the front yard and helping out my grandmother with her memoir. None of it gave me pleasure, but keeping busy filled up my time and headspace.

George and Jorge brought home their second child, Miranda. Their foster-to-adopt process, just like the one before with Jack, was moving fast. Miranda's two older siblings had already been adopted by another gay couple, PopLuck members as well. At the club's mid-summer meeting, I snapped a photo of all of them: Miranda, her two siblings, and their four dads.

At the meeting, when I picked up the soft, copper-haired baby Miranda, Marianna's face turned sour.

"Sweetie, I'm not the baby's Pappy," I explained to her. "She is Jack's baby sister. She is not coming home with us, okay?"

"But if twenty years from now, our Marianna marries your Jack," Jon remarked *sotto-voce* to Jorge, standing watch nearby. "Our grandkids will have four grandfathers."

Jorge grinned. "I call it a perfect match!"

Happy for my friends, I couldn't help feeling a pinch of jealousy about their relatively painless adoptions. The luck of the draw.

"So what do you think?" I asked Kim Dally.

Tall, tanned, and clad in shorts, the licensed occupational therapist was sent to us by the regional center looked more like a beach volleyball player, which she very well might have been.

"You were right to be concerned about Gabriella. Look—"

Kim placed several Cheerios in front of Gaby. The little girl slid them in her mouth one by one, her jaw shifting back-and-forth.

"No lateral movement, see? At this age, 14 months, she's behind in tongue mobility and rotary jaw movement which you need for chewing. We'll have to work on that. I also noticed some gross motor delays: she can lift herself up to standing, but she doesn't seem to know how to move sideways, nor to sit down. And then there's this. C'mon sweetie . . ."

Kim bent down. Gaby grabbed on to Kim's index fingers and took several uncertain steps.

"She is almost walking," Kim commented, "but her supported walk is wobbly. She mostly uses her right foot and sort of drags the left one along."

"Is she autistic?" I asked anxiously.

"I wouldn't say that. Her cognition and other mental functions test out okay."

That was good news. I sighed with relief, yet I wouldn't have loved her any less had she been developmentally disabled, and if we got to keep her, I'd have done all I could to support her.

§

Jackie called to schedule her monthly visit—*monthly*, yet her first in three months. I insisted that we meet at the daycare because our kitchen remodel was now in full swing. The last thing she needed to see was a twenty-foot trench cut through the center of the floor and three construction teams turning the kitchen into a Babylon of languages: a Cambodian crew rebuilding the floor and installing tiles; a Mexican crew working on the cabinets, and a Chinese crew installing new countertops.

With the kitchen out of use for weeks to come, Jon and I arranged for a temporary split: I would be first taking Marianna to see my family in the Bay Area, and then to a house we'd rented in Idyllwild, an alpine village two hours east of LA. Gaby was to remain home with Jon, sustained by formula and disposable Gerber food, she had no need for a working kitchen.

§

When I arrived at Playtime Learning, Jackie was in Marianna's group room, talking to Estela, the daycare director. Marianna rushed to hide behind me and wouldn't say much besides "my Pappy."

"Is she verbal?" asked Jackie.

"Verbal? You kidding? Marianna—" I turned around.

"What?"

"Be a nice girl, say hello to Ms. Jackie. She came to see you."

"Mm." For some reason, Marianna was acting fearful of Jackie and wouldn't say a word. What on Earth had gotten into her?

"Normally, she's a real talker, Jackie, believe me. She can string sentences of up to six words, she's just a little shy today."

I brought in Gaby from the dining nook and set her down on the floor. She immediately crawled toward Marianna, and they started to play, crawling in a circle, giggling, yelling.

Jackie's face grew long in surprise. "I've never seen the baby being so lively."

"It's because of Marianna. She loves being around her big sister."

"How are the visits with Tony going?"

I chose my words carefully. "To tell you the truth, not so well. He tries, but he doesn't seem to know much about parenting."

I provided her with details, which she already knew from Vernon's reports. Two daycare workers and Estela, standing within an earshot distance, were listening in.

Jackie brushed it all off. "He's doing his best. The good thing is he's been complying with the judge's orders, so it's just a matter of time before he gets his daughter."

"I have nothing against him, Jackie. I'm sure Tony means well, but these visits are very hard on Gaby. She is very agitated when he's around because she doesn't know him."

"I know. That's why we should increase their frequency to, at least, twice a week, and maybe more later. She needs to get to know her father and get used to him. They need to have more visits to develop the bond."

"It's not just about Tony," I again phrased it carefully, "I *am* concerned about the kind of environment Gaby might be moving into, and how this would affect her."

"I wouldn't worry too much about that. We've checked him out, him and his family. They're a family like any other."

I decided not to argue with her. There was no point. As Jackie was leaving, I gave her a recent photo of the four of us, together as a family. Maybe not "a family like any other," but a family, nonetheless. And I added a second photo—just of the kids, Marianna hugging her baby sister. To give Gaby to Tony, Jackie would have to rip the sisters, like that photograph, apart.

Hidden Photographs

"*Mariannochka* has grown quite a bit," Grandma pointed with her chin to Marianna doodling on the paper stacked by the printer. "But where is the baby? I was so hoping to see our *rebyonochek* (little child)."

Grandma looked frailer and thinner than last summer, leaning, like a windblown pine, to one side.

"Sorry, Babushka, I had to leave her at home because she might have a visit."

Babushka's Palo Alto apartment was furnished with simple but tasteful Danish furniture: bookshelves with hundreds of books, related newspaper clippings stuffed between covers, the obligatory display of crystal vases in the china cabinet, a Renoir reproduction on the wall. It was comfortable, welcoming, and a bit formal, doubling as an office. Grandma was still seeing clients, writing them prescriptions that their relatives would fill in Russia and mail back here.

The afternoon breeze was blowing through the lace curtains. The air in the Bay Area felt very different from SoCal: cooler, more humid; the trees at once greener and familiar. Palo Alto was, after all, my original home in California.

There is a Russian saying that the feast table prepared for the guests should lean under the weight of its offerings, and Babushka had indeed put out a feast to celebrate our visit: chopped liver, gefilte fish, and sautéed, garlicky eggplant. Yet Marianna refused to eat the Old-World delicacies.

This upset Grandma greatly. "I've been really trying, cooking the whole week . . . and *Mariannochka* wouldn't touch any of it."

"I'm so sorry. She's not used to this food. It's my fault; I should've told you."

"But what *does* she eat?"

After surveying the contents of the fridge and the pantry, we settled on the more familiar chicken, rice, tomatoes, and cucumbers.

Still, I was touched. Grandma, at 85 and barely walking, had gone out of her way to receive us.

Before putting Marianna to bed, we gave her a bath, changed her into her PJs, and walked her to bed, holding one hand each. There Grandma tucked her in and sang her a Russian lullaby. Lying on her side, Marianna started crying quietly: a strange song, a spooky room, an unfamiliar bed. Grandma couldn't hear it; she'd taken out her hearing aids.

I took over, humming a wordless lullaby, a melody of a Russian lullaby I grew up watching on TV since no one sang it to me, the same one I'd hum to her and Gaby every night. Hearing the familiar tune, Marianna calmed down and dozed off.

§

Heading up Highway 280 from Grandma's apartment in Palo Alto to see my mother in San Francisco brought so many memories of driving that highway daily. First to grad school, then to my job at Stanford News Service. The nightly rides home through the fog, thick and fuzzy like a blanket, rolling over the forested hills and down to the lakes nestled in the San Andreas Fault. A memorable ride in the motorcade of the Czech prime minister from his speaking engagement at Stanford to the Fairmont Hotel high on a hill in the city, police stopping traffic at the intersections to let us pass. Jon and

I were already an item by then, so from Fairmont that night, I drove to his house in Twin Peaks.

By the time Marianna and I reached the Outer Sunset, an oceanside neighborhood of San Francisco, the sun just barely started to break through the low clouds and the cold, moist air. Summer in the City is typically colder than January in LA.

We left our bags at my mother's apartment, and the three of us—Mark was at his relatives' party—headed out to a playground nearby.

Back at the flat, our cheeks reddened by the chilly wind outside, my mother mentioned Mark's new grandson.

"He's such a big, healthy boy. You want to see his photo?"

"Sure," I said.

Reaching into the entertainment center, Mom pulled out a thick family album. She brought it to the couch, and we sat down to leaf through its crinkly plastic pages. There were photos of Mark's daughters, grandchildren, relatives on the East Coast, family anniversaries, trips and cruises out-of-town, Natalie's wedding, my photo, taking Mom and Natalie to Fort Ross twelve years earlier, a year after they came from Russia.

The album ended without a single picture of Jon, Marianna, or Gaby.

"Where are they," I swallowed, my throat suddenly gone dry, "our pictures?"

"Oh, I have them. I've got them all. I can show you."

From the same drawer, she produced a pocket-size album, containing all those photos I'd mailed her over the years, and a few she and Mark took visiting Jon and me before and after the kids: at the old house, at the new house, at Gaby's first birthday party, at Natalie's wedding, at the beach . . .

I sat there glaring at her, not saying a word. My heart was beating hard.

"Your situation with the kids is so uncertain," my mother said, looking down at the little album in her hand, "I didn't want to put the photos in, only to take them out a year later."

"Is that so?"

She paused.

"You know I couldn't bear Mark's relatives asking me questions about the two of you."

"Mark's family knows! I told them everything myself—at his birthday party, years ago. There is no secret. They're fine with it."

"Alright, I didn't want them in there with the rest because of your letter."

"My letter?"

"From five years ago."

"Ah, 'The Letter' . . . you mean when you wanted to break up with Mark? When you thought you'd quit your job, leave him, and move down to Long Beach to live with us? And I wrote to you suggesting that you sort it out, reconcile, rather than upend your entire life over some petty squabble? And look at the two of you, together, content, all these years later . . ."

My mother got up and went to her bedroom. Mad, I supposed, as mad as I was. Staring at Marianna lining up her beanie babies on the rug beside the couch, I felt the urge to grab her and run. It terrified me to think we were going to be trapped in my mother's apartment until the next morning.

In a minute, my mother returned . . . with a map of California.

"So, where's this Idyllwild with the *dacha* you've rented?" she asked calmly.

"I'm sorry?"

"Remember, you invited us to stay with you at the *dacha*? Well, we've been talking, Mark and I, we could come down for a few days—take a Greyhound to Riverside, and you could just pick us up there."

Like nothing happened. I couldn't believe my ears.

"You still think it's a good idea?" I asked, just to confirm.

"Why not? We're not going anywhere. And it's so gloomy here in July. You can see it for yourself," she waved towards the gray, cloudy view outside the window.

"What do you want from me, Mom?"

She looked away without answering.

"You ask me to do things for you; you come down to see us, but then you hide my partner and my kids from whoever might come to your house. And now you're asking to visit us in Idyllwild? What for? A cheap vacation?"

Now the fight erupted for real. In the barrage of accusations she threw at me, there wasn't a single, remote apology for the little photo album lying between us on the table. It was all about her, how she'd been pushed around all her life—by her parents, her ex-husbands, her in-laws, and, of course, by me.

"You blaming me?" I asked. "You left me, remember? Left me when I was seven!"

"I had no choice!" she yelled.

"You made your choice!" I yelled back. "You met a guy on the rebound, moved in with him, and left me behind like discarded baggage. And you know as well as I do how little your parents wanted me in their home, the kind of place it was, you know it because you grew up there yourself!"

She didn't reply, biting her lower lip.

"That's how it was—don't rewrite my childhood for me. You left me, but I got over it." That was a lie, but saying it made me feel stronger. "My whole adult life I've been helping you: bringing you to this country, pulling you out of one trouble after another, even helping you find Mark, helping you move in with him into this very apartment! When was the last time you helped me? But still I'm here, and look." I slapped the photo album hard. "I still do not exist!"

I noticed Marianna staring at us shouting in Russian, looking shocked, bewildered. Here she was, in the home of my mother, an embodiment of love, of commitment between Jon and me, and she was yet excluded from my mother's family album.

"We're leaving. It's better that way. We don't need to stay here with you. Marianna," I switched to English, "put your beanies in the backpack, sweetie."

My mother threw her arms to the sides, eyes wide open. "Why leave now? The dinner is ready!"

The tone of her voice—high-pitched, thin, desperate—betrayed a genuine hurt. It cut through everything she'd said.

Might there still be something there, at the bottom of the well, I wondered? Love, or just a loveless attachment?

I couldn't tell. But I felt profoundly sad for her, for myself wanting to hear that tone, for both of us. That one genuine note was enough to deter me, to bend my will. Maybe, I thought, we shouldn't leave, at least, not yet, not like this.

We went to the kitchen. Marianna enjoyed her dinner: fried potatoes, chicken, cheese, boiled carrots. I had no appetite.

Why was I there? I wondered. I had so many friends and cousins all over the Bay Area, everyone wanting to see "the ladybug," every day packed with fun, outings, smiles to share, glasses to clink. All I had to do was make a call.

And yet I stayed.

§

In the morning, still icy to each other, we went for a walk over the ocean dunes, conversing carefully about safe, trivial things. Back at the apartment, Mark was playing the piano for Marianna, who absolutely loved it. Mom taught her some simple origami. It looked almost normal, but I knew she couldn't wait for me to leave.

After loading the car to go, I turned to my mother and gave her a peacemaking hug. She didn't embrace me back, just stood there stiffly, her arms straight down at her sides.

Part 6
The Legal and the Human

Edmund D. Edelman Children's Courthouse, County of Los Angeles
© Lane Igoudin, 2023

An Idyllwild Interlude

Fourth of July in a bucolic mountain town surrounded by miles of pine forest. Up by the side of the road, overlooking the parade, was the American Family 2.0: Jon, me, and two little kids.

"Look it, loud, loud!" Marianna was screaming with delight, jumping up and down in a red-white-and-blue summer dress as a yellow-and-blue tartaned pipe band was marching past us, bagpipes screeching in unison up front, drums pounding behind. She'd grown lovely, her thick, golden-brown hair curling up at her shoulders, her creamy-smooth face and arms lightly tanned.

Gaby, sitting in her stroller and pulling at the tips of her soft shoes, was watching the colorful procession with befuddled amusement. She was in shorts, a tank top and a bucket hat embroidered with little flowers. When the firefighter trucks revved up their engines and sirens, Jon clamped his hands over Gaby's ears. Marianna did the same to hers, her face intent: what's next, what's next?

Next came the American Legion veterans, a truckful of summer camp kids in cowboy hats, a volunteer troop of mountain rescuers who demonstrated how to stabilize an injured climber. They were followed by the belly dancers and a line of elderly lady quilters, show-stopping the parade with a can-can.

What a difference it made to be away from LA. An alternative reality had opened up, one in which Jon, the kids, and I were simply enjoying a summer vacation.

Our roomy, two-story house was set in the cul-de-sac of a quiet country lane, overlooking a vast canyon, its chaparral alive with butterflies, blue jays, cottontails, and occasional coyotes. Every sunset was glorious, the sky above the pine-dotted ridge turning vivid shades of pink and strawberry, deepening to purple and royal blue before melting into the distant Pacific.

During the week, only Marianna and I were in Idyllwild, and would only get *off-the-hill*, as they say there, to drive to the visits and restock the groceries. There was no TV reception, so Marianna got to watch her Teletubbies, Barney, and Elmo tapes, often asking to repeat the same episode with "Again! Again!" Together we were discovering the town and the many activities it offered: the playground, the Nature Center, the library story time.

The reduction of our household to just the two of us brought me some calm. During the first week, all I did was take care of Marianna, read books, drink pinot on the deck, and sleep as much as I wanted. My cell phone died because I forgot to bring the charger. At first, I panicked; what if . . . ? But then I relaxed as I got pestered less.

Jon would still call, at least three times a day, on the house landline. He'd always talk to Marianna if she was up; he was missing her.

In the same way, I was missing Gaby, her aura of delicate sweetness. In LA, at times, I felt distant from her. Was it because of the legal drama or her deeper connection to Jon? I couldn't tell, but I was putting up walls. Here the walls dissolved. I thought of her constantly.

§

A biography I brought with me into the mountains offered an unexpected insight into our situation. An illegitimate daughter of an eighteenth-century Venetian mother and an English father, the stateless heroine, Giustiniana Wynne, spent decades, trying to acquire permanent citizenship in several European countries. Their absurd, endless legal processes framed Wynne's life. Meanwhile, her marriage and income prospects came and went, wrecked by her unsettled legal status.[24]

And yet, in the shadows of those court hearings, Wynne enjoyed life—a grand romance, music, food; she made right and wrong choices. In other words, she lived.

So should we, I realized. The kids' court cases may frame our existence, but within them lies our real life, one in which we take care of these children, play with them, delight in their joys, reprove if they misbehave, watch them change subtly, moment-to-moment. Only this life with the kids—a rich, fully lived family life with its daily changes, interactions, and memories—is real and meaningful.

§

I returned to the dusty midsummer LA for Marianna's rescheduled parental rights termination hearing. Waiting by Judge Hooke's courtroom door, I spotted the steel-blue silhouette of Margaret McPherson gliding purposefully towards me.

"Ms. McPherson?"

"Good morning, Lane. I wanted to let you know in person that I am no longer representing your kids," she said with cool politeness. "I had too many cases, so I had to let go of a few. You can speak to Stephanie Fiore. I'll see if she's available."

Stephanie Fiore? Who is Stephanie Fiore?

I stood perplexed, frozen in the hallway, while just like that, McPherson walked away from the years of the court drama, the unwritten knowledge of the players, the ins and outs of our children's cases—the children, whom she'd never met. Piles of files, was all that was left. Someone new would be reading them, making their own conclusions, following their own biases. In the ominous shadow of the three-ring binders, court stenographer records, faxes, court orders, doctors' evaluations, agency reports, database entries stood the birth parents, the kids, and us. We remained.

McPherson emerged from the closed doors of the courtroom

with an unfamiliar woman—young, curvy, with reddish-blonde hair tied in a ponytail, and a pleasant wide face.

"Steph, this is Lane; Lane is Marianna's and her sister's foster dad."

"Good to meet you, Lane."

"Me too."

"Lane, I know this is sudden for you," said McPherson without a tinge of sadness, "but I just had to split my workload. I'm leaving you in very capable hands."

"I understand. Well, thanks for everything you've done for Marianna and for Gaby."

I meant that, despite my disappointment about her leaving. I knew that she, like all children's attorneys, was overloaded and overworked.[25]

"I've taken a quick look at the case," said Stephanie as we sat down by the hallway window. "Anything new I need to know about?"

I walked Stephanie through the most recent developments: Gaby's Regional Center assessment, Tony's losses of his apartment and of his job, his three-week absence from the visits, Jackie remaining staunchly pro-Tony. We talked for about 20 minutes. Stephanie came off less rigid, warmer than McPherson.

"You think we'll be done before lunch?" I asked.

"You mean Marianna's termination? Um, there's something you need to know, Lane. We won't be terminating today. Last Friday, Jenna filed a motion 'to have the child come home' as we say. She is asking to reconsider the termination of her reunification services for Marianna from six months ago."

"Oh, for God's sake! Are we starting another round?"

"I really have no idea. It does seem strange to appeal so far into the case."

Why on earth is Jenna doing it? I wondered. In five months, she only asked to see Marianna once.

"Judge Hooke will sustain Jenna's motion," said Stephanie, "and set it for a trial. She'll tell you that herself when she calls you in."

"What can you do?"

"Get the earliest court date possible so we can deal with it ASAP."
With that, Stephanie went back into the court chambers.

§

Around 2 p.m., Stephanie came out again. The hearing had taken place. At Jenna's request, I was excluded.

"I am so sorry—it is as I said. The judge scheduled a trial for September 12 to investigate Jenna's relationship with Marianna," she said and paused. "It's better if you don't attend it."

"Not a problem," I replied. Not that I really had a choice. I didn't ask Stephanie if she was able to use any of the information I'd given her before lunch, nor any other questions. I felt I needed to pull back. This was our first interaction, and I already showed enough involvement.

"One more thing, Lane, just so you know. At the upcoming August court date for Gaby, I am going to ask to terminate family reunification for both birth parents."

My eyes lit up, "Will they contest?"

"They most certainly will."

"And you're going to make DCFS mighty upset, too."

"Probably." She gave me a sly smile. "We'll see what happens."

I liked her. Barely a day into the case, she was already going on the offensive. And she wasn't keeping her cards close to her chest.

§

Marianna crawled up close to a foot-long desert tortoise than an Idyllwild Nature Center volunteer had put down on the floor.

"*Gurgle*, hello, hello!" she patted the turtle on the hexagonal ridges patterning its shell. Then she stood up and stretched out one foot.

"Don't step on her!" I caught her just in time to prevent the disaster. "She'll get an owie. You have to be nice and gentle."

Marianna plopped back on her knees, and, bending over the turtle, touched it with two fingers. "I touching . . . nice . . .

gurgle lay like that." To illustrate, Marianna lay down cheek to the floor. Next, her fingers grasped the mustard-colored shell, trying to pick it up. The turtle's head retreated inside.

"I think the turtle wants to go to sleep. Why don't we put her back in her house?"

Carefully, I took it out of her hands and returned it to the safety of its Plexiglas case.

"C'mon," Marianna pulled me by the hand towards the Center's display room.

"Where are we going?"

"C'mon. Walk. Lookit—kitty-cat." She pointed at a mountain lion posed mid-step.

"Uh-huh."

"Birdie," a motionless hawk spreading its wings.

I loved the way she said "bir-die"—with a smile that broke out in the second syllable.

"Look it." The finger moved to another display box, "Doggie, right there."

"That's a gray fox."

"*That* a fox too?" She pointed at another taxidermied animal.

"It's a coyote."

"Like doggie?"

"Yeah."

Her attention shifted again. "That a doggie. Right there up in the tree."

"No, sweetie, that's a raccoon. Let's go outside, do the nature walk before it gets too hot."

I returned to Idyllwild somewhat demoralized by the setback with Marianna's case, but Marianna and I were no longer alone. Our friend Caryn Davidson came up from Joshua Tree to see us. Marianna, with her baby doll tucked under her arm, first chased Caryn around the house, and later sat listening attentively to Caryn reading *Cactus Café* and *The Tortoise and the Hare,* the same books Caryn, a Joshua Tree park ranger, would take to local schools to introduce kids to the park.

On the weekend, my younger sister Rina, up from San Diego, was circling the living room on all fours, Marianna lying on top of her back, arms clasped underneath, legs bent, feet up in the air, screaming, "Horsey! Horsey!"

Natalie came up too, hers and Rina's presence, as well as dinners with new friends in Idyllwild, calls and emails from all around the country and abroad, made me feel validated. Our friends could do little to help us win these cases, but their empathy, like a collective prayer, was fortifying.

§

When Jon brought Gaby the following weekend, we witnessed a miracle. Replacing tapes in my portable video camera, I heard Jon exclaim: "Baby just made her first step!"

I spun around, camera rolling, just in time to capture Gaby getting up off the carpet with Jon's help: "Up, up, up, it's okay ..."

She elevated herself unsteadily, stood in a precarious balance, made another uncertain step towards the coffee table, one more, and collapsed on her bum.

"Good job!" Jon encouraged her.

"July 21," I reported excitedly into the camera, "she just took her first two steps! She'd never walked before!"

The number of steps, after those first few, increased daily. Gaby still crawled most of the time, but occasionally, with encouragement, tried to walk.

The four of us now ventured further out—for swims at a local pool; for a frosty milkshake at a date farm down in Indio, where I'd point out to Marianna the desert plants that she saw in Caryn's books—*cholla*, *ocotillo*, *yucca*; to Lake Fulmor hidden in the mountain ridge, where we did our first hike, circling the lake—Jon carrying Gaby in his arms, Marianna bumbling ahead, climbing granite rocks, pulling down cattails to stare at blue dragonflies swarming at the water's edge.

Those beautiful summer weeks with the kids, I was enjoying them so much, and knew that I'd be missing them, each day slipping like a golden coin through my fingers.

The Pendulum Swings

Trying to keep vacation interruptions to a minimum, I grouped all visits in LA into one day: Vernon at 8:45 a.m., Stephanie's representative at 9:45 a.m.—a twice-a-year obligation, timed to help Stephanie prepare for Gaby's upcoming court date, then Tony at noon, and Jenna at 3 p.m.

By the end of the day, I felt completely worn out, which I hadn't felt in a long time. Away from it all, I'd forgotten the toll it took.

Everything was now focused on Gaby's August 10 hearing: the court would review her parents' progress and decide, in particular, on Tony's readiness to take her.

Based on Kim Dally's assessment, Harbor Regional Center approved therapy to improve Gaby's motor skills. They sent the assessment and the approval to Jackie. I faxed my copy to Stephanie, along with Vernon's visit observation report, and a note stating that "No visits with the baby's father, Tony Girona, have taken place in 7 weeks since June 21, 2007. Neither we nor the foster agency have heard from him, despite Dr. Vernon Brezins's multiple messages."

Hours after this information was shared with other parties in court, Tony called Vernon asking for a visit.

"What's the rush? Let him have his visit after the court date," said Vernon.

"Vernon," I said, "he can have his visit any time he wants. And doing it now will only highlight his long absence."

"Alright then, I'll give him a call."

Tony didn't call him back.

Both Jenna and Tony showed up for the hearing, Stephanie updated me afterwards. And Jackie's report about Tony was . . . "scathing."

Scathing? I couldn't believe my ears. Had I misread Jackie? Or was DCFS finally bowing down to Stephanie's pressure and the judge's skepticism?

I'll never know. The fact remains that DCFS, the same DCFS that had been railroading Gaby to him for months, convincing all of us this was the only choice, was now aligning itself with Stephanie to end his family reunification.

Tony contested the DCFS report, and the judge set the trial for October 4.

"The bad news," Stephanie continued, "is that Jackie submitted a great report on the mother's progress and asked the court to continue her services, 'with the eventual readiness to assume parental responsibilities by next March'."

"No way . . ."

"She reported that Jenna has been consistent in her visits . . ."

"That's not true!"

". . . her AA meetings, therapy, and so on, so she's doing great. Apparently, Jenna has made some breakthroughs in therapy."

"Does the report say anything about her relationship with Gaby, that Gaby really doesn't know who she is?"

"Nope."

"What about the regional center eval, the delays?"

"No, none of that. But I have it—from you, and I will use it. So now, with this glowing report from DCFS, Jenna asked for unmonitored visits. I objected on the grounds that her home staff, which monitors the visits, didn't submit their report, but

Judge Hooke overruled me and approved Jenna's request. She allowed Jenna unsupervised visits, for two hours, and with the social worker's discretion to increase them to four hours."

"Unbelievable . . ." I breathed out.

"I'm with you. This is way too premature. I contested on Gaby's behalf, and we set that hearing for the same day in October as Tony's."

"What do you think is going to happen in October? Jenna's about to emancipate, but emancipate and go where? Where will she be taking Gaby?"

"It's all very complicated. If Jenna emancipates when she turns 18 in September and moves out, she's going to lose most of her services. If she doesn't, she can't have the child. I have no idea what the county wants to do with her, or if they have any place prepared to transition her into . . . What's most important though is that Gaby is turning 18 months in December, and her social worker, Jackie Willis, will have to make a final recommendation to the court about what to do—give Gaby to a birth parent, or place her in the adoption track. There is no third option."

§

Jenna won something tangible this time—time *alone* with her daughters. She asked Jackie for a photo of both kids, which I was dutifully delivering to the visit, along with the kids, a double-stroller for her to use, as well as cookies and milk for her to give to them.

In the library parking lot, I caught sight of Jenna through the open windows of her orphanage van, next to her new counselor, Morgan—a large woman in a sweatsuit, reclining in the driver's seat, listening to the radio.

Waiting for the end of the visit, I left a message for Jackie asking to let me know what happened in the court. Of course, I already knew, but I was hoping to glean some nuggets Stephanie might have overlooked.

Jackie returned my call, not on my cell, but as usual, on my home voicemail. The one new detail that came to light was that the judge, at Stephanie's insistence, asked DCFS to provide information about the mother's current and anticipated living situation. Stephanie was following through.

Jackie and I finally talked—three weeks later.

She called me at 1 p.m., as I was about to start a class. "Lane, it's the end of the month. I need to see the kids. Are they at daycare today?"

"Yes, until 4 p.m."

"Good, I'll stop by—" she was about to hang up.

"Jackie, hold on. We'd like to know what's going on with the kids' cases." I nodded to my students filing past me into the language lab.

"Well, we're going to try to terminate the parental rights for Marianna in September."

"Yes, I know. But what about Gaby?"

Jackie reiterated the facts I already knew: "they ordered . . . they found . . . what can we do . . ." as if it wasn't her own report that was sending Gaby to Jenna. Then, finally, came the news: "I'm looking to place Jenna in a transitional home by December."

"Which accepts children?"

"Which accepts children."

"And Jenna has made so much progress that she'll be ready to parent by December?"

"If she goes at the rate she goes, you never know."

"But how can she take care of Gaby? I can't imagine her living independently, even alone."

"She won't be alone there. They have counselors."

"Will those counselors be helping her raise the child? Drive Jenna to the stores to buy food for Gaby, feed her, bathe her, read to her, play with her, wash her clothes, change her diapers seven times a day, potty train her? Who will watch Gaby when Jenna goes to work? And this is Jenna we're talking about—still very much a teen, with all her issues!"

"Sure, Jenna had a difficult past, and we still don't know how well she can take care of herself, but—"

"Then how can you advocate for giving her a child? Especially one who doesn't really know her and possibly has medical issues?"

"Do you think Jenna would harm the baby?"

"Not intentionally, no, but through lack of experience and neglect. And what about the harm to Gaby from being removed from the only parents she has ever known, and from her sister? Is that *not* going to be traumatic?" I appealed to her, "Jackie, you have kids. You know what it's like to take care of them 24/7. It's so much more than playing with them and feeding them snacks twice a week. Would you entrust your own children to someone like Jenna, even for a day?"

Jackie didn't answer, but she didn't hang up either. In that pause, I sensed Jackie's ambivalence. DCFS was inclined to send Gaby to Jenna because it was the easiest solution, but it was the wrong solution, and Jackie knew that: she's known Jenna for five years.

"How are the visits going? How is Jenna interacting with the baby?" she asked.

We were still talking then.

"Can't tell you much. I leave right after I bring her over."

"What about Vernon?"

"Vernon doesn't monitor Jenna's visits. The judge removed the monitors from her visits, remember?"

Jackie's voice softened. "You know that the court's job is to reunify."

"I thought it was to do what's best for the *child*, Jackie." My voice trembled, "I'm happy about the progress Jenna has made, I really am, she's gone through a lot. But from that to being a parent is a gigantic step. Aren't you concerned about Gaby's safety?"

There was no answer.

I took a deep sigh. "I just hope the court will take pity on this child."

I don't know where those last, melodramatic words came from, maybe from too many Italian operas I'd seen, but I actually said that.

We parted neutrally. Was there something I said, something that could sway her opinion just a tad? Everything seemed set. All the court needed was Jackie's recommending the placement, and Gaby would be gone.

I entered the classroom, closed the door behind me, and tried to focus my agitated mind on explaining the essay topic for the day. One student, an older Salvadorean woman, gave me a peculiar look. She was scanning my face compassionately, like my grandmother, maybe even guessing the reason for the turmoil.

Suzanne offered to give Jackie a call—the farthest our supposed advocates were prepared to go. Other than that, the agency was washing its hands of Gaby, the child for whom it had been paid handsomely for 15 months. I knew the exact amount: DCFS, in its typically messy fashion, sent us its contract with Our Bright Futures, the contract which I later forwarded on to Suzanne.

"Fine," I said, "go ahead, call."

"Are You My Mommy?"

"What resilience!" exclaimed Françoise, a friend from my Paris days, responding to my update. "Your American process is *complètement fou* (completely crazy). How do you deal with it?"

Simple: drugs. I took Babushka's advice. My physician started me on Paxil the previous month.

Little white pills, I found, are miracle workers. They take the edge off and allow one to interact with others in a relatively calm, almost serene tone. Paxil enabled me to get up in the morning, go to work, take care of the kids, manage the household, and continue the fight. The county should've sent them along with foster payments.

"Which Lane do you like more, before or after the pills?" I asked Jon one day.

"The new Lane, the happy Lane. Definitely. You were so tightly wound up before, blowing up at a moment's notice."

The "happy Lane" slept better and felt less.

The "happy Lane" could handle his mother.

After our disastrous visit in June, I made several Sunday calls, trying to repair our relationship. I felt obligated to do so. Someone had to be an adult in this relationship.

My mother sounded reluctant to talk to me, not asking a single question about us, but also being atypically quiet about herself.

Soon, a letter, written in a neat Cyrillic cursive, arrived to take care of the problem.

I am asking you not to call me anymore unless it is an extreme emergency. These calls of duty throw me out of balance for the entire week until the next such call, causing insomnia, headaches, hypertension, not to mention the effect on my general mood. I have no interest in idle chatter about daily news, knowing full well what you really think of me. [. . .]

I am closing this topic forever. But exactly because I can never forget how you dragged me through the dirt, your warnings and refusals, I am asking you to spare me the unnecessary phone calls, just so you could check the box next to the line called 'relationship with my mother,' as well as spare me your wishes and congratulations for any holidays, birthdays, and other occasions.

I understand that from time to time we will have to communicate out of necessity, and for the sake of the others, I will remain outwardly polite. Of course, I will lose the contact with the grandchildren, so indispensable at my age and so common among my friends, and it would not hurt your children to have a relationship with me either, but the price is too high to pay, so it will have to be minimized.[26]

She signed her letter with her first name, not with "Mom" or "Mother."

The letter was meant to wound, each multi-clause Russian sentence a blistering bayonet. If anything, it was a desperate act. She couldn't deal with it—my sexuality, my family, my drama with the kids—so she tried to bury it all, just like the photographs, by cutting me off, by slamming the door.

"So dramatic. Who does she think she is—the Queen of England in a Section 8 apartment?" quipped Natalie, reading it later. And yet, the letter shook her up; she downed a glass of wine when she put it down.

I didn't have to drink; I had Paxil. The little white pills cushioned the blow, digested and compartmentalized the pain.

We all have an image of what a mother should be. Often, as in Jon's life, the image and the real person are one and the same. But not so much in mine. My whole childhood, I longed for my mother to be present in my life, to synchronize with the Ashkenazi archetype—that of a strong, vibrant, protective mother, under whose absolute control, even if smothering at times, the rest of the household feels safe—a *Yiddishe mame*, forever enthralled and entwined with her son.

Occasionally, my mother would match that fantasy, be fully present for me, but these moments would never last. She got full custody after the divorce and took me with her to live with her parents, my maternal grandparents. Barely two years later, when I was 7, she moved out to live with her second husband (not Mark, he'd be her third), leaving me with my aging grandparents, who would be raising me more out of a sense of duty, not love.

My mother didn't abandon me completely: she'd take me out to see a play, or an opera, to ski or skate in the winter, to go on vacation in the summer, and so I owe much of my cultural exposure to her. Yet starting at age 10, even these visits would change: like Gaby with Tony, I'd be the one doing the visiting—a tram ride once or twice a month to her apartment to see her, my stepdad Leonid, and my half-sister Natalie. I never spent the night under her roof; not a single item of mine would be left behind once I boarded the tram back. I didn't know what was sadder—pretending to be more than a guest there or returning to my grandparents' home where I wasn't wanted.

In my adult years, our connection grew even more distant and uncertain, our relationship flipping, with me sponsoring my mother's immigration to the US, settling her in, managing her finances, and so on.

How could I truly feel the loss or shock of her rejection? A loss of what exactly? The ties she was cutting were so tenuous, so frayed.

Instead, I came to see that it wasn't so much my mother's rejection, but my own expectations of her, and the absence of a true substitute parent, that made me suffer. Had I been raised in love by adults, related or not, it would've mattered little who they were.

In the end, it was the love I was missing, the unconditional, accepting, supportive, warm love. Just the kind of love I was hoping to give to Marianna and Gaby.

§

By the start of the fall, Gaby was walking in earnest. She looked super-cute, pulling herself up and puttering unsteadily forward on her bowed legs—a biological instinct finally kicking in.

Biological nature had its costs too. One Sunday morning I walked into the kids' bedroom to find Gaby, upright in her crib, greeting me with a mischievous smile, one hand holding on to the crib rail, and the other—"Oh my God! Jon, come here now!"—squishing poop. Her diaper lay open on the bed; the excrement smeared all over the crib walls, Gaby's legs, arms, nightgown, face, and even hair.

Standing at a safe distance, Marianna was gurgling with laughter, one index finger in her drooling mouth, the other pointing at her baby sister. "Daddy, look what *baby tita* did!"

"Oh, I can see it alright, Marianna," said Jon. "Why the heck didn't you call us?"

Grabbing Gaby by the shoulders, I carried her like a dirty kitten to the bath; Jon ran ahead of me to start the water. We scrubbed her for a good forty minutes. She was having a wonderful time throughout.

Trained by Kim Dally, we were teaching Gaby to chew by placing a potato or vegetable fry in the far corner of her mouth. To move it to the front and split it into smaller chunks, she had to engage her tongue, jaws, and back teeth. Sometimes she choked, and we helped her get the food out, but more and more, in slow, jerking movements, she'd been squishing and moving the fries to the center as she should.

Another development—complete words. Since her first one a month before—"*da-da*" (Jon), my ears have recorded her "*boh*" for "ball;" "*woo-woo,*" "dog;" "*ba-wu,*" "balloon;" "*wa-wa,*" "water;" "*uh-oh,*" for dropping things, and the reduplicative "*na-na,*" for her sister. These words—"father," "sister," "ball," "dog," "balloon," "water"—circumscribed her world and her immediate interests.

How precious were those fleeting moments with her next to me—feeding her those fries or talking about "*bob*" or "*woo-woo,*" or feeling her play with my hair or ears with those light touches of her tiny fingers, or burying herself in my embrace.

Isn't this why we want to be parents? Ultimately, we don't know what will happen when they grow up, if we even make it there, but that moment, that warm tenderness, was real.

Afraid to lose Gaby, this time to her mother, Jon and I were showering a disproportionate amount of affection on her—and Marianna was noticeably unhappy. We shouldn't have, but we couldn't help it. The bittersweet mixture of love and loss belied our attentions as we cherished our finite time together, the warm rays of a setting sun.

§

On her third birthday, Marianna looked like a little lady in her sleeveless lavender dress with a matching purple necklace, white socks and white patent-leather shoes with a little heel. Jon had combed her soft brown hair into a ponytail, over which he clasped a sparkling purple hairpin.

When the six-foot Elmo, Marianna's favorite TV character, walked into the front door, most kids ran to him, but Marianna bolted to the back of the living room—to Jon. From there, she watched incredulously as the six-foot figure in a red, furry outfit rallied some forty kids and adults crowding our living room.

"Everybody stand up! Stamp your feet! Now everybody shout *hur-ray!*"

"Hurray!!!"

"We're going to sing a very special song for a very special birthday girl. Are you all ready? Everybody, look at the birthday girl, look at Marianna!" Heads turned. Marianna wouldn't budge from Jon's lap, "Are you all ready to sing Marianna 'Happy Birthday'?"

As Elmo led the crowd in the toddler sing-along, Marianna warmed up. Cautiously, she stepped up closer and eventually joined the other kids.

In the evening, Marianna was rearranging the furniture in her dollhouse.

"My Elmo came to see me," she told me.

"Did you sing?"

"Yes."

"Did you dance?"

"Yes."

"Did you give Elmo a hug?"

"No."

"Why not?"

Marianna paused. "Elmo has a big tummy."

She didn't elaborate, and we left it at that.

§

A few days later, Stephanie notified me that the termination of Jenna's parental rights to Marianna was postponed again because DCFS failed, again, to provide Jenna with the transportation to the court.

I took it calmly. I'd gotten used to living with uncertainty. In fact, hearing the TPR had indeed gone through, on this third try, would've left me more surprised, fearful even, as it would've brought us into a new and unfamiliar reality. Humans get used to living in bondage, imprisonment, abusive relationships. Couldn't the possibility of an exit, exciting as it was, also be frightening? Fear of liberation overcoming the dread of the known?

One outcome of this new delay got me concerned, though. The previous week, Jenna missed her monthly visit with Marianna. A fluke—she did show up, but without first confirming the visit with Vernon. Had the termination gone through, there would be no more visits. Now she could ask again.

This termination was long overdue, as Jenna's ongoing presences and absences kept confusing Marianna. Back in the Bay Area, she called my friend Robin "Mommy," hearing her daughter refer to her that way. Now Marianna tried the same label on Jon's niece visiting us, after hearing her daughter Trinity call her "Mommy."

Trinity strongly objected, "She's not *your* Mommy. She's *my* Mommy!"

Marianna pursed her lips, trying to figure out what it all meant. Clearly, someone had to be *her* Mommy.

"Are you my Mommy?" Marianna asked me, sitting up in the bath while I was shampooing her hair.

"No, sweetie, but I am your Pappy. You saw your Mommy last month."

"I saw Mommy?"

"Yes, at the park, you had a visit, remember?"

Marianna frowned, neither affirming nor denying the information. "So where is Mommy now?"

"She doesn't live with us. She lives in a different place. But your Mommy loves you very, very much. I'm sure of it. She just can't take care of you."

What I really wanted to say was I understand your confusion, kid, I really do. This is all we get. You will never get the mother you want, and neither will I. There is nothing you can do, except to accept the fact. And then to realize that you will always have me. I hope that you and I will learn to become our own mothers—understanding, caring, and kind, raising our kids in love, unconditional and responsible; better mothers than the ones we've been given.

§

DCFS requires notification every time a foster child has to leave the county. We were heading to Palm Springs for a special LGBT family weekend organized by Family Equality, so I had to notify Jackie via a fax. But I also added a bit more: a two-page update on Gaby's recent immunizations, her first words, Jenna's visitation, as well as Dr. Goldfarb's new letter, written on his medical office stationery. In his previous letter, he recommended Gaby's developmental evaluations. In this second one, Dr. Goldfarb urged not to move Gaby out of our home and away from her sister, stressing that "for the child's best interest, she should be with a stable set of parents without change, attending the same daycare/preschool. Disruption of this pattern, along with a changing set of primary caregivers, would make a negative impact on her."

Once all the papers had gone through, I put them back into the feeder and dialed a second number—Stephanie's.

§

On a warm September day, a group of three-year-olds were scavenging the sidewalk in front of a wide-arched, modern synagogue. Among them were Marianna and Benji Goldfarb, Dr. Goldfarb's son and Marianna's playmate from Playtime Learning.

The rambunctious bunch scurried back into the temple with a bounty of fallen oak and sycamore leaves, strips of tree bark, and some red berries. Leaving the sukkah decorations on the classroom tables, parents and children, including Marianna, Gaby, and me, gathered in a circle on the rug. Gaby woke up and sat up in my lap, rubbing her eyes.

"Why do we observe Sukkot?" asked the Jewish school teacher, leading this parent-and-me class.

"To celebrate fruits and vegetables?" ventured Benji.

"Right," she confirmed, widening her eyes enthusiastically, "to celebrate harvest. In ancient Israel, at this time of year, the Jews would bring their best fruits and vegetables to the Temple to celebrate a good harvest."

As a family, we did what an affiliated Jewish family would usually do: celebrate Shabbat every Friday, light the candles on Hanukkah, go to the family services at our synagogue and the kids' events at the JCC, and so on.

None of it was a given, though. Growing up Jewish in the Soviet Union, I never had a bar mitzvah. The Communist doctrine essentially prohibited religion, and few Jewish families dared to practice Judaism openly, at least, none that I knew. The elderly grandparents who raised me were of the generation that severed connections with the *shtetl* past and religious observance. They passed on many subtle ways of what it meant to be Jewish—the values, the dos and the don'ts, the food, the deep connection to the family near and far—but steered clear of religion, the heart of the Jewish tradition.

I heard my first Kol Nidre at the Conservative temple of our American-born relatives shortly after our arrival in the US as refugees. There I got introduced to the Jewish holiday cycle and the basic liturgy. At Stanford, I attended Conservative services as well, and moving to LA, joined a Conservative temple near my home. I had much to learn yet, but at the moment, the priority wasn't my, but the kids' Jewish education.

"Why raise them Jewish?" I'd been asked by a few well-meaning people.

Why wouldn't I? I was Marianna and Gaby's day-to-day, factual, and hopefully soon-to-be-legal father. Naturally, I wanted to pass on my heritage to my children, but it was more than that. A sense of roots, I strongly believed then and now, is even more important for the kids whose own have been cut. I wanted to share my roots with them, graft them onto the branches of my ancient tree.

The traditional Jewish law, *halakhah*, provides no legal mechanism for adoption, though it does allow a child, like an adult, to become a Jew through formal conversion, including an appearance before the rabbinical court (*beit din*), circumcision (for a boy), and an immersion into the ritual bath (*mikvah*) for both boys and girls. After conversion, the child is considered as Jewish as one born to Jewish parents.

Watching Marianna learn her first words of Hebrew, I hoped one day to have the joy and the honor of bringing her before a *beit din* and submerging her in the living waters of the *mikvah*.

The Coming Storm

Jackie received my fax, but I heard from her for a completely different reason.

"Thanks for the travel notification, it's fine, of course, but I want you to know that I'm not on your case anymore. I've been reassigned to another unit in our department. You'll be getting a new social worker, Lynette Huckaby."

"Okay." I was stunned, trying to digest this new cast change. "Is this Lynette also going to be handling Jenna's case?"

"Yes, all three clients."

"Okay, we'll work with Lynette, no problem. If you don't mind me asking, Jackie, what do you think is going to happen to Gaby?"

"Hard to tell. I know you're going to tell me how much she's grown attached to all of you."

"Dr. Goldfarb wrote to you that such separation will have a negative impact on her."

"That may be so."

"You can see from my reports that Gaby, after 16 months, really doesn't know who Jenna is. Seeing a child twice a month for a couple of hours does little to build a bond."

"Well, it's not entirely Jenna's fault. She's been busy, she doesn't have the time for visits. Just so you know, she just had a good interview at Holy Names. I'm proud of her."

"Really? For a church job?" I pretended not to know what Holy Names was.

"No, no," she laughed, "for an apartment! Holy Names is a Catholic home for teenage moms and homeless teens. It used to be her home, hers and Marianna's that is. She can live there again, with Gaby. Her home staff will supervise her baby while she's taking classes or going to work."

I caught my breath. That was what she kept hidden from me, and what she was going to report to the court next week.

"When is she moving in?"

"We haven't set a date yet."

"So you're going to recommend Jenna's placement there, at Holy Names?"

"Mm . . ." she made an uncertain sound, "it's not that simple. She needs to transition to living on her own, but she still needs help. The court will need to see reports from Jenna's group home, therapist, school, and so on, before they can make a decision."

Was DCFS, in fact, going to recommend such a placement? From the tired but determined tone in Jackie's voice, I felt she was ready to let the court deal with it.

But then, what were Jenna's chances of getting an apartment at Holy Names? Wouldn't some teen picked off the street be more of a priority? Or another girl, teenage and pregnant, like herself not so long ago, needing to be moved from her foster placement?

Jackie had to have very few options if she was trying to return Jenna to the very place from which she allegedly had to be removed last year. Still, I figured, if DCFS was throwing its full weight behind it, she might get it and take Gaby with her.

§

Marianna got difficult. She demanded changes to daily routines, refused to eat meals, ignored what we'd tell her to do. She behaved no better at Playtime Learning. One day, she earned three pink slips: for biting one kid, hitting another, and pushing the third.

It might have been age-related, the delayed "terrible twos," or simply reflecting the tension at home ahead of the upcoming court hearings for both kids.

I no longer knew what to expect. Jon predicted that the attorneys would eventually divide the kids—a plea bargain of sorts. He broke down at a department store, buying Halloween outfits for them. Of all places, it hit him there, in the festively decorated aisles, looking at toddler-size costumes, that we might not have Gaby on Halloween.

I asked Kim Dally if she too could write something to advocate for Gaby. She agreed and sent the following letter to Stephanie.

I am writing this letter to state my respectful and professional opinion that removing Gabriella from the only family and home that she had ever known could likely leave lasting and detrimental psycho-social effects that could further impede her global developmental progress at this time. Gabriella has already demonstrated mild delays in receptive language, gross motor skills, and oral motor skills. Her current level of developmental functioning is attributable to the attention, devotion, and love that her caregivers have provided her.

Since the treatment began, Gaby's foster parents, Lane and Jonathan, have shown excellent follow-through with therapist recommended treatment activities and exercises. They have shown to be dedicated and committed parents for which I highly commend them.

In this very impressionable and fragile stage of her development, I do not feel that removing Gabriella from her current home is in her best interests. It would also likely be a very traumatic separation for Gabriella's sister as well.

Kim attached her four-page developmental evaluation of Gaby to the letter. If asked, she said, she'd gladly testify in court on Gaby's behalf.

§

Vernon, Gaby, and I were taking a slow stroll around the parking lot waiting for Jenna's van. Gaby was waddling along, holding on to my hand. It was just her today. Jenna didn't ask to see Marianna.

"Jackie called me this morning," Vernon growled in his husky baritone, "asking for a last-minute report on the children."

"Today? The day before the court?"

"Oh yeah. Organization isn't her strong suit."

I learned to appreciate his quiet sarcasm. Somehow, it felt more reassuring than all the empty words I heard from the others. I knew whose side he was on.

"I had to push everything away, but I got it done. I threw in my own recommendation not to move Gaby. I've known Jenna for much too long. It would be catastrophic for the child. Three years into the process, the case was still entirely about Jenna, not her children."

"Well, Vernon, thank you for that."

I doubted that the opinion of a contracted foster-to-adopt agency social worker would carry much weight in court, but even so, any witness, any support would help.

"Lynette, this new DCFS social worker, is supposed to be here today," I said.

"You talked to her?" Vernon asked.

"Yes, she called." I remembered a distinct, if softened, twang in her speech. "She didn't seem familiar with the case."

The van with Jenna eventually arrived, but not Lynette. Vernon stayed on, and I left.

At the pickup time, just as Gaby and I were about to get into the car, Jenna rushed up to me with something in her hand—a purple bear.

She handed it to me, looking away. "Here's something for Marianna—I missed her birthday."

"Thank you," I said, "I'll give it to her."

That was all, but imperceptibly to others, the light had subtly changed, and a quiet descended. She was letting Marianna go, I knew it instinctively. That's why she hadn't asked to see her, as a matter of fact, hadn't asked any questions about Marianna in weeks. She was letting her go.

The Legal and the Human

"Marianna had a court hearing on Friday. We just found out the results," I was typing an email to my friends and family on October 15. "Marianna's birth parents' parental rights have been terminated on the fourth attempt, which opens up the road to her adoption by us."

It was done. I hit "send," and within hours, congratulatory replies flooded my inbox. Natalie and Dad called, as did Jon's sister, happy, just happy for us.

Of course, Jon and I were happy too: it was such an important milestone in Marianna's case. At dinner, we uncorked a bottle of champagne, but refrained from explaining the news to the kids who were busy emptying their juice cups. In reality, this long-awaited court decision didn't change anything fundamental in our life as a family. They were the same to us, and we to them, as the day before. To me, it underscored one essential problem with the whole system: the ambivalence about being fost-adoptive parents, the tension between the legal and the human.

Were we foster, or were we adoptive? Were we there simply to support the birth parents' needs and take care of their children as state-paid nannies, or were we in it to grow our own family? These were two completely different roles that we were somehow supposed to play simultaneously and harmoniously.

How attached should we have been to the kids we were raising? Did the court expect us to love Marianna less while she was under reunification and more now that she became available for adoption? Conversely, were we supposed to be less attached to Gaby, still under reunification with her birth parents, but be ready to crank it up a notch if it fell through?

This entire premise is nonsense. The parent's heart doesn't change simply because a kid's legal status is amended in a courtroom 20 miles away. We loved Marianna and Gaby that day the same way we always had and always will.

No one actually informed us of the court orders. I called every number I had but heard nothing. We were, after all, in legal terms, just the "non-relative non-guardians" to these kids.

The first to respond was Stephanie Fiore, four days later. She'd had to stay home Friday with an illness. Margaret McPherson stepped in to cover, and her familiarity with Marianna's case might have helped the termination to finally sail through.

Jenna apparently cried in the courtroom, saying she loved Marianna and didn't visit because "she never knew when the visit would be."

I knew that she loved Marianna. The excuse for not visiting though was rather flimsy. All Jenna had to do was ask. But she hadn't—in two months. After she missed Marianna's birthday visit, I expected her to complain, to demand a reschedule, but she made no mention. My hunch at the park proved right.

A victory? Not yet. Jenna had sixty days to appeal. And appeal she might—she'd changed her mind before, and being a destitute dependent of the court, it'd cost her nothing financially.

The news took time to settle in. One part that I was able to absorb was that there would be no more visits between Jenna and Marianna. *Lo que pasó, pasó*, and now Marianna could begin to move past her traumatic start the best she could, and with our help.

At the same hearing, Judge Hooke continued Gaby's case, siding with Jenna's attorney, who now blamed Our Bright

Futures for her missed visits. After Jenna's multiple cancellations and no-shows, the agency had demanded that Jenna confirm her visits before Vernon could put them on his schedule. The agency's lack of flexibility thus "did not make the child available."

To make up for the lost mother-daughter meetings, Judge Hooke ordered DCFS to double the number of visits with Gaby to twice a week. With increased visits, waitlisted for housing, emancipation on the way, Jenna was being readied for a new chapter in her life—a life with her baby. Well, not so much a baby anymore, a pre-toddler.

Where was it all heading?

I felt I knew the answer, I knew it for some time. We would have one child, but not the other. The system was splitting up the sisters—giving Marianna to us, Gaby to Jenna. Jon had been right all along.

My thoughts rolled back to our time in Idyllwild, that one golden summer we had with both of them—a sepia picture of a carefree, perfect childhood in the open air, among oaks and pines. I wished I could keep only that one season in my memory and erase all the rest because that's how it all should have been.

Fires and Smoke

As our struggle to make our family permanent started to tip towards a favorable outcome, so did the LGBTQ community struggle for full equality in marriage and family rights across the US. In California, a wide array of civil rights, religious, and professional groups, along with the state's largest cities and bar associations, filed an unprecedented 30 *amicus* (friend-of-the-court) briefs in support of marriage equality.

In April 2007, New Hampshire and Washington passed civil union and domestic partnership laws, respectively. There would be no other acts recognizing same-sex marriage or its substitute forms for the rest of the year. But in September of the same year, Maryland's highest court ruled that the state did not have to recognize or sanction same-sex marriage—a replica of many such measures already passed around the country.

What was also unprecedented, and exhilarating, was to watch Hillary Clinton, Barack Obama, and four other Democratic candidates debate LGBTQ issues live on "The Visible Vote '08: A Presidential Forum," hosted by Human Rights Campaign on August 9, 2007, on the Logo channel. Clearly, we'd come a long way if our support was being courted openly.

§

In LA, ashes were falling softly all day long. The air was foul; the morning sun ascended into twilight. We had to cancel a visit because the air was so toxic. Most schools and businesses were closed as well.

Two hours away, in San Diego, at 4:30 a.m., police ordered my sister Rina to evacuate. Rina had already dropped off her dog and cats at a friend's house, packed her belongings, and drove herself to a shelter. The fire passed within a mile of her condo.

Those October 2007 fires, raging from Santa Barbara to the Mexican border, were indeed historic: close to a million people ordered to evacuate, 1,300 dwellings destroyed, 600 square miles burned.[27] And yet they were expected—the right sort of year, the right sort of weather. In SoCal, we are used to natural disasters. The region's ecology, as the historian Mike Davis observed, is shaped by the annual cycle of out-of-control wildfires, floods, and earthquakes.[28]

November brought a respite. With cooling weather, and overcast skies, the fires had been mostly put out, and the evacuees, including my sister, returned home.

As arranged, I started to drive Gaby twice a week, Tuesday and Thursday afternoons, to her unconfirmed and unmonitored visits with Jenna 30 miles away.

At her first post-court visit at the park, Jenna emerged from the van with a stroller and Tupperware with baby food. She didn't rush to get the child. Instead, leaning on the stroller, she walked around the van to the rolled-down window of her driver and counselor Morgan, yelling something about $600 in some savings account. So here we were: Jenna taking her time ranting by the van, and me holding Gaby in my arms across the parking lot.

I expected Jenna to carry herself victoriously—the county was finally looking for a home for her and Gaby, just as she had hoped. Yet Jenna looked surprisingly glum.

But at the next visit, just as inexplicably, her attitude changed. At the pickup time, Jenna started recounting to me, in a somewhat frantic but friendly manner, what she did with Gaby during their two hours together. I kept my response to a minimum, our distance intact. These wild swings of attitude, I sensed, had nothing to do with me. Lynette, the new social worker, could have enlightened me, but she missed that visit just like all the ones before.

Driving back, sadness overtook me, breaking through the Paxil barricade, the copious doses I'd been taking to numb myself to handle it all. Waiting for the light to change, I glanced over my shoulder at the little child curled up in the car seat; I turned, took up her tiny, soft hand, my face twisting up in a spasm. Gaby's eyes, shiny brown buttons, were staring back at me in confusion.

Might she have any idea of what was going on, any idea at all?

I hoped not. She'll be home soon enough, I thought, home with us and her sister. At least, for now.

Lynette called later that night to reschedule seeing Gaby.

"We missed you today, Lynette," I told her.

"Well, something I told Jenna last time I saw her at the group home got her real upset, so I thought I should give her some time to cool off."

How I wished to know what it was, to see through the smog covering the case.

"Jenna must be so happy she'll be moving in soon, with the baby," I ventured casually. "I heard you guys gave her a glowing report."

"Report? I didn't write that last court report. Jackie Willis did, and attached my name to it without my knowledge."

The note of resentment in Lynette's voice made me wonder. I thought DCFS was greenlighting the handover; it was just a matter of weeks. What had Jackie reported to the court that Lynette found so disagreeable?

She wouldn't say, but through morsels of information picked up here and there, I gathered it concerned Jenna's high school.

§

My father flew down to San Diego to check on Rina in the aftermath of the fire, and then brought her and her dog to us in Long Beach for a visit. The "cocker-poo" was most eagerly awaited by Marianna, who chased it around the kitchen with peals of laughter. Gaby, at a safe distance away, was watching the doggie curiously, covering her mouth ladylike, and holding on to Jon's knee, which was level with her head.

We drove to Seal Beach for a stroll on the pier. Out there, the California coast was gorgeous in its rough, winter beauty: pewter-grey ocean waves cresting high, dotted by scores of surfers in black wet suits; above them, the sun breaking intermittently through the low clouds.

Marianna ran ahead with Rina and the cocker-poo. My dad carried Gaby on his chest, keeping one hand over the hood of her rain jacket to protect her from the chilly wind. He really took to her, which, given her sweet, calm demeanor, wasn't hard.

§

Marianna's adoption process was getting underway. Having ended family reunification, the court's next step was to sever Marianna's biological parents' rights over her, clearing the way for the final hearing to place her with an adoptive family—us. It sounded simple, straightforward.

Yun Hee called to schedule a meeting to sign the initial paperwork. She was discussing our post-adoption payments. In the middle of her talk, I caught myself thinking I was dreaming. I couldn't accept it; I couldn't allow this good news into my conscience. It felt too dangerous to believe this would actually happen. I could accept that we were less likely to lose Marianna now, but not that she was about to become fully ours.

We might have been a bit ahead of the time, as back then in 2007, we were adopting Marianna as two unrelated, single adults in the eyes of the federal government. Our flimsy domestic partnership meant nothing outside of the state borders. Full marriage wasn't possible yet.

November 12. The morning started, as usual, in the bathroom. While I was changing Gaby, Marianna took the initiative in removing her gown pants herself, diaper, gown top, and, finally, the onesie. Then she pulled up her Curious George "underwears," a skirt, pushed her head through a T-shirt, and, after several tries, put on her red fleece sweater, backwards.

"Yay!" I applauded. "You did it all by yourself. The first time ever! What a big girl you are."

Marianna beamed, wrinkling her little nose.

That day marked two years since she came to live with us.

Twelve or Eighteen?

Despite a relative calm, clouds were gathering. Lynette called me to go over some details she needed for her court report. I reminded her to include the letters and reports from Gaby's physician Dr. Goldfarb and Kim, her occupational therapist.

"I don't believe I got them on file," she said.

"Oh . . . didn't Jackie pass them on to you?"

"Nope, don't remember seeing those."

"Vernon has a copy of both letters. I can ask him to fax them over to you."

"If you want."

If you want. Why such a lack of interest? Why wouldn't Gaby's social worker *want* to know what the child's doctors had to say?

"Okay. Anything else?" She was clearly wrapping up.

I decided to ask her point blank, leaving aside our habitual dance of hints and inferences.

"Lynette, what are you recommending to the court?"

"Well, Lane, we still got a few things missing. Let me get all the facts in order . . ." and so on and so forth.

She mentioned Yun Hee stopping by to see her about Marianna's adoption paperwork. That gave me an idea. I left

Yun Hee a message, and just as before, she came through.

"You asked me to check with Lynette about Marianna's sister Gaby, right? She said she's still working on her 12-month hearing report."

"You mean her 18-month review hearing report?"

"That's not how I remember it. She said the 12-month hearing report."

"What do you mean? Gaby is almost 18 months."

"Right, hm . . ." she sounded puzzled. "All I know, if I recall it correctly, is that this hearing had something to do with their mother's being denied services for Marianna's sister."

I thanked Yun Hee and immediately dialed Stephanie. "It's urgent," I said.

§

"It's true," Stephanie confirmed, "Jenna is contesting Gaby's 12-month review claiming DCFS did not provide her with reasonable services to have the baby come home. The court has to address it before it can move on."

This delay held water legally, but it also subverted the spirit of the federal law and the state's welfare code, which limited the reunification period for a small child like Gaby to six months, not a year, and certainly not a year and a half. Delays and postponements—this was Marianna's story being played out all over again.

"And she is very close. That's what Jackie Willis reported to the court: Jenna has completed most of the reunification order requirements—rehab, drug testing, parenting classes—all except therapy. So her new social worker, Lynette Huckaby, tells us that since Jenna is complying with the court orders overall, she feels she'll have no choice but to recommend Gaby's placement with her."

Now I could see through the veil of Lynette's politeness and evasiveness, I could see why she'd been keeping me in the dark.

"Jenna's therapist, however, thinks that Jenna still has a lot of issues to resolve before she can competently parent."

"Sounds like Jenna's therapist is afraid to sign off on the county plan."

"Could be, or maybe he just states the facts. Either way, I'm going to fight to end reunification now, at this postponed 12-month review hearing. Gabriella is turning 18 months in two weeks. We can wait for that hearing, but what can Jenna achieve in two weeks that she couldn't in a year and a half?"

"Sounds logical, but what if the judge still decides to hold this 18-month hearing?"

"Then it will go up for a contest by either me or the mother's attorney. The judge will have to set it for a trial, and those proceedings won't start until January . . ."

". . . and that will give Jenna another extension to comply."

"Yep, we don't want that to happen."

I knew what she meant. Ron Griggs's children's court procedure pamphlet noted that "in rare circumstances," family reunification can be extended for yet another six months past the 18-month hearing. There had been no shortage of *rare circumstances* in these kids' cases.

"You see, Stephanie, we've been having problems dealing with Lynette Huckaby. To me, it sounds like she is having a conflict of interests representing both the mother, whom she clearly supports, and the daughter, who seems dispensable to her. Can anything be done about it?"

"In other words, you want me to get the kids' social worker fired?" Stephanie laughed.

I laughed back, waiting intently for her answer.

"Don't hold your breath for it, Lane. This issue has come up a few times before, and the courts, at their highest levels, believe it much more efficient to have one social worker in charge of a dependent family, even if the worker herself isn't exactly impartial. Ultimately, it's the court's, not the social worker's responsibility to decide what to do with the child. So you're stuck with Lynette. Find a way to deal with her."

Lynette's name popped up again when I stopped by Playtime Learning to pick up the kids in the afternoon. She'd dropped by earlier in the day, unannounced, telling Estela it was easier for her to do than to see the kids at home. Why not at home, I wondered? She hasn't been to our home—the kids' home; she hasn't met Jon or me—the kids' foster parents.

"I was . . . disappointed," said Estela indignantly, "by how this lady was praising the mother that we've never seen, while we've been watching these kids grow up here, right here. I also didn't like that she didn't want to hear what great parents you guys have been to these girls, and how terrible it will be for the baby to be taken from you. It's like she got it all wrong!"

§

Saturday morning, fighting off a cold, I attended the meeting of the regional chapter of the state's ESL faculty organization, now as its community college chair. My voice gone, I had to stay out of the discussions, but no matter. I felt grateful for having something going on in life to get me out of the house besides household chores and grading. I was also making travel arrangements to fly to Germany to attend the World Congress of Applied Linguistics, the tri-annual Olympics in my field. Having spoken at the previous congress, I had two new studies to present this time. The children were my top priority, yet other aspects of my life were still going on. They kept me sane.

§

Wednesday, November 21, we reached another milestone in Marianna's case. Yun Hee and an Our Bright Futures representative came to our house to witness us sign Marianna's preliminary adoptive placement documents. The foster life was officially over for Marianna; she was now in an adoptive placement, though not legally ours, still the ward of the court.

Yun Hee gave us a thin folder with information about the birth parents: Jenna's mostly redacted, zero about the father, and the pic of Marianna when she first went into the DCFS care—a seven-month-old infant with a headband over shortly cropped hair, big chestnut eyes staring unsmilingly at the camera.

I'd expected to feel happy, but I didn't. It could have been

Paxil bulldozing my emotional highs, or Gaby's situation weighing heavily on me. Either way, I just felt pleased that we'd made it to that day, all four together, our family intact, and that was that.

Untying the Knot

November 27, the morning of the court hearing, I called the orphanage.

"Hi, Morgan, it's Lane, calling about Jenna's 3 p.m. visit today."

"Oh . . . don't you know she's in court?"

"I do, but I need to confirm, just in case I have to drive." What I was really confirming was whether Jenna had made it to the court.

"Well, she's not here. Why don't you call again after 1? We should know by then."

"Sounds good."

Around 1:00 p.m., Morgan called me back herself.

"Just heard from Jenna. Sounds like her case will be heard in the afternoon. We don't expect her to return until after 5. So, no visit today."

The cancelled visit opened up my afternoon. After teaching at Los Angeles City College in Hollywood, I headed out to Amoeba Records nearby, my favorite music store. That was where Stephanie, around 4 p.m., caught me on my cell phone—in the World Music section lined with CD bins.

"Good news, Lane. We terminated Jenna's family reunification with Gaby."

"Oh my God! Really?" I shouted in disbelief. "Incredible, wow!" My shouting was catching stares from people in other aisles. "How did it happen?"

"It's because of Jenna's high school. To be eligible for transitional housing where they accept babies, like Holy Names, she has to graduate from high school. She's fallen behind in her studies. At this point, she is looking at graduating in spring, but it's just too late. This is what I've been working on since October—Jenna's had a year and a half to reunify, but she still has no home for the baby to "return to." Jenna's therapist also doubts her parenting skills. So, in essence, she's not ready to take care of the child—not at some point later, *right now*, it has to be *now*. That's the court's finding.

"Judge Hooke spoke to Jenna a few times, saying 'I have to wear two hats.' She said she was really pleased with the progress Jenna has made—staying clean, staying in school, continuing therapy; but, as she said, 'putting on another hat,' she didn't see Jenna 'ready to be a mommy.' In that second capacity, she explained to Jenna as gently as she could, she had to protect the baby's rights first."

I was stunned. This turn in the case came as a complete surprise.

"Wow, Stephanie. I don't know what to say . . . I thought I knew it all, but it seems that it's Jenna's graduation delay that is ending her reunification. That wasn't even on my radar."

"Yep, as far as the judge is concerned, Jenna reached her limit. Even if her social worker disagrees."

"What do you mean?"

"Lynette Huckaby asked to extend the family reunification services until next December."

"A whole other year?"

"I know. It doesn't make sense. Gabriella can't wait that long. Even the county counsel, Bertha Moore, argued against Lynette's recommendation, siding with me, which helped a lot. Lynette did submit your fax and Vernon's report, but there were no letters from Gaby's therapist and physician."

"Vernon sent them to her. I know it for a fact!"

"We were fine without them. I had your copies just in case

we went down that route. But we didn't need to; Judge Hooke terminated Jenna's reunification in one day, one hearing, rather than continue to an 18-month review. We don't need to go any further, contest anything. Jenna simply ran out of time to get her act together."

I exhaled. "So this is it?"

"Um . . . not quite. Jenna is interviewing for several transitional programs which potentially accept babies. If all goes well, she'll be moving into one of them by March. At that point, she might file a modification petition arguing that her circumstances have changed since the termination order. If she does, she'll need to prove that it would be in Gaby's best interests to resume the reunification process, rather than allow her to be adopted by you and Jonathan."

"Does she have a chance?"

"There's always a chance, of course, but to me, the difficulties she'd have to prove it would be overwhelming."

I knew what she meant. Now that reunification had failed, the alternative concurrent planning track, including adoption, was taking precedence. To redirect the process back into reunification, Jenna, the birth parent would have to prove "a preponderance of the evidence to show that the child's welfare requires such a modification."[30] To Stephanie, Jenna's potential move to transitional housing wouldn't merit the reversal of the entire process. Yet, the possibility that Judge Hooke, who had been so supportive of Jenna over the years, would consider it remained.

"For the time being, the judge ordered to continue unsupervised visits with Gaby, but reduce them to once a week."

"No problem."

"That's not all though." The tone of Stephanie's voice changes from relaxed and confident to tight and determined.

What else can there be? I thought.

"Jenna filed an appeal of the termination of parental rights for Marianna."

"Oh . . ." I felt more disappointed than shocked or angry. Signing the placement papers had seemed too unreal, as if we didn't deserve it. Too quick for a happy ending.

"What's your take?" I asked.

"The appeal is general; there's nothing concrete in it. So far, I see nothing she can really latch on to. It's just the continuation of her denial. She even told the judge, 'I can't understand why you're not letting me see Marianna,' but the judge just ignored her. Still, the appellate court will have to read the entire case and see if there was some problem, procedurally. Marianna's adoptive status won't change, but it'll just take longer for you to finalize. I can't tell you how long, but longer. Just sit tight. Appeals move slowly."

"We'll ride it out, Stephanie. Gaby's news is the real deal. I was so afraid again that we were going to lose her. It's the fourth time we came close . . . I can't thank you enough for not letting it happen."

"Well, I'm glad it finally came through. She deserves a stable, permanent home, with her sister and you two. We set the preliminary date for the termination of her parental rights for mid-April. We'll be in touch."

Part 7
Dads and Daughters

Lane and Jon's marriage, San Francisco City Hall, July 2008
© Lane Igoudin, 2008

Lynette

In the two weeks after the hearing, my mood improved considerably. I went off Paxil, which had its advantages: my sex drive was back to its normal highs, and I gained back some of the 30 pounds I'd lost at the height of the drama. Yet something inside me felt unsettled; we'd turned the page in both kids' cases, but the finish line remained elusive. Our daily life under the microscope, the calls, and the weekly visits went on as before.

Jenna's first visit after the court fell on a sunny, yet chilly, winter Tuesday. This time, stepping out of the van, she was wearing sunglasses. I couldn't see her eyes, but I noticed how much she'd changed. The pounds she'd gained during her second pregnancy remained. Her facial features, still retaining some soft bloom of youth, had sharpened, setting her face in a guarded expression.

Gaby no longer cried when I handed her over, she just kept looking at me. By now, she had apparently accepted it as a regular routine—being left for a short while with this young woman, with the assurance of my return.

While Jenna was wheeling Gaby to a picnic table behind a row of sycamores, I stayed behind and walked over to the driver's side of her van.

"Whoa, that baby has grown!" gushed Morgan, her gaze following Jenna and the stroller up the ramp into the library. I leaned against her side of the van.

"Oh yeah, quite a bit. Anything new with Jenna?"

"Oh, the same, trying to make it to graduation, hanging out with the girls. She's learning to cook, by the way. A counselor has been teaching her and other girls at the emancipation cottage. Jenna now gets to cook one day a week."

"Have you seen Lynette?" I asked. "I keep hearing about her coming to the visits, but haven't seen her yet."

"She's been visiting Jenna at her cottage. Last time she stopped by, she sat a long time talking with Jenna, apparently, to get through her head what's going on."

"Really?" I asked.

According to Morgan, Jenna was in deep denial about the loss of both children, of the necessity to think through her career plans after emancipation. In other words, of the end of the life she'd grown accustomed to since coming into the system reportedly at age 12. Coming to grips with reality was going to be hard. Real life was about to begin. No more county handholding.

I listened and nodded.

"This appeal on her older child, Marianna," I changed the subject, "is it Jenna trying to get at us? Why's she doing it?"

Morgan shook her head. "I don't think she's spiteful; that's just not her. Though she sure can be confused about things. You know what Jenna is like: one day she wants one thing, another day she wants another."

"Is she moving soon into transitional housing?"

"No idea."

"Really?"

"We'll be the last to know. She's going to have to, at some point. She can't live with us forever."

§

In a few days, I heard Lynette's familiar twang.

"I've got this new court order here. It concerns you, Lane. It tells DCFS 'to coordinate with the caretaker to keep the mother updated about Gaby's medical appointments.'"

"Sure."

"Glad we agree. You got any doctors' visits coming up? I'll see when Jenna's available."

"Now, wait a minute here . . ."

It sounded illogical that Jenna would suddenly start getting involved in Gaby's medical appointments after her reunification with Gaby was cut, and her parental rights were next up for termination. What was the point? Didn't she see how intrusive, logistically difficult, and just plain awkward it would be?

"Sweetheart, that's what the judge ordered. Jenna is still Gaby's mother, she has the right to attend her daughter's appointments if she chooses to do so."

"That order you read to me says to 'keep the mother updated,' not to get her to participate in doctors' appointments. I'll be happy to keep you and her *updated*. She doesn't need to come to any of them."

"Well, it's not me. It's the county counsel," Lynette's mellow voice sounded less than sincere. She was trying, it seemed, late in the game, to build up the case for Jenna's parental involvement. No wonder Jenna was delusional—Lynette was fanning the flames. "Check with Gaby's attorney if you don't believe me."

"That's fine. If we have a doctor's appointment, I'll be sure to let you know. When are we going to meet you, Lynette? You've been on this case for months now."

"I got a lot going on, Lane," she said curtly. "If I'm available to see the kids, I'll let you know. Are the kids alright?"

"Of course."

"So there's nothing for me to worry about."

§

In the weeks leading up to Christmas and Hanukkah, our house was buzzing with activity. Jon was mounting red and green wreaths on the windows outside to the sounds of Yolanda Adams and Patti LaBelle's holiday records. The kids were decorating the Christmas tree in the living room. Meanwhile, I was lining up the toy dreidels around the fireplace menorah.

Marianna helped me stick stamps on a stack of holiday cards piled high on the dining room table. On the card, the kids were dressed in matching pink fleece sweaters with fuzzy wintry-white trim around the hoods; Marianna grinning wide, showing a full set of teeth, and Gaby—included for the first time—smiling at the camera, her tongue sticking slyly out of the corner of her mouth, "A ball of sweetness and warmth, with a little pinch of mischief thrown in," as I would describe her in one of my emails.

With the calendar year ending, the doorbell kept ringing. In the week before New Year's Eve, five people paid us visits: a regional center social worker, the agency rep for the annual home inspection, Kim Dally for her therapy session with Gaby, and Vernon, like a bearded Santa in cowboy boots, bearing brightly wrapped gifts for the kids.

The last person to pay us a call was . . . Lynette.

The morning of December 31, she rang me up. "Hi Lane, I'm having lunch in downtown Long Beach with my husband. Thought this could be a good time to see the kids since you guys are so close. I've got to see them once a month, you know."

"Who does she take us for?" Jon was fuming behind my back. "Cutting into our New Year's Eve like this, like our house doors are ready to swing open 24-7 at anyone's convenience. Why can't she schedule her visits ahead of time, and on a weekday, like everyone else? She had a whole month to do it!"

I muffled the phone and told Jon that I agreed, it was disrespectful, but we didn't want to give her an excuse to complain to the court. And I was curious to finally meet her.

Lynette arrived on time. A middle-aged woman, touches of country from her long hair and bangs to her boots, she observed us politely, coolly. She complimented us on how well Gaby and Marianna looked, steering the conversation away from the case to local attractions and our plans for the new year. She didn't stay long, didn't ask to see the kids' bedroom and playroom, didn't actually venture into our house ten feet past the living room armchair.

She didn't like us, that much was clear. Polite and experienced, Lynette gave off the unmistakable homophobic vibe, to which any gay man is as attuned as any Black man to covert racism. It was in the avoidances, the lack of eye contact, the cold, insincere smiles that put me on guard. This would be the first time in our foster-to-adoption process I felt we were viewed differently.

In the way Lynette talked about Jenna, I sensed empathy, but of a particular kind—the kind you feel for a wayward relative. She probably understood Jenna better than any of us, knowing all too well the dysfunctional milieu that would produce and ravage Jenna, feeling for Jenna like for a misbehaving daughter or niece, scolding her while doing her best to protect her and build her up, to turn the all-but-lost case in her favor.

Jackie, a middle-class Black woman, had none of those biases and saw Jenna for what she was. We lucked out with Lynette coming on the case so late. Her belief in Jenna's redemption would have taken the children out of our home months ago.

"Picture Time!"

After the holidays, the visits with Jenna moved from the park back to the Santa Fe Springs library, more appropriate for chilly winter days.

"Look what I brought you, mama." Jenna rattled a plastic bag with Christmas toys in front of Gaby. Christmas was a month ago, but she had no presents then. She must have saved them, expecting Gaby to come to live with her. The termination court changed that.

Gaby looked withdrawn, indifferent to Jenna and her toys, her eyes tinged with redness. She scrunched up her tiny potato nose and, after a couple of seconds, emitted a half-hearted sneeze.

"Ooh," purred Jenna, "we got little sniffles . . . is she okay?" she asked me.

"She's sick. The fever is mostly gone, but she's still a bit weak, and her nose is still running."

Jenna didn't respond, but regarded the little girl with concern and tucked in her blanket.

§

The visit cut into the middle of a very long day. What made that week crazier than usual was the overlapping semester schedules in the multiple colleges where I was teaching hourly courses: in Orange County, the winter courses were still on, while in LA, the spring semester had already started. This overlap resulted in sixteen-hour days, with classes running from eight in the morning until ten at night, with the kids' visits squeezed into the afternoons.

I had no choice; this is how an educator makes a middle-class living in a tight labor market while trying to parent. And it wasn't just about settling into a new career. The 2007 Playtime Learning pre-school bill alone came to $19,388. That was about half of my income that year. The county's foster payments covered less than a half of the actual costs of raising the kids. While Jon's salary contributed a larger portion of our family budget, it simply wasn't enough. I had to keep teaching bloated course loads at four colleges until I finally landed a full-time professorial position at Los Angeles City College in 2010.

§

Stephanie's call came at 6:55 p.m., right before my fourth, and last, class for the day, and in the midst of trying to locate the section transfer form for Thuy, an ambitious young student who aced the diagnostic test and was eager to transfer up.

The first news was good. A special court-appointed attorney reviewed Marianna's 1,000+ page case and found no grounds for the reversal of the termination of Jenna's parental rights.

"So then the appeal is dead in the water?"

"Not yet. The appellate court still has to review it."

"How long will that take?" I asked.

"At least two months, but it may go up to six. Only after that can we get a court date on the books for your adoption proceedings."

And that was how the "good news" dissolved into the usual drag.

"There's something else."

Her tone made my gut tighten.

"About Gaby. Jenna is filing a writ before the appellate court to show cause for the termination of her family reunification."

"Could you explain it to me?" I muffled the phone with my hand. "Thuy, go to class. I will talk to you in a minute, okay?"

"Jenna is trying to prove the court made an error in ending her reunification with Gaby. So far, her attorney requested the case records, but what the court clerk sent her was incomplete, and she is awaiting the full transcript. In the meantime, this writ may postpone the termination of Jenna's parental rights to Gaby, which we scheduled for April, and if it proves that something was done in error, it can thwart the entire process."

I sighed. "It never ends, does it? What should we do, Stephanie?"

"Nothing really. Just wait and see what Jenna's attorney is able to find that she can actually contest."

The elderly department advisor was eyeing me across the long hallway, furiously. Our meeting before class—I'd completely forgotten it! He was probably thinking I ditched him to chat on the phone.

"Thanks, Stephanie." I hurried to end the phone call. "Like you said, we'll just wait and see."

§

Soon, low clouds turned into a hard winter rain. One morning, as I was getting the kids ready for daycare, I sat Gaby up in my lap to tie her fuchsia rubber boots. Her hair was growing unevenly—Jon wouldn't let me cut it, so it just framed her face in a sort of chocolate froth.

When I finished, I bent over to help Marianna put on her rain boots, too. She kept trying to do it herself, but couldn't get one loop around the other.

"Can I sit in your lap, Pappy?" asked Marianna.

"Yes, sweetie."

She climbed up noisily and exclaimed, stretching her arms out, "Picture time!"

Gaby leaned over to Marianna and gave her a hug around her waist, putting her own head on Marianna's shoulder. I hugged them both and kissed each on their foreheads.

This unscripted moment diffused the morning rush out the door, the routines. It stopped the clock. For a second, I tried to imagine my life without these kids in my arms—just Jon, work, projects, and friends, like it used to be.

I couldn't. These two little girls, their happiness together and mine with them, were by far the most significant thing I had ever done. How could I feel unfulfilled? Without them, the longing in me would have been much greater than anything else could ever fill.

With the wipers shoveling rivulets of rain left, right, and off the windshield, I drove the kids to daycare, then on to my last winter class at Coastline College, then to two more at Cypress College; their spring semester had started.

Jon surprised me when I got home.

"Are you okay, Lane?" he asked. "I'm really concerned about how you're dealing with all the stress."

I liked his attention. I liked it so much I didn't know what to say.

I put my bag down and looked at him. "Why are you asking?"

"I'm afraid that one day you'll drop dead of a heart attack or leave me."

My eyes popped out. "Leave you? I'm never going to leave you, Jon. Nor the kids. Don't ever think that."

"You still have to do something to relax. Every night when I see you, you look exhausted."

I couldn't argue with that.

"I'm fine with the kids in the evening," he continued. "Surely you've noticed that. You can always grab a bite to eat instead of having dinner with us. Maybe you could cut some classes too."

I was touched by his thoughtfulness. He was right, of course, but I didn't want to change anything.

"That winter class I taught this morning was the last one. It should get a little easier now; I'll just have my spring schedule to teach. So thank you, dear, thank you for thinking of me, but I think I can manage."

Cycles

Gaby picked up a couple of French fries from her plate and put them in her mouth. Her jaws were gnawing them in a circle, no longer just sliding them back-and-forth as she did four months ago when the therapy had started.

"Looking good," said Kim Dally, nodding her head.

"Now that she can chew properly," I said, filling up Gaby's sippy cup, "we're starting to feed her table food, chopping it rather than blending it."

"Plees." Gaby stretched both hands out towards her cup.

"Here you go." I handed it to her, tightening the lid.

"T'ak you."

"Wow," said Kim. "She knows these words already?"

"Yep, we can hardly believe it ourselves. With Marianna, we're still working on 'thank you' and 'please.' Gaby says all those, and also 'hi' and 'bye-bye,' and all in the right situations."

"What are you drinking, sweetie?" Kim asked Gaby, pointing at her cup.

"Jush," Gaby replied, shooting Kim an inquisitive glance from under her eyebrows—this facial expression, like many others, completely, originally hers.

"No-o," said Kim, "water!"

"Jush!"

Kim shook her head in disagreement.

Gaby cackled, picking up on Kim's game.

"Jush! Jush! Jush!"

"Okay, juice. Marianna's juice?"

"No Nana jush. Ga-bee, Ga-bee jush."

Then she offered it to Kim.

"Good news, Lane. I'm not noticing any signs of delays." Kim looked pleased. "My job is done. I'll be sending my final report to the county next week."

§

Marianna's synagogue class was learning about *Tu B'Shvat*, the Jewish holiday of trees. The teacher and the kids recited the blessing of the Lord who creates the fruit of the trees, and then tasted apricots, dates, figs, and nuts from the paper plates on their tables.

"Why do we need trees?" asked the teacher.

"They give us food to eat," said one boy.

"They are big and pretty," said another girl.

"They make homes for birds and bears and tigers," said Marianna and looked at me.

I nodded in approval, good answer.

The teacher then spoke about what makes trees grow and explained that in the land of Israel, late winter is the traditional time for planting trees.

"Who wants to plant a tree?" she asked.

All hands flew up.

This class, which I was observing with Gaby dozing off in my lap, was a welcome interruption in the task-to-task race that characterized my days. It reminded me to notice something very essential I'd lost and regained only when outdoors, hiking, kayaking, just being out—the sense of connection to nature, to its change of seasons.

In Moscow, where I grew up, each season was sharply defined—freezing winter; fragrant, awakening spring; lush, wet summer; rainy fall. In LA, with its comparatively minimal fluctuations in weather year-round, and amidst our very hectic life, I'd rarely been in touch with this fundamental cycle of seasons—birth, growth, death, rebirth. But I glimpsed it there, amidst our "process," as I was watching Marianna, like other kids around her, stuff a hollowed-out apple with seeds and dirt, spray it with water, and put it in a Ziploc bag. The seeds were supposed to sprout, and then she'd plant the apple tree embryo in our backyard. It was spring, time to plant.

Tu B'Shvat, I thought, means *Purim* isn't far off, followed by *Pesach*, *Shavuot*, then summer, then High Holidays, *Sukkot*, and then we start again. This year-round Jewish cycle overlies other cycles in which we exist—Easter egg hunt and Christmas tree, national holidays, school calendars, our birthdays, the anniversary of our union. These are the cycles in which, if God wills it, our kids will grow up.

Some cycles were destined to end, however. Roger and Inga were splitting up. The divorce proceedings were underway; their house was slated to go on the market. Inga, still beautiful and impetuous, took off for Vancouver to prepare to move her son and her business up there.

"It's her fault." As usual, Babushka's judgment was fast and final. "The woman has her ways to control her man; she should be the smart one in a marriage. If a marriage falls apart, it's because the wife let it happen."

"Grandma, it's not Odessa, 1925."

"And what of that? You think women have changed much since then? They haven't."

I was supposed to rebut her. From the American standpoint, this assumption was ludicrous. But in the Old World—not so much. Men were expected to misbehave and women to control, cajole, and cater to them. And that's where she and Inga were from.

I didn't respond. We were already sad for Inga and Roger's falling out, for us losing the neighbors we loved so much, for Marianna losing her playmate Tommy.

Absences, Witnesses, Summons, and Appeals

Marianna couldn't identify her Mommy, but Gaby apparently figured it out. "Nya-nya," my original code name, got transformed into "Ma-ma," and no amount of correcting that I was "Dada" or "Papa," and not "Mama," had any effect on her. Jon and I just chuckled and hoped it would pass, as parenting books say it should.

Unfortunately, her naming preference went public under the worst circumstances.

At a visit, awoken from her nap by the handover from the car, Gaby went into an instant overdrive, reaching out to me, screaming, "Mama, mama!"—right in front of Jenna.

Jenna flashed me an angry look. In a huff, she yanked the stroller away from my car, then wheeled Gaby up the library ramp, but the little one just wouldn't stop screaming.

Jenna froze at the library door, unsure what to do, embarrassed in front of the audience of Morgan, library patrons, and me. If she took Gaby inside, they would disturb the patrons. Jenna went inside.

I returned an hour later, at 2:30 p.m., Gaby's frantic screaming, which apparently had ceased, restarted the second she saw
me, and didn't stop until Jenna rolled her out, brought her to
my car, and silently walked away. Only then did Gaby's crying
drop down to spastic breathing, and eventually, deep sighs.

I left Stephanie a message, asking her to please, please, please
check on Jenna's deadline to file a writ.

"So glad you reminded me," Stephanie said, returning my call. "I
just checked. Jenna had until January 21. That was three days ago."

"Have you seen it?"

"Nope, so I assume nothing got filed. If so, without this writ,
Jenna's appeal of her termination of reunification with Gaby
will have to be dismissed."

"When will we know for sure?"

"Probably within the next two weeks."

§

Gaby was shrieking in Jenna's arms at the next visit as Jenna
and Lynette were trying to soothe her in soft voices.

"It's just some teenagers," shrugged Lynette, "they gave
her a fright."

The moment I took over, Gaby downscaled to sighs, jerking
her head sideways, until she calmed down completely.

§

The week after, the scene repeated unvaryingly. Gaby started
crying the moment Jenna picked her up. Her cry followed me
inside the library where I dropped off books and headed to the
computer lab past the two of them, the crying Gaby and the
hapless Jenna, sitting at a table in the café area. Gaby's wails
came through just as loudly behind the flimsy screen, partition-
ing off the computer area. I hesitated in front of the lab assistant, realizing I wouldn't be able to check my email with the
child crying so close to me, while I could do nothing to help
her. I turned around and headed back to the library.

Inside, I grabbed a book off the New Arrivals shelf and situ-
ated myself in an armchair at the far end of the stacks. I could

not read a word. Gaby's cry cut like a distant siren through the thick door.

I called Lynette, who didn't pick up the phone.

I called Morgan—same result.

I rubbed my temples, asking myself how much longer, how many more times I could go through this. Lynette Huckaby, Judge Hooke, Jenna's attorney, and whoever else was advocating for reunification should have been right where I was, tied to a chair, forced to listen to these screams.

A few minutes later, I saw Jenna wheel the stroller out into the drizzle. She had to be taking Gaby to the car, I figured, thinking that with Morgan, she'd somehow calm down.

Sure enough, in a minute, my cell phone rang.

"Hey Lane, could you come and get the baby?" asked Morgan. "She just won't stop crying."

I ran outside. I took Gaby into my arms, and instantly, as though flicking a switch, she fell silent after forty-five minutes of hysteria, save for those deep sighs and head twitching. I carried her to my car in a tight hug, kissing the brown locks covering her forehead, her reddish, swollen cheeks, her little nose.

§

Gaby was due for a physical. In the doctor's waiting room, where after years of bringing the kids in for shots, check-ups, referrals, and emergencies, the staff knew me by my name, I got nervous.

What if Jenna turns up? She knew about the appointment: I dutifully notified her via a phone call to the orphanage and a fax to Lynette. What if she'd had her transportation arranged and was on her way? How awkward it would be having her here, discussing Gaby's health, immunizations, suddenly putting my authority as the child's factual parent, my decisions about her health, on trial.

I squirmed thinking about it. Every door opening in the patient lounge made me jerk my head—was it her?

Jenna did not show up. Gaby and I made it through the growth measurements, head-to-toe physical exam, and three immunization shots. There was no reason for concern. The only prescription I left with was a refill for the diaper rash cream.

After the physical, I dropped off Gaby at daycare, drove to Orange County, taught two courses, returned home, picked up the visit bag, and drove back to daycare to pick up Gaby. In the process of parking, a text beeped in from Morgan: "I just found out we'll have to cancel the visit. I'm so, so sorry."

No problem. I drove home with the gift of a couple of hours of quiet before the night class. I used the time to write a fax to Lynette, recapping Gaby's health assessment this morning, Jenna's absence, and then the last five visits: the drama, the cancellations, the witnesses present, including her.

"I do not know what you can do to alleviate the situation," I concluded, "but it seems to me that these weekly visits have turned into a form of emotional torture for Gaby."

I interrupted my typing. Ultimately, what *could* Lynette do?

A lot, I realized. If Lynette took up Gaby's side, *she* would be doing what I was doing: alerting the court, fighting to curtail the harmful visits, encouraging Jenna to transition out of a reunification fantasy and into the real world, a tough, unwelcoming world into which she was supposed to emancipate within weeks and somehow survive.

I got no response. But I did get a call from Stephanie who received a copy of my fax.

"Thanks for alerting me, Lane. I'm going to use it to file a petition tomorrow morning to decrease the visits to once a month. No matter how long it will take us to get Gaby's birth parents' rights terminated, there is no reason she should suffer these visits."

"That's what I think too, Stephanie. Jenna is trying to have a relationship with Gaby, she really is, but it's not working, and it's not doing anybody any good."

"Jenna probably won't give up the visits without a fight. Can I subpoena you, along with Lynette?"

"Of course, no question. I stand by every word I put down there. Or you can ask Morgan, Jenna's counselor; she's seen pretty much everything I've seen."

"Jenna, by the way, didn't file any writs to contest the end of reunification with Gaby, and the deadline has passed."

"Wow, so there goes the appeal . . . is there anything else she can do before the termination on April 11?"

"If she gets moved into transitional housing, she can file that modification petition I told you about. The judge may deny it, or order a hearing. Jenna may also claim a special relationship with Gaby, although the baby crying around her will pretty much kill that. But just so you know, these motions can be filed even as late as the day of the termination hearing, as long as they come before the termination order is issued. If Jenna files, the trial may continue into the summer and go on for quite some time. So don't hold your breath for April 11."

§

I was in the middle of giving a midterm in a grammar course. While most students were busy doing their work, some were trying to cheat. A couple of instant Fs later, they grudgingly fell into line. A watchful eye, clear instructions, and immediate consequences—for their own good; it never ceased to amaze me how similar managing an adult classroom at work was to parenting at home.

My phone vibrated, and I took the call standing by the open door, my feet in the hallway, but my eyes facing the students, who were beginning to stir.

"Oh hi! Glad I got you on the phone. It's Donna here! Yeah. I'm really confused—why should that girl be getting our baby? She's way too young, she's got no one. Got our Tony into all this trouble, and now blaming him for—"

"I'm sorry, who's this? And who are you calling?"

"Thought I wrote it down right, your cell phone number . . . is this Lynette?"

"Lynette? No. It's Lane. And who are you?" It took me a few moments to realize who this Donna was. My heart shrank.

"Oh… Oh, I must've called the wrong number," she rasped. "Now wait a minute, Lane? Lane, you that professor guy taking care of my great grandbaby? How is she?"

"She's doing great, Donna. Let me get you Lynette's number—"

"She walking yet? I ain't seen her in a long time. You gotta bring her around to my house sometime. Tell me—"

"Right. Here's Lynette's number. I can't discuss any of this with you. Call Lynette. But just so you know, the baby is doing fine. I have to go now."

"Alright, you go. Thank you. Thank you."

I broke out in a sweat.

Oh my God, I thought, *is he back, back after nine months? Back to claim Gaby?*

To us, Tony was a distant memory, a phantom gone. The court cut his reunification with Gaby during his nine-month absence. Everyone assumed his parental rights would be cut *in absentia* as well at the upcoming April hearing. Why was his grandmother calling Lynette? She must have received a letter from the court. Hearing the baby left in the system was going away for good probably caused a stir, hence the call.

Could Tony halt the process? He still had a whole month, and like Jenna, he had the right to file a modification petition claiming changed circumstances.

Would he?

§

"What's with Tony's Grandma? Why was she calling me, or Lynette Huckaby, to be exact, after all these months?"

I posed this question to Carl, the dependency court investigator, at our house to write a report on the children's progress.

"You mean Ms. Donna?" Carl chuckled. "I actually *made* Lynette hand-deliver the court appearance notification to her. Donna's house was our last-known address for Tony. Oh, she didn't like that, Lynette, having to drive all the way there. Those court letters bounced back—some problem with the street spelling. So that's where Lynette saw Donna, his grandmother. Tony himself, turns out, is still in Portland. Seems like his mother lives there. Grandma promised to let him know, so Lynette had her sign Proof of Service. And then he called."

"Did he?" I jumped.

"Yep. Just a couple of hours later, and said he's going to come to court. Lynette took his current address and sent him another copy, this time directly to him. That's how we found him."

Homophobia

"*Chag Purim, Chag Purim, Chag Gadol la-Yehudim* . . ." a kids'
choir was singing on the synagogue stage.

Dressed primly in princess frocks as two Queen Esthers, Gaby
and Marianna were watching the *Purim* play from the sanctuary seats. The din from the dozens of noisemakers going off at
the mention of Hamas, the villain, disconcerted Marianna. She
clung to me while Gaby, less interested, slid down from her seat
to the space between the rows to explore the contents of my om-
nipresent visit bag, spreading the diapers, wipes, and extra underwear for her and her sister on the floor in a sort of *ikebana*.

She was all calm and smiling, a huge difference from
the morning.

That morning, we were awoken by the *gevalt* coming from
the kids' bedroom. Gaby emptied her crib of linens, ripped the
embroidered *arpilleras*, Peruvian tapestries hung above it on the
wall, and threw them on the floor. Marianna, sharing in the
festivities, was hopping in Gaby's barren crib as if in a jumper.

I put them both in time-out, one for pulling down the *arpilleras*, and the other for cheering her on. Marianna, seated on
the bottom stair, predictably stomped her feet and vocalized
her displeasure at the top of her lungs.

Gaby, a few feet away, responded differently. Rarely put in time out, she acted like an offended princess: keeping mum and staring at me with an accusatory pout.

I came over and asked, "Gaby?"

Gaby defiantly swung her head to the right, chin out, mouth tightened into a thin line, acting very much like offended royalty.

"Are you going to listen to Daddy and me?"

Silence.

"Okie-dokie . . . sit here then till you change your mind."

The screaming resumed the moment I turned to walk away. But when I returned, Gaby pointedly ignored me, head, chin, and mouth set back in full attitude. I had to leave and come back a few more times until she began to cooperate.

Irritated as I was, I liked Gaby's newly discovered attitude. No longer just a cuddly, loving baby, her personality was expanding into new dimensions. In her, stubbornness was endearing.

§

High in the mountains above Big Bear Lake, the last spell of winter often comes in early April, and it made Marianna jump with excitement: snow, real snow, the first snow in her life! She went around the camp playground searching out and stomping joyfully on the sooty, slippery patches hidden in shaded spots under oaks and pines.

And for me, what joy it was to be planning nothing, doing nothing, just sitting there and watching her play.

The much-anticipated April 11 hearing was just two weeks away, but up there, two hours from LA at a family weekend organized by the LA Gay & Lesbian Center, it didn't feel real or important. The mornings would start with a tug-of-war and a marshmallow-spaghetti house building contest; the rest of the day packed with fun stuff—all very lighthearted, a place where we could just be ourselves.

Later, during a group hike through the forest, another toddler launched a snowball, which hit Marianna in the cheek. It didn't hurt as much as shocked her with its sudden freezing sensation. Marianna let out a scream, but then, still screaming, she ran ahead, not wanting to stay behind other kids. The hike turned quite strenuous as we scrambled down a steep, muddy slope to the bottom of a creek, and then up again. As the sky was turning dark, we completed the loop, cheeks reddened by the unfamiliar cold weather, proud to make it back, and hungry.

After dinner, the camp staff turned down the lights, inviting everyone to the family dance. I stayed behind while Marianna climbed on stage and went swaying and jumping to Rihanna's "Please Don't Stop the Music."

"Your daughter's really into it, she's got good rhythm," commented Aliza, the Jewish half of a Black-Jewish lesbian couple, much like ours. Marianna befriended their mixed-race daughter on the hike.

"Oh yeah, she does," I agreed.

Aliza struck me as culturally so like me: her close watch, her hands-on interaction with her daughter, her eyebrows raised critically at other parents letting their toddlers roam the icy grounds in flip-flops and shirtless.

It was way past her bedtime, but Marianna refused to leave the party, delivering her first big tantrum that weekend. I prevailed, and once she was back in our cabin, teeth brushed, PJs on, she fell asleep instantly, with all the lights on. As the temperature outside dropped below freezing, heat and cold in the room alternated in volatile jumps. In the middle of the night, the bang from the heater turning itself on woke her up. Marianna sat up and smiled drowsily, still halfway in her dream, and I massaged her back in a circle to help her fall back asleep.

§

The entire drive back from Big Bear, and for days afterwards, I felt anxious, unsettled. This puzzled me—Marianna and I had had such a wonderful, relaxing time together; the camp was fun, the staff and the families couldn't have been more friendly.

I didn't arrive at the origin of this anxiety until the following weekend, deep in meditation with my Zen group.

My mother's birthday passed the weekend we were at the camp. I didn't call her. Quite unusual for a family where birthdays are of paramount importance, in part because there are so few of us. An uneasy sensation was hovering over me—I knew I was supposed to do it, but I just couldn't.

Diving deeper into the swirl, I touched the true source of my resistance to calling her—thick, pulsating, ugly—my mother's disapproval of my sexuality, of the way I live my life. That's what kept me away from her. I could neither accept my mother's rejection nor deny it, so I blocked out her and her opinions altogether—I rejected the rejector. And it worked well, most of the time.

Yet at the camp, her disapproval came back, manifesting itself in an insidious sense of strangeness I felt among the lesbian moms, who outnumbered gay dads four to one. Masculine features peeked through some faces, male body posture in others. When they didn't, their union looked even more strange.

There was one family I caught myself staring at—two long-haired, wholesome-looking women from a small town in the Central Valley with three kids. Consciously, I was accepting of them, admiring them even for raising three kids, but somewhere deeper, I wondered why they'd want to be with someone like themselves.

Then, logically, why would I want to be with someone like me, say, Jon? The disorienting, infectious doubt.

There is a term for this—*internalized homophobia*. Poisonous, insidious, learned mostly from the people whose opinions matter, people you love. You know who you, your partner, and your kids are, but then, abruptly, this stable norm is abruptly removed, swept away by a dizzying apprehension of living a life that is a fraud.

I rarely feel that way because I am, nearly always, comfortable with who I am, but on those rare occasions this feeling hits me, it leaves me disoriented.

What restored my balance, reaffirmed my identity, was, of all things, a movie. Returning home from the meditation, still under the shadow of anxiety, I joined Jon watching *Brokeback Mountain*. Beautiful and touching, the tenderness between

Ennis and Jack echoed my feelings for Jon. My sensitivity dulled by our real-life drama, I'd been afraid to allow myself to really feel, to be vulnerable. The movie pierced the armor.

Feeding Gaby afterwards, putting her to bed, I thought again how lucky I was, compared to Ennis, Jack, and millions of other men like me, lucky just to have these moments, lucky to hope to keep this child in our family.

I remember then going upstairs, siding up next to Jon, and holding his beautiful, warm body tight in my arms. Like Ennis and Jack, except with a happy ending. Too often I take Jon for granted, I realized, and I shouldn't. How blessed I was to find him, and to spend so many happy years, so many blissful nights and ordinary days, in the constant glow of his presence.

Relishing his warmth, his love, brought back the sense of who I am. The pendulum stopped swinging. My anxiety passed.

The Hammer Strikes

"Lane, you need to hear this!" Jon put on the speakerphone, eyes beaming.

"Hello, Lane and Jon." Stephanie's voice on her voicemail message was confident, cheerful. "Finally, finally, finally, I've got some good news for you. It's about Marianna. The appellate court notified me that the appeal in her case was withdrawn. It's not clear if the appellate judge threw it out, or someone convinced Jenna to withdraw it for lack of merit. Whatever the reason, it's gone. Gone, woo-hoo!" Click.

Jon was looking at me, ecstatic. "It's over, you hear it? It's all over! No one can mess with Marianna's adoption anymore!"

Slowly admitting the news into my consciousness, I didn't share Jon's joy. I felt afraid, afraid to see this hope destroyed like so many before. I couldn't let down my guard, not yet. To me, the Wall was going to come down, the fireworks would light up the sky over the Brandenburg Gate, only when it was really over, all of it, and the court and the system were gone from our lives forever. The fact that the last roadblock to Marianna's adoption had been removed was encouraging. Encouraging— that I could accept.

The week of Gaby's court date, by a stroke of luck, I caught Stephanie in her office.

"Everything is on track. I'll attempt to terminate Jenna's parental rights this Friday, and we'll probably go to trial. I'm already aiming for May 15 as the trial date. You should also know that I filed a petition to cut Jenna's visits down to a half-hour once every two weeks."

"Good."

"I attached all your faxes about the visits. I know I asked you before, but are you still willing to testify? I can put you on the stand. What do you think?"

"If it helps, absolutely. Should I cancel my class?"

"Let me think . . . let's see how things go in the morning—the case might not even be heard until the afternoon anyway. So just make yourself available, okay? I'll call you if we need you."

"Will do. Is Tony coming?"

"Tony, Gabriella's birth father? Why should he?"

"The county found him, through his grandmother."

"Really?" She paused. "That's news to me. It might complicate things."

"Nobody told you?"

"No . . ." She sounded baffled. "Well, I suppose if Tony was planning some action, I would've heard it by now. So we'll see."

§

Three days before the court hearing, Gaby and I were sitting on the library steps waiting for Jenna. Gaby was in my lap, inside my big puffy rain jacket, safe from the gusts of cold wind. I was using the time to clip her nails.

"Whose little fingers are these?" I asked her.

"Ga-bee," she replied.

"And these little feets?" I squeezed them gently.

"Ga-bee."

"And this little nosie?" I tapped her on the little knob in the middle of her face.

She laughed.

Twenty minutes into the scheduled visit, Jenna was nowhere to be seen. I put away the nail clippers and called Morgan at the group home.

"She's not there?" Morgan sounded surprised. "I just got here myself, my shift just started. I didn't know she didn't get transported . . . well, I suppose I could take her."

"How long will it take you to get here?"

"To Santa Fe Springs? Half an hour, at least."

"Just so you know, I'm supposed to take Gaby home in 40 minutes."

"Well then, never mind, we'll just call it off."

Five minutes later, Lynette rang my cell.

"Lane, Jenna called me just now about your cancelling the visit," she started out in an accusing tone. "I want to know what happened today. I want to hear your side of the story."

"I don't know what to tell you, Lynette," I said calmly. "I've been here, at the library, the whole time. Still here, matter of fact, in the library's bathroom, changing Gaby before we go home. Jenna is the one who's absent."

"Jenna says she had a scheduling problem," Lynette replied, a bit more conciliatorily, "but she just didn't have your cell number."

"All she had to do was ask her 'staff.' They've got my number, they've got the foster agency number, they've got your number. How many people does it take to get Jenna to the visit?"

Lynette backed off. "Don't get mad at *me*, Lane. She doesn't drive, you know that. Though I agree; Jenna should take on at least some of the responsibility to schedule her appointments and make sure she has some way to get there."

"What frustrates me, Lynette, is that Gaby and I just drove 30 miles here—for nothing."

"Yeah, yeah, I understand," Lynette replied. "Well, you can go, I suppose."

"Alright. Hope she'll get her transportation worked out for this Friday's hearing," I said, pulling up Gaby's jeans and standing her upright.

"Don't you worry. I'll make sure she will."

I expected Lynette to end the conversation, but she suddenly added: "Tony will be there too. He confirmed. He called me up this morning and asked if Jenna was still seeing their child. And I told him, 'Yes, young man, that's what parents do.'"

That was interesting. I moved the phone to my other ear. "He did? How did he take it?"

"Don't know, hard to say . . ."

"So now he is planning to go to the hearing?"

"Yeah. That much is clear."

§

Awaiting the hearing that was to decide Gaby's future, I should've been mostly worried about its outcome, or at least of having to testify, but what unnerved me the most was Tony's presence in the courtroom. I was expecting him to bring up all kinds of excuses for his long absence, to contest his separation from Gaby, to force the case to go to trial, like Stephanie said. In the meantime, the judge, while taking time to untangle his claims, would order visits, and we'd be back in heavy rotation with him and Jenna, and no end in sight.

§

Friday morning, April 11, 2008, as agreed, I went to work. No calls came during the class. Afterwards, having heard nothing all morning, I drove to a department store, assuming the court was in lunch recess for at least an hour, an hour I could spend stocking up on kids' diapers, shoes, and summer clothes.

Still no call. I quickly packed the bags and the boxes in the trunk and decided to drive to the gym on my way home. If Stephanie still needed me to testify, I could throw back on my teaching clothes and rush to the court.

The car parked, I was walking up to the gym entrance when my cell suddenly beeped. I had a message. Apparently, her call came in while I was driving through a dead spot on the freeway. It went straight to voicemail.

Stephanie's message was short: there was no need for me to go to court as the parental rights for Gaby's birth parents—both birth parents—had been terminated. The end, total and complete.

"Yes! Yes! Yes!" I shouted, jumping up and down in the gym parking lot. "It's over! Oh my God, it's over!"

People walking the treadmills behind the glass wall were looking at me like I was deranged.

I ran back to the car, hitting the redial.

"Congratulations, Lane!" Stephanie picked up the phone on the first ring.

"I don't know what to say . . ." I breathed out, "oh yes, I do: Thank you! A huge thank you from the kids and from us!"

"You're most welcome!"

"Did it get ugly, in the courtroom?"

"Not really. Jenna agreed to have her rights terminated," she said.

"Formally? She actually said it?"

"Yes."

"Wow!"

I was too stunned to believe it. I expected Jenna to fight to the last and the trial to drag out until the fall. I was so wrong.

"Jenna told the judge she realized she couldn't take care of Gaby and wanted to have her adopted with Marianna. She'd made the same statement before the court."

"So wait, Stephanie—are you telling me you knew that going in?"

"Yes, but I didn't want to get your hopes up in case she'd change her mind. She's done it before."

"Gaby's rejection must've had some effect on her, I think."

"That came up in court too. Lynette Huckaby's report described Gabriella's persistent crying in her mother's presence. Instead of testifying as a witness, or asking you, Lynette interviewed that third party you've mentioned—Morgan McCoy, Jenna's counselor, who drove her to the visits. Morgan stated that sometimes the baby cries, sometimes she doesn't. But, she said, Jenna can't stop her crying and sometimes cuts her visits short. If anything, you'd expect Morgan to support her client, right? Her statement made it very difficult for Jenna to claim a 'strong relationship' with Gaby. So Lynette's report also supported termination. Except not expecting it to happen so quickly, she asked to continue the visits, just reduce them to once a month until the matter settles."

"I bet she was hoping something might change in Jenna's living situation in the meantime."

"Maybe. But she was also very complimentary of the care Gabriella received in your home and at Playtime Learning, and of Gabriella's successful completion of Regional Center services. This time Lynette attached all her medical and dental documents. Not one negative word about you guys in that report."

"Interesting," I said. "I don't know what to think about it . . . she somehow warmed up to us, I guess."

Stephanie was asked to leave the courtroom during the hearing of Jenna's own case—which came after Gaby's. From what she heard afterwards, Jenna wasn't doing so well in her own progress: she got fired from a job for shoplifting and was moved back to the pre-emancipation cottage at the orphanage, a step down.

"And Tony?"

"He showed up. Alone, actually. None of his family came. I made it clear to the court that he had no reason to claim a parental relationship with Gaby after being gone for ten months. Tony still made a 'legal objection to his TPR for the record' and was quite emotional in court."

"Burst out crying?"

"Uh-huh."

"Not surprised. I've seen it before. And Jenna?"

"Jenna didn't cry. She looked quite relaxed actually, smiled even. They can appeal their terminations, you know. I'd put my bet on Tony, though you never know with Jenna either."

"What's there left to appeal?"

"The only ground she can claim now is 'ineffective counsel.'"

"Well, that'd be a joke. She's had an excellent attorney; stood by her all these years."

"Yes, Janine's been very effective. Just so you know, Judge Hooke allowed Jenna one 'goodbye visit' with Gaby. Probably unmonitored, but the judge didn't specify."

"Of course, but can we make sure there's a social worker present, Lynette or Vernon, whichever? Just like after Gaby's birth, I don't want to be the one taking away her child the second time. Nor do I want to be remembered by Jenna with hostility. Judge Hooke and DCFS terminated her rights, not me."

"That's reasonable."

I will dress Gaby up nicely, I decided, for Jenna's sake. Jenna will want to have nice photos from her last visit with her child.

§

Still standing by my car in the gym's parking lot, I called Jon.

He was simply overjoyed. "This is it, babe! We're done! You can relax now."

We'll see. Before getting in the car, I left quick messages for Babushka and Dad.

Arriving home, I saw Inga, back from Vancouver. She was coiling up the garden hose on her porch, watching Tommy push his truck down the front steps. Their house was in escrow. Roger had moved out.

I shared the news.

"Pozdravlyayu! (Congratulations!)" Inga said in accented Russian and gave me a warm hug. "Funny," she continued in English, "how we're always here when something big happens."

"C'mon over then," I invited her, "Jon said he'd put a bottle of champagne on ice and have a cake ready."

"I won't say no to that," she smiled.

In a few minutes, Inga and Tommy were knocking on our door, carrying juice and mangoes for the kids. Behind them stood Natalie, in her office clothes and a laptop case under her arm, coming for the Shabbat dinner. Inga told her the news, and Natalie screamed and clapped her hands.

We sliced the cake and the mangoes in the kitchen, and clicked flute glasses with Inga and Natalie, celebrating the breakthrough in the case. The cause of the celebration, her head in a swirl of mahogany curls, was rubbing her eyes, tired after a long day.

The Hyphenated Name

Marianna's adoption hearing was set for May 7, 2008, less than a month after Jenna and Tony's termination of parental rights. Everything seemed in order when on Monday, April 28, during dinner, we received a call from Mark, the adoption attorney recommended to us by other PopLuck dads.

"The county counsel asked me to cancel our adoption finalization date. She says that Judge Hooke has not received the *remittitur*—"

"The what?"

"The document from the appellate court that transfers jurisdiction over the case back to the trial court—back to Judge Hooke. They were supposed to issue it at the same time as they dismissed Jenna Sewell's appeal of the termination of her parental rights to Marianna, but for some reason, they haven't."

"This hearing has been on the books for months, Mark!"

"Right, but now the county says we've been allowed to proceed with scheduling finalization 'erroneously.'"

"Anything else missing from the file?"

"Not that I know of."

"Okay, let me see what I can do, but do not, I repeat, do not cancel the date!"

§

I went on the Internet to learn more about this new obstacle. The appellate court generally issues a *remittitur* 61 days after the appeal ruling, setting aside that time for challenges. Sixty-one days, I calculated, was April 29, which was the next day, eight days before the finalization. I immediately set to work: emails, phone calls, messages.

By the end of the week, the *remittitur* still hadn't reached the Children's Court. Stephanie said there was still time to get it into the court file before the Wednesday hearing. She would neither notify Judge Hooke, nor cancel the hearing.

Tuesday night, May 6, when Stephanie left the court, it still wasn't there.

The morning of Wednesday, May 7, we dropped off Marianna and Gaby at Playtime Learning on our way to the courthouse. We'd made the decision not to take Marianna with us to the court. As much as her adoption finalization meant to us, we didn't want to draw her attention to it, to remind Marianna one more time that she'd been abandoned, and that we were somehow not her 'real' parents. To Marianna, we believed, there should be no difference between her being part of our family that day, the day before, or that memorable day two and a half years earlier when she came to live with us as an infant.

We arrived at the courthouse excited and uncertain. Jon was carrying a thank you card and a festive bouquet for Stephanie, just in case it would all go through. I carried a briefcase with files, including, as instructed, photos of Marianna, should anyone ask.

"They've got the *remittitur* this morning," said Mark, after greeting us by the courtroom door.

I exhaled. We went in.

Every available surface in the courtroom was taken up by stacks of files. There were several open boxes of stuffed teddy bears in the corner.

Judge Hooke looked about the same—a dry, imperious face,

but older. That didn't surprise me: shut out of the process, we hadn't seen her in nearly two years.

"Okay," she said, holding two thick files, "here we have Marianna and Elizabeth."

"There is no 'Elizabeth,'" Stephanie corrected her. "Marianna has a sister, Gabriella, whose parental rights we terminated last month. This is not her hearing."

"Oh, Marianna, Marianna…isn't she Jenna's child?" Hooke asked.

I nodded. At least she remembered Jenna, even if she didn't remember the kids.

Judge Hooke was staring at me over her glasses. Clearly she was beginning to remember me now too, from all the letters and faxes that had gone into the children's files.

Hooke then looked down at the adoption order, verifying the spelling of our names and of Marianna's adoptive name. Hearing Hooke pronounce, for the first time, Marianna's new last name, which hyphenated Jon's and mine, felt surreal, overpowering.

"I can't believe we're finally doing it," I whispered to Stephanie, who was standing next to us as we were signing the adoption documents.

Jon got teary-eyed while we were waiting for the papers to be stamped and brought back to us. He squeezed my hand, "Thank you, babe! It's all your hard work."

I had nothing to say in reply; I just couldn't stop grinning.

The First Weddings

June 16, 2008. I hadn't slept a wink the night before. The tension had been building for months. On May 15, the California Supreme Court ruled to allow same-sex couples to marry. Once the marriage decision came down, the right-wingers opposing gay marriage asked the court to stay it, but the judges rejected their motion. Anticipating it, the same conservatives had collected enough signatures to qualify for the November 2008 ballot as a state initiative; the so-called Proposition 8 that would overrule the court decision and prohibit same-sex marriage in the state.

All eyes, in the state and nationwide, the night of June 16 were on the weddings of the original plaintiffs in the case: Phyllis Lyon and Del Martin, a lesbian activist couple in San Francisco, and two other community leaders, Diane Olson and Robin Tyler, here in LA. If those two first marriages were allowed to go through, the next day the doors of all registry offices in the state would be flung open for all gay couples.

§

The Tyler-Olson wedding was set up on the steps of the Beverly Hills Municipal Courthouse, complete with a table with champagne glasses and a three-tiered white wedding cake topped with a pair of brides under a cascade of whipped cream roses.

The crowd of about a hundred people included sixty-some guests, two dozen protesters, police, and security. The rest were all media, a lot of media; I counted nine TV trucks, both English and Spanish-speaking channels, BBC, and NHK, and spotted reporters from *Los Angeles Times* and the Associated Press.

I arrived dressed in a suit and carrying a simple sign saying "*Finally!*"

"Who're you with?" a tough-looking gatekeeper bellowed over the din.

I told her the name of an attorney friend of the couple who'd invited me and was waving at me, with her partner, from behind the police line.

"Go in the back!" she jerked her head over her shoulder.

People loved my sign and took pictures of it. There was no shortage of other signs made up in block letters, some six-foot high—"Repent!" "Homo sex is sin!" "Sodomites and lesbos, hear me (sic) true JUDGMENT and HELL for what you do!" Those were held up by a semicircle of the protesters a short distance from the courthouse staircase.

At 5:01 p.m., in the courthouse lobby, in the presence of a county supervisor, the Beverly Hills mayor, and their attorney Gloria Allred, Diane Olson and Robin Tyler signed their marriage licenses. Watching them through the glass walls outside, the crowd roared joyously.

The newlyweds came out of the doors with Allred, holding up the license papers to more ovations. They weren't young, but looked vigorous and radiant—Tyler with her short dark hair, and Olson, a long-haired blonde, both in white linen suits. The rows of white chairs set up outside emptied out as the wedding guests flocked to the couple, surrounding them. I lifted my sign.

Olson and Tyler descended halfway down the steps to the *chuppah*, the four posters of which were being lifted by their relatives and friends. Photographers and headphoned video crews swarmed the *chuppah*, thrusting their cameras directly in, just inches from their faces.

I stood two cameras behind Tyler, which allowed me to catch snippets of Rabbi Denise Eger reciting the vows: "Do you take . . . for your lawfully wedded wife . . . to love and cherish . . . from this day forward . . . for better or for worse . . . in sickness and in health?"

"Yes!" said Tyler.

"Absolutely!" affirmed Olson.

Then they crushed the glass (Tyler after several tries), signed the *ketubah*, and kissed.

"A-bo-mi-na-tion!" chanted the protesters. "God hates you!"

Allred grabbed the microphone and hollered back, holding up the licenses, "If She was here, She would approve!"

The ceremony now completed, Olson and Tyler walked over to the cake table and thanked all who came. The public officials spoke too, while the newlyweds had a line of reporters waiting. But I was heading home where I would put up my sign in the front window.

Those were exhilarating, groundbreaking days. The Olson-Tyler and Lyon-Martin weddings dominated national news, as California became the second state in the Union, after Massachusetts, to allow full marriage, and not only to the gay couples who live here, but to *any* gay couple wanting to get married. For several days, news stations broadcast images of hundreds of exultant couples streaming into registry offices throughout the state. I felt the public opinion shift as millions of people were absorbing the non-verbal joy, happiness, and love emanating from the newlyweds.

Our PopLuck mailing list, our phones, and our emails were abuzz with sharing news and tips about wedding locations, officiants, caterers, and marriage license dates. Our excitement, though, was tinged with uncertainty whether the marriages would actually stand, or be annulled by a court decree like after the 2004 'Valentine Revolution' in San Francisco.[31]

§

We too will get married, Jonathan and I decided.

We drove to a jewelry store at a mall nearby to buy rings and ended up with a matching pair of yellow and white gold bands. Buying them was a chaotic experience: the girls were running around the store while Jon was trying to catch them, unable to pay attention to what we were choosing.

"You like these?"

"Yeah, get them," Jon responded, barely turning his head, while pulling Gaby down from the glass counter she was trying to climb.

The rings felt heavy in my hand, solidifying 11 years of our union into perfect, luminous objects.

Seven Blessings

The rings were packed.

The public marriage appointment was set for July 3 at San Francisco City Hall.

A dear friend took out a license to officiate.

I was drafting the wedding script.

San Francisco was a natural choice for our marriage ceremony: this is where we'd met, where many of our friends and some family members were still living.

Getting a marriage date was hard. Despite the expanded calendar, all of San Francisco County's June and July dates were booked solid. In the post-Supreme Court decision wedding stampede, the county clerk's office apparently turned off its phones (I called five times), did not answer emails (I sent three), and the online reservation system (which I checked daily), had zero openings.

Then one appointment opened up online—the last one before the county would be closing down for the Fourth of July—and I seized it.

We met everyone for lunch at an old Italian restaurant a short walk from the City Hall—friends mostly, my college friend

Robin brought her daughter Syann. We appreciated them coming in the middle of a workday for a makeshift celebration. "We are not planning a full formal wedding," said our email invite, "because after 11 years together, and two kids, there is really no point."

I didn't invite my mother: we were no longer on speaking terms. Our contact narrowed to birthday card exchanges and tense meetings at Natalie and Devlon's whenever she and Mark would pass through LA on their way to a cruise or a hot springs resort.

I had to let go of the fantasy of having a real mother for myself and a grandmother for my kids. It wasn't right, but it was alright, easier that way.

My father and stepmother were on a cruise to Alaska. I didn't want to force them to change their pre-planned vacation on super short notice. To my father's credit, he sounded excited on the phone and sent us a generous gift.

We had stopped to see Babushka on the way up to San Francisco. She was the one family member who really wanted to witness our *gei svad'ba*, gay marriage, but the logistics—the drive, the walker, the absence of Dad—were insurmountable.

Still, we spent a wonderful day with her, the kids bouncing on her couch, playing beach ball with her, and enjoying her homemade lunch.

"*Posmotri, nichevo?* (Look, not too bad?)"

With a mischievous twinkle in her eye, Grandma handed me a stack of papers. This was the draft of "A Fair Law," her article written for a widely read Bay Area Russian weekly—an enthusiastic response to the legalization of same-sex marriage in California.[32]

"The editor has promised me a two-page spread!"

She'd backed up the facts with her half-a-century psychiatric expertise—the kind of information that doesn't often reach her deeply homophobic émigré readers. At 86, Babushka was again in hot water and loving it. She was ready for the vitriol she was about to get.

I hugged her. Her article was the best wedding gift I could ever hope to get.

§

So there we were, Jon and I, dressed in suits—Jon's charcoal and mine off-white—adorned with matching boutonnieres handmade by a friend, enjoying our wedding lunch with friends, Gaby wrapping her head in a table napkin, Marianna blowing me kisses from across the table, and laughter and clinking of glasses all around. I hadn't expected it to be so lighthearted, so laid back. I felt no burden, just radiant joy as if carried on a cloud.

We'd be married in a couple of hours in the city of our youth, a short cab ride away from where we had first met. Outside, the city was overcast and chilly, wrapped in its typical midsummer gloom. The night before, after taking the kids to a new playground in the Castro, the city's gay neighborhood, we had dinner in Chinatown and stayed with a friend in North Beach, with a view of Coit Tower rising in a moonlight blur in the fog. Being there was like bringing together the fringes of the prayer shawl, all four corners of our world, of our lives and histories, into one perfect union.

The county clerk's old-fashioned office had high ceilings, but was also small, like a principal's office, barely enough for the four of us and a couple of friends. Gaby got fussy, so we sat her up on the counter.

Going over our names and the birthplaces of our parents (Arkansas, Oklahoma, Russia) on an application which no longer listed "husband" and "wife," but the gender-neutral "party 1" and "party 2", cemented in legal terms to everyone who we were to each other. With our signatures and the state's official seal, our union, which began as an improvisation there in San Francisco 11 years earlier, became a true, legal marriage.

Like Olson and Tyler, we emerged from the doors holding up our marriage license to the cheers from our friends and family. The kids, freed from the confines of the clerk's office, escaped down the gilded, palatial hallway of City Hall, playing hide-and-seek behind the marble statues that line it.

We walked a few feet down to a marble landing with the vast Beaux-Arts expanse of the City Hall behind us, the same place where the wedding of the other marriage case plaintiffs—Phyllis Lyon and Del Martin—took place three weeks earlier.

Here our officiant, Jan Elise Sells, took over. To me, Jan has always represented California: a free Berkeley spirit with flowing golden curls, an accomplished therapist, a modern dance teacher, and Jewish. I couldn't have wished for anyone better to marry us.

Jan read a poem, introduced each of us, and went over the vows in our script—all in her signature warm, down-to-earth manner. She then brought out our wedding bands and passed them to our friends, asking each of them to bless them.

"I now present these rings to Jonathan and Lane," she said, "and as they exchange their rings, I'd like them to tell us what it means to them."

"Okey-dokey," said Jon, and as he put a ring on my finger, he stuck out his tongue jokingly, and read a short poem he'd written for the occasion.

When I, in my turn, put a ring on Jon's finger and read my speech, he cried. And then we kissed, maybe longer than customary, but oh well.

Gaby was getting tired—she was missing her naptime—so Jon picked her up, and she immediately stuck her thumb in her mouth. Marianna too reached up, so I picked her up as well.

With our daughters in pastel silk dresses swept up into our arms, we listened to Jan reciting our *Sheva Brachot*, the seven blessings Jonathan and I wrote together:

"May all people live in peace and free from suffering, illness, and violence.

May all gay people, African American people, Jewish people, and all other oppressed minorities achieve justice, equality, and respect.

May you always follow the path of wisdom and courage in your work, relationships, and everywhere else.

May all your friends and relatives remain in your lives for many years to come, and you in theirs. Without their love and support, you wouldn't be here now.

May you always share the love of your children, who brought a new light of happiness into your lives.

May you open your hearts to accept yourselves and continue to help your minds and souls grow, as you age and face the challenges of life.

May you always change, but your love remain unchanged."

"And," Jan added, "may Obama win!"

"A-men!" Everyone clapped.

The Aftermath

"I see birdie outside," Gaby said, pointing to the window of her bedroom.

A simple sentence, yet it embodied so much: a subject, a verb, an object, a locative, a reference to something I could not see. I went over to the window—a hummingbird was circling the blooms on the honeysuckle vine below her bedroom window.

"Yes, sweetie, little birdie. It's drinking juice from the flowers, see?"

Gaby nodded.

"You want to play Winnie-the-Pooh cards with me?"

Gaby nodded again.

"Okay." I pulled one card out of the stack. "What is Pooh doing here?"

"Pooh read book." Gaby enunciated each word with a lot of stress and very seriously, like a newscaster.

She was right. "How many books is he reading?"

"Four, five, six!"—her default answer for any question about a number.

Jon left to visit friends in New York. I insisted on it; he needed a break after a very stressful year.

Gaby got clingy the first day, getting upset when I'd leave the room. When Jon called at bedtime, Gaby stared at the phone and exclaimed, "Daddy! Where's Daddy?"

"Daddy is not here," Marianna said matter-of-factly from her bed. "He's not coming back."

"He is," I corrected her. "Daddy will be back soon. Friday you'll go on a field trip to the park, then we go to the shul for the Shabbat dinner, then you go to bed, then you get up Saturday morning and we'll all go to the airport to pick up Daddy. See, he'll be home soon."

They were very, very good the entire time of Jon's trip. Even the schoolteachers at Playtime Learning commented on how well they were behaving.

Our friend Debbie stopped by and brought some lipstick which got them very excited; she put it on both of them. Gaby tried to eat it off her lips, but Marianna understood its purpose and kept checking herself in the mirror from different angles.

One night, Gaby managed to climb out of her crib and we found her in her sister's bed. In the morning, I rushed to the store to buy her a toddler bed. The first night, unfamiliar with the new bed, she ended up sleeping curled up on the floor with her head resting on the bed.

§

On Jon's return, just a few days after Gaby's second birthday, we signed her preliminary adoption placement papers. Yun Hee Park, the county adoption social worker, arrived on time, but Amanda Truong, Our Bright Futures' representative, was a half hour late.

"Hello," Yun Hee greeted her with a stiff, formal smile. I could tell she didn't appreciate being kept waiting.

"I'm so sorry. The traffic was bad."

"Oh, that's too bad."

"Do we need to sign the county documents first?"

"Oh, don't worry," said Yun Hee in an even voice. "We did it while we waited for you."

Amanda's face tightened just a tad, but I noticed it after three years of teaching first-generation Asian American students. The reprimand was noted.

With the signing of the docs, Gaby was now formally out of foster care. We were no longer the agency's clients and would report directly to the county until Gaby's adoption was finalized. Besides signing the papers, there was no other recognition, formal or informal, of the end of our three-year relationship with Our Bright Futures. No cards, no thank-you, not even requests for referrals. I thanked Vernon, though, with a gift at his last visit. He said he was retiring.

§

At her monthly visit with Gaby, Lynette again got chatty. Now that we were close to the end of the process, she was finally warming up to us.

"Would you believe it? Tony just called me the other day, asking how Gaby was. Said he needed someone to talk to. It sounded like he was tearing up or something. 'Well,' I say, 'she's doing just fine, young man, she's very well taken care of.' When he heard his baby is okay, he calmed down some. 'You should be talking to a counselor, not to me,' I told him. 'You need to find yourself a good therapist to work through your issues.'"

"You think he's going to appeal the TPR?" I asked

"No, I don't see that coming. He just wanted to know how his baby is doing, that's all."

"What about Jenna?"

"I don't think she wants to appeal either. She's been really focused on her graduation this month. She got herself enrolled in Job Corps and wants to be a chef."

"Is she still living at that group home?"

"Yes, and she'll be staying there until the court reviews her case and decides what to do about her. Legally, once she's out of school, she can petition to emancipate. But they'll also need mine and her therapist's recommendations . . ."

I didn't ask what her recommendation would be.

"But get this," Lynette said, "her mother is coming to her graduation."

"Whose—Jenna's? You found her?"

"Oh yes, up in Oregon. She left Jenna when she was very little, and just a few months ago, our locator person tracked her down. That one phone call turned Jenna's life upside down. She's no longer alone! She asked for permission to go visit her mother, but the judge said no. First, she said, graduate and emancipate, and then you can leave the state. So they've been talking on the phone—a lot, especially about her Mom's coming to her high school graduation, and Jenna sure is excited about that. 'Don't set your sights too high,' I said to her, 'this woman showed no interest in you for a very long time, so if you don't see her showing up, don't be surprised.'"

"Does Jenna ask about Gaby?"

"No, not at all. All she talks about is graduation and Job Corps and getting the hell out of California."

§

The appeal deadline on Gaby's parental rights passed with no filings from Jenna and Tony.

In August, Lynette came for one last visit before Gaby's adoption hearing scheduled for September 11.

"Jenna is gone," she told me matter-of-factly. "Her mother, like she promised, came out to LA to her graduation. Jenna wanted to leave with her to go to Oregon, but I told her she had to wait a couple of weeks until her emancipation hearing, so she stayed on. But once the court emancipated her, she got on the bus and left. She worked for a bit at a Carl's Jr. here in LA, and they liked her, so her restaurant manager called some Carl's Jr. location over there and they promised her a job. Personally, I don't think it was good for her to leave like this. What does she know about her mother? What's waiting for her out there? Here she could've had free transitional housing, her job, therapist, all kinds of support, at least, until she is 21 . . ."

This all sounded reasonable, but I thought I understood Jenna. She wanted to escape the foster prison, and leave behind her nightmarish childhood. If she had to walk to Oregon, she would.

"Did she ask about her children?"

"Nope. She didn't ask me, for sure. All she said was that she was moving on with her life and looking ahead. Well, good luck with that ... Tony is gone too. He also has some family out of state, so he went to live with them. He asked for a picture of Gaby, though. So I sent him one."

"I do not doubt his love for Gaby, but sending him her photo four months after his parental rights were cut?"

"Yeah. Don't worry, Lane, it won't hurt you or the baby. Maybe it'll help him get a bit more stable."

I wasn't comfortable hearing that, but if Lynette had already sent it, what was I supposed to do?

"Which picture?" I asked, just to know.

"One I took at Jenna's visit last fall."

"With Jenna in it?" It sounded hard to believe after all that had gone on in court between them.

"I didn't have any other I could spare. Well, he's got it now. There's nothing else I can do for him but pray."

§

Gaby's adoption order was issued on Thursday, September 11, 2008, bringing our three-year saga to an end. The country was in mourning, commemorating the seventh anniversary of the deadly attacks. We put off the celebration until the next day, when Jon and I took the kids to Disneyland.

And then it all flowed like water through a breached levee. Happily, unstoppably. A flood of emails and calls.

Ahead of us were new birth certificates, new Social Security numbers, travel passports, and school registrations.

Behind us were the years of legal arguments, visits, reports, rumors; of details—personal, banal, or sordid—evaporating off the court transcripts into the smoggy heat of LA. The cleaning crew was propping open the tall doors of the empty courtroom, ready to vacuum the worn-out carpet.

Grandma, calling me after the court, observed: "Had you not gone through all this struggle to keep these children, you wouldn't have grown so deeply attached to them."

She was right; I knew it in my heart. But even more so, in my body. Even though these kids were not my flesh and blood, my bond with them was deep enough to make me lose sleep and endure chest pain and migraines. Tobias Wolff once described feeling the physical pain his baby son felt when the nurse kept jabbing him with a needle, trying to find his vein— I can relate.[33]

§

Saturday night Natalie was watching the kids. Jon and I headed to Frank Romero's studio in Highland Park, not far from the foster home Señora Teresa still ran for emergency placement babies.

We ended up bringing home something tangible to remember the journey's end—a still life by Romero that we hung above the fireplace in our living room. This work portrays the pleasures of a warm, welcoming home—a guitar, a cat curled up on the rug, books. You can almost smell the cookies being baked in the oven and hear the kids clapping to nursery rhymes.

I felt the sense of an ending, a crossing of the threshold. But my celebration, like the crossing of the Red Sea in Exodus, was tarnished by the awareness of someone else's loss. It seemed that we won, but that would be a misreading of our story. Our kids' birthparents did not lose the children to us, but to their own shortcomings. As they battled the court, each other, and their circumstances, struggled to gain control over their parental abilities and rights, we were waiting on the sidelines for the outcome. We were, after all, the concurrent track, an alternative in case the main goal—reunification—failed.

During the process, I understood Jenna, commiserated with her, tried to take her side, and, I won't deny it, despised her at times. But those are many feelings, and none that are mutually exclusive. Once the court decisions came down, the animosity, in particular, evaporated like night dew on a hot summer morning. I was trying to recall it, but I felt none. What came up instead was the overpowering sorrow for Jenna's damaged life, but also hope that she would find some stability, some degree of happiness in the future.

For some reason, I didn't feel much of the same compassion toward Tony, maybe because he was an adult all along.

"Pray," is what Lynette said she would do for Tony. I prayed, and I still pray to this day, for Jenna, for her healing.

Through these children, I feel connected to her, to "our Jenna," as Grandma once called her. She entered motherhood as a victim: an abused orphan, a lone teenager who earnestly wanted what she couldn't have. Those three years brought us close, and even though our relationship ended with the court cases, our connection never will.

"I still have a hard time calling them 'my daughters,' isn't it strange?" I wrote in my diary after Gaby's adoption became final. "Still referring to them with other people impersonally as 'my older one, my younger one.'"

Many years later, I do not have this problem. But sometimes Marianna turns her face, and her facial expression—anger, irritation, or smile—reminds me of the same expression I used to see on Jenna's face, as if her mother's ghost has passed between us.

We Have the Future

Proposition 8 passed, leaving our marriage in limbo: legal in California, yet illegal in most states and—thanks to DOMA—in the eyes of the federal government. Its validity, along with that of all of California's 18,000-plus same-sex marriages consecrated earlier that year, was now in the hands of the California Supreme Court.[34]

All through the late summer and fall of 2008, despite teaching 24 units at four colleges and keeping the house afloat, I fought to stop the Prop 8 assault—emailing and calling friends and acquaintances, talking to my students, demonstrating, putting up street signs (that would often disappear overnight), donating, and so on.

The night of the vote, after teaching in Orange County, I drove deeper into this conservative county to volunteer with the "No on 8" campaign at a polling place in Stanton, California. Our small group stood there on the street corner with signs and pamphlets, talking to whoever was willing to talk. Some drivers would slow down only to roll down their windows and yell homophobic slurs. But I made sure to make eye contact with each of them, and with the voters coming into the station.

I wanted them to see me, a real person they were going to discriminate against, to confront their conscience.

Not all people were against us though. I noted many friendly honks and waves from women, which reminded me that our rights were an offshoot of the feminist revolution, another step away from patriarchal uniformity towards equality and inclusion.

And still, I felt crushed by the passage of Prop 8. It won decisively throughout the state, even in the more progressive Los Angeles County. Barack Obama, whom we'd fervently supported, also won, but left us on the fence: during his campaign, he pledged to repeal DOMA, but also stated, repeatedly, his opposition to gay marriage on religious grounds.[35]

I didn't fail to notice that on the same Election Day, halfway across the country in Arkansas, another voter initiative passed, making it "illegal for any individuals cohabiting outside of a valid marriage to adopt or provide foster care to minors." The Arkansas measure was an eerie echo of Anita BJackt-inspired 1977 Florida's ban on gay and lesbian adoption, still in effect in 2008. Was this a sign of things to come? Legal bans on gay and lesbian fostering and adoption popping up around the country to prevent gay families from becoming a new normal?[36]

We, gay families, aren't visible enough, I surmised. After the November vote, I took to wearing a two inch-wide, impossible-to-miss rainbow bracelet anywhere we went as a family—beach, restaurant, zoo, the Barnum & Bailey Circus. Let everyone see, if it weren't clear enough already—we exist.

I also made a point of telling anyone who'd listen about Jon, me, and the kids. An acquaintance at work encouraged me by saying that as a woman of faith, she was initially against gay marriage, but getting to know me personally changed her mind and her vote. This may take years, I thought, but without acceptance by the straight community, we are never going to win this fight.

§

"You can apply for a new Social Security number for your adopted child . . . Marianna, isn't it?" asked the clerk, a middle-aged white woman, behind the plexiglass window.

"Her birth certificate is valid, but," she gave me a sympathetic look, "you can only have one father on it."

The federal SSN application, unlike the newly issued State of California birth certificate, did not have a "Parent 1" and "Parent 2" option. Only "Mother" and "Father," plain and simple. In the eyes of the federal government under DOMA, Jon and I, now legally married in California, were still two single men. Neither our marriage nor our joint parenting claim to Marianna was valid.

"What can we do about it?"

"One of you could put your own name down there, or you can leave 'Mother' blank."

"I'll take that," I said.

"Which option?"

"I'll be the mother."

I felt sadly amused. The prohibition was mocking itself, with its antiquated, heteronormative idea of parenting. Symbolically, DOMA was forcing one of us, Marianna's legal parents, to take the place of her biological mother, and who would be better suited to do it than me? Had I not been a substitute all along?

§

2008, the unforgettable year, was winding down. We spent its last week in Palm Desert. With Hanukkah and Christmas overlapping that year, we lit the menorah every night of our vacation, watching the row of candles growing right to left next to Jon's portable Christmas tree.

I'd say the blessings and distribute *Hanukkah gelt*, a.k.a. "the chocolate money," to Gaby and Marianna, and afterwards, we'd sing the traditional "*Ma'oz Tzur*" and spin dreidels on the kitchen table. Something about dreidels fishtailing in different directions and colliding with each other would set off Marianna and Gaby in the paroxysms of laughter, infecting us too, and we'd all laugh around the table.

One windy winter day, the kind when the tumbleweeds roll along the railroad tracks in the desert, and the air carries tiny, linen-colored particles of sand scented with sage, mint, and the rainy odor of creosote, we took Marianna and Gaby to a large playground in the Palm Desert Civic Center. Noticing a sign for an open-air Holocaust memorial nearby, we walked over to explore it.

There, our kids touched the life-size statues of the Holocaust victims—one dying silently alone, another standing defiant, a mother and two children pleading for mercy. They brought up the images of a death camp or a ghetto in Eastern Europe, but glancing at Jon, I thought it could have been Elaine, Arkansas, as well.

Jon and I were trying our best to explain, as gently as we could, what these bronze figures meant, but the girls weren't listening. They ran off, chasing each other among the statues, their voices filling the solemn memorial with joy and laughter.

Their laughter, I realized, was consecrating the place. Our adversaries may come and go, but we are still here—together and now married. And with these two beautiful beings, who have become part of us. The four of us might have come from different cultures, histories, religions, even different parts of the world, but through this journey, we have all added up to something wonderfully new, and that something new is our family.

In our kids' joyful laughter, I heard our future.

Epilogue

In 2011, at the request from Courage Campaign, a legislative nonprofit, Jonathan and I submitted a written testimony to the US Senate Judiciary Committee in support of the Senator Dianne Feinstein-sponsored bill to overturn DOMA (SB 598 "The Respect for Marriage Act"). In it, we documented examples of unfair treatment and specific harm caused by DOMA to our benefits, finances, and taxes. We cited an IRS audit triggered by the discrepancy between our filing taxes as married in the state, while single on the federal return (though with two related but separately claimed kids)—the kind of absurd everyday discrimination married gay couples had to endure under DOMA. Senator Feinstein's bill failed, but the proceedings attracted significant media attention, and our testimony became part of the Congressional record.[37]

Prop 8 remained in effect for close to five years. It was first declared unconstitutional, in 2010, by the US District Chief Judge Vaughn Walker, and again in 2012, by the federal Ninth Circuit Court of Appeals. On June 26, 2013, the US Supreme Court ruled that the Prop 8 proponents did not possess legal standing to defend the law in federal court, and thus left Judge

Walker's decision intact.[38] Two days later, same-sex couples began to marry again in California.

Exactly two years after it annulled Prop 8, on June 26, 2015, in *Obergefell v. Hodges,* the US Supreme Court affirmed same-sex couples' right to marry under the Fourteenth Amendment to the US Constitution, and mandated all states to perform and recognize the marriages of same-sex couples on the same basis as those of opposite-sex couples.[39] With that, marriage equality finally became a reality in the entire country.

In 2018, our testimony about Marianna and Gaby's public adoption was included in an *amicus* brief filed by Family Equality, the nationwide LGBTQ+ family advocacy organization, alongside ACLU, in *Fulton v. City of Philadelphia*—a case that would allow Catholic Social Services (CSS), a provider of foster care for the kids in the taxpayer-funded child welfare system, not to place children with same-sex couples.[40] The City of Philadelphia had previously suspended its contract with CSS in adherence to its non-discrimination policy, arguing that the agency's faith-based choice about whom it wants to serve could potentially discriminate against LGBTQ+ parents and prospective parents of other faiths.[41]

The problem for us lay not only in the immediate discrimination against prospective gay parents but also in using faith to justify it. As Jonathan and I wrote in our testimony, *"Our religious beliefs have provided an important spiritual foundation to our initial decision to adopt children from the public foster system, and to raising them as ethical human beings."*

The next year, we submitted another *amicus* brief testimony in a similar case in Michigan, where another Catholic social services agency sued the state for the same right to reject LGBTQ+ applicants in violation of the state's non-discrimination policy.[42]

Although two lower-level federal district courts sided with the City of Philadelphia in the Fulton case, the US Supreme Court ruled in June 2021 in favor of the Catholic foster agency, stating that the City of Philadelphia violated its religious freedom protections under the First Amendment.[43] The Fulton ruling created a new legal precedent that will continue to have consequences far beyond gay families and public adoption.

This setback, however, has been offset by the passing of the Respect for Marriage Act, the same one Dianne Feinstein first sponsored in 2011. Signed into law by President Joe Biden on December 13, 2022, the Act finally voided DOMA, conferring federal rights and protections for same-sex couples and mandating all states to honor the validity of same-sex marriage licenses.

To be married and to have children are viable options for same-sex couples today. A recent Gallup poll showed that 61 percent of same-sex US couples living together are married.[44] Meanwhile, Family Equality estimates that between 2 and 3.7 million American children have an LGBTQ+ parent, and 29 percent of LGBTQ+ adults are raising a child who is under 18.[45] And as before, same-sex couples continue to raise adoptive children at a disproportionately higher rate than straight couples with children, 21 vs. 3 percent, respectively.[46]

Since Gaby's first steps there in 2007, the alpine village of Idyllwild, California has been our second home, where both kids have spent every summer and winter break. In 2022, Marianna graduated from high school and enrolled in the Administration of Justice program at a local junior college. Her sister Gaby is a star student at a college prep school, who has her eyes set on studying public administration. They still play, tease, and compete with each other, but also laugh at themselves playing pranks on screen in our home movies—memories of the time they were babies, a childhood away.

Our family, June 2021
Photography by Dakota Fine

A Prospective Parent Resource

Demystifying Child Welfare Policies for Foster-to-Adopt Parents

By *Lane Igoudin*, 2021
Reprinted with permission from Adoption.com

When considering adopting kids from foster care, prospective parents are usually concerned about childproofing their home, completing the required classes and background checks, and in so many other ways, becoming ready for the arrival of a human being they will be responsible for around the clock. What these parents might not be as aware of is the complex legal landscape they are about to enter. This article, written by a foster/adoptive parent, presents an overview of public opinions, legal viewpoints, and legislative mandates which have shaped child welfare policies today.

Natural Family Preservation

Common wisdom dictates that children, no matter what, belong to their natural (biological) parents. Parents are their children's guardians. Parents take care of their kids and raise them to adulthood. Kids are safe with their parents.

For most children, this premise holds true. Though, not so much for 424,000 kids in America who enter foster care because of abuse, neglect, or abandonment: the three basic criteria for children's removal from their family's homes.

What should be done about them? What does their future hold?

Most Americans agree that if kids have to be removed from their biological parents and placed in foster care, their parents should be given the opportunity to reform or recover so that they can regain their ability to raise their children. This general belief is mirrored in legislative acts and child welfare policies at both federal and state levels.

Law strongly supports biological family preservation. It presumes that biological parents possess the fundamental right to direct the care and custody of their children, and that, by default, they act in their children's best interests. A historical chain of federal legislative acts— The Indian Child Welfare Act of 1978, the Adoption Assistance and Child Welfare Act of 1980, the Adoption and Safe Families Act of 1997, and Family First Prevention Services Act of 2018—all speak in favor of family preservation and view child removal as a necessary, in some circumstances, but temporary measure.

A series of US Supreme Court cases (e.g., Quilloin v. Walcott (1978); Santosky v. Kramer (1982)) also recognized the supremacy of parents' rights to parent their children, and required clear and convincing evidence of their inability to do so before their rights can be suspended or terminated.

Those bonds, however, have limits. As Fred Wulczyn—senior research fellow and director of the Center for State Child Welfare Data at the University of Chicago—noted the Supreme Court repeatedly acknowledged "the interest of the state to protect and promote children's welfare and to assure that children have permanent homes. The exercising of this authority emphasizes that a child is not the absolute property of a parent, although state action is limited to situations in which parents are proven unfit or unwilling to perform parental duties and obligations."

When a child is legally removed from his or her family, he or she becomes the ward of juvenile (children's) court, which holds the so-called dispositional hearings to "determine whether the child can remain at home and, if not, where the child will live" (Children's Bureau, U.S. Department of Health & Human Services). To preserve natural families, children's courts order local child welfare agencies, like the Department of Child and Family Services in the Los Angeles County where we live, to provide reunification services to the birth parents so they can assume responsibility for the children removed from their homes. But for how long?

Without a clearly defined time limit for reunification, a large number of children used to be trapped in a continuous drift through foster homes, sometimes returning to their parents or relatives, yet often reentering foster care. Meanwhile, the kids' psychological stresses would compound, and their chances for a future with another adoptive family would dwindle to zero through no fault of their own.

In California, my home state, even ten years after the introduction of reunification limits described below, foster youth would spend, on average, about six years in the system with nearly two in five kids returning to foster care at least once. "Most troublingly," noted a report from the Public Policy Institute of California, the state's largest policy-setting think tank, "nine percent of all youth who emancipated in 2007, first entered state care when less than a year old, meaning that they had spent their entire lives in the system. Roughly an additional 1,000, or 19 percent of all who emancipated, first entered between ages 1 and 5." In other words, more than a quarter of children leaving foster care in California that year spent all or most of their childhood in it.

At the end of foster care, then and now, comes emancipation, which means that upon reaching a certain age, 18 in most states, foster children have to leave foster care and live on their own.

To compare, while the young adults in the general population can continue to rely on their families well past 18, foster care youth, traumatized by the removal from their original homes, separation from their birth families, and multiple foster home placements are somehow expected to become fully independent and self-sufficient in time to be cut off from state care at 18.

What happens in real life, as Donaldson Adoption Institute experts explain, is that "these youths, lacking permanent families to help them transition into adulthood, are at heightened risk of negative outcomes: emotional adjustment problems, poor educational results, and employment prospects, and inadequate housing and homelessness; furthermore, they are more likely to become involved with the criminal justice system."

The Adoption and Safe Families Act (ASFA)

Concerns about the universal application of the reunification policies, resulting in virtually indefinite confinement in foster care and multiple home placements, led to the passing of the federal Adoption and Safe Families Act in 1997. The act was an important step in shifting the focus from family preservation and reunification towards efforts to achieve permanency and stability for children, in part through adoption.

ASFA required states to make reasonable efforts to preserve or reunify families, limited the timeframe for dispositional reviews to 12 months, and mandated the states to terminate parental rights for children who have been in foster care for 15 of the most recent 22 months. After ASFA, children's courts no longer had the leeway to continue children's cases indefinitely.

One might assume that most children in the nation's foster care system are in some stage of reunification with their biological parents. Not quite. The Children's Bureau reported that only 55 percent of foster children nationwide were undergoing reunification in 2015, and a similar number—one half—were able to reunite with their birth parents that year.

This is definitely good news for those kids who can return to their families, but what about the other half? How can these children ever find a permanent home?

Here, in another groundbreaking change to child welfare policies, ASFA directed states to engage in concurrent planning, i.e., planning family reunification simultaneously with other, out-of-home options for permanency, such as kinship care (placement with a relative), adoption, and guardianship. In the post-ASFA world, when a child is removed from the home and detained by the court, the state sets in motion a two-pronged process: family reunification services and an alternative track for the child's permanency in case reunification fails.

ASFA created a paradigm shift in the way child welfare is run in this country. By setting a clock on reunification, ASFA put pressure on states' child welfare systems—and on biological parents—to comply with the court orders, or release the children into alternative tracks towards permanency.

While still prioritizing reunification, the Children's Bureau warned that "child welfare agencies may find it challenging to help families achieve timely reunification, while at the same time preventing children from reentering foster care." What this meant is that held to tight deadlines, these agencies, especially the overstrained ones like the Los Angeles County DCFS which oversaw 21,303 children in out-of-home placements in June of this year, would be hard-pressed to adequately support the biological parents' efforts to get back their children and not return them to their biological families too early.

Child psychologists concur with the concern about early reunification. Unless the harmful environments from which the children were removed have changed, it is risky to send them home. Chances are family reunification in those cases will lead to further abuse, and a likely re-entry into foster care.

This foster system reentry, governments realized, is not only emotionally damaging to the children, but also costly. In 2014 alone, federal, state, and local government agencies spent $13.5 billion on the removal of children's out-of-home care, nearly half of all of child welfare expenditures.

Concurrent Planning, or Alternatives to Reunification

Concurrent planning is still a relatively new phenomenon in American child welfare. The idea that a child could be placed with a pre-adoptive foster family originated sometime in the 1970s. It wasn't until the 1980s that Lutheran Social Services in the state of Washington developed the first concurrent planning model for the children placed in its care, one that favored reunification, but also encouraged the child's foster family to adopt him or her should reunification fail.

With ASFA, concurrent planning became a national mandate, and beginning in 2000, the Children's Bureau has started awarding grants to states to promote it. With the federal government providing the overarching goals, policies, and funding, states were expected to develop their own statutes detailing their concurrent planning policies.

The implementation of concurrent planning was not instant. In 2002, five years after the passing of ASFA, only 37 states had these statutes, and like state adoption laws, those statutes varied (and still vary) from state to state.

Current concurrent planning guidelines from the Children's Bureau set the seven main goals:

- Ensure that the child's first placement is their last.
- Expedite sustainable permanency.
- Minimize a child's separation from parents, relatives, and caretakers.
- Keep siblings together.
- Empower [birth] parents by involving them in alternative placement plans when reunification is not possible.
- Engage the family's relatives and support system immediately for potential placement and permanency plan discussions and actions.
- Communicate with parents . . . regarding their children's need for permanence, case plan progress, and the agency's concurrent planning policy.

These guidelines lay out the benefits of concurrent planning to the children—such as fewer placements and quicker case processing, and achievement of permanency—and to the system itself through "reduced court involvement" and cost saving.

If a child is placed in a foster-to-adopt home rather than in a purely foster emergency placement or a group home, the child's foster parents are presumed to be his or her future adoptive parents—a plan B option from the get-go, in case the return to the birth family fails. In the same document, the bureau cautions these foster-to-adopt parents that the kids they are fostering might still "be reunited with their birth family," and that "only when the court terminates parental rights are foster parents considered as prospective adoptive parents . . . There are no guarantees this will happen."

Family First Prevention Services Act (FFPSA)

The most significant recent development in the child welfare policies has been a renewed emphasis on the natural family preservation, which can be summarized as a "keep-them-at-home" approach. Signed into law in 2018, FFPSA has dramatically increased federal funding to states for services that partner with natural families to prevent children from entering foster care while also addressing safety concerns at home.

As explained in a Children's Bureau-promoted guide to FFPSA, "parents or relatives caring for children who are 'candidates for foster care'" are eligible for federally funded prevention services to address mental health challenges, substance abuse treatment, and improvement of parenting skills. "The clock starts the day a child is identified in a 'prevention plan' as a candidate for foster care."

Note the word "relatives" in the definition above. In the cases when birth parents are unable to comply with prevention service requirements and the child is already living with a relative, the act appears to encourage long-term custody arrangement with that relative.

In another important provision, FFPSA also limited, with some exceptions, federal "room-and-board" payments for children in "child-serving institutions that hold 25 or fewer children," (i.e., large group homes), to 14 days.

Increased funding for foster care prevention services in FFPSA comes in part from the cuts to spending on adoption assistance, specifically on the federal payments to the states towards post-adoption services. North American Council on Adoptable Children (NACAC) raised concern about these cuts, calling it "a step backward." For a more detailed explanation of this new funding mechanism, please see "Re-Links Federal Title IV-E Adoption Assistance Eligibility to Birth Parent Income" in the NACAC review of the law."

Stay Informed and Keep the Faith

Child welfare policies are always evolving, but do not let their complexity scare you. Getting certified to be foster/adoptive parents, my partner and I were often told there was a child for us out there; and despite all the challenges we met along the way later on, our parenting dreams came true.

Ultimately, the system tries to accommodate—within the law—what it views to be each child's best interests. So arm yourself with knowledge about the legal side of the process and the needs of the many parties involved in the foster/adoption process. Once you understand it well, set limits for yourself as to what you can and cannot do. While the federal government and the states continue to favor natural family preservation and reunification, concurrent planning alternatives available today provide many opportunities for you to find a child who needs a permanent, loving home.

Notes and References

1 *California Welfare and Institutions Code (WIC)*, Division 2, Part 1 "Delinquents and Wards of the Juvenile Court," Article 7 "Dependent Children—Temporary Custody and Detention," §311(a) and §319, and Article 8 "Dependent Children—Commencement of Proceedings" §332, amended 2018.

2 Health and Human Services Agency, Department of Social Services, State of California. *"Child Welfare Services: Manual of Policies and Procedures (CWS-93-01),"* July 1, 1993, 8.

3 Francine Uenuma, "The Massacre of Black Sharecroppers That Led the Supreme Court to Curb the Racial Disparities of the Justice System," *Smithsonian Magazine*, August 2, 2018.

4 *County of Los Angeles*, "Team Decision Making (TDM) Meetings: Policy Guide," (Pub. 0070-548.03), updated July 1, 2014.

5 *Bottoms v. Bottoms*, 457 S.E.2d 102 (Va. 1995)

6 English is not my first language, but it is my primary language, the one in which I have learned to express myself fully as an adult. Russian, my first language, stayed with me, reserved primarily for my parents, while I'd communicate with my younger sisters in English. I am also fluent in French, Hebrew, and Spanish.

7 29,948 to be exact per U.S. Department of Health and Human Services, Administration for Children and Families, Administration on Children, Youth and Families, "Adoption and Foster Care Analysis and Reporting System Data for the Fiscal Year 2004 (10/1/03 through 9/30/04)," 2006.

8 Published by California Teratogen Information Service and Clinical Research Program, University of California, San Diego.

9 This parent-requested temporary transfer of a child's custody to social services with a service and return plan is defined in California WIC §16506 and §16507.3.

10 *California WIC, Division 2*, Part 1 "Delinquents and Wards of the Juvenile Court," Article 6, §300(g), amended 2018.

11 *'Disposed'* is derived from the same root as *'disposition'*, which is a legal term for the final settlement of a matter brought up in court. In juvenile dependency (children's) courts, *dispositional* hearings "determine whether the child can remain at home and, if not, where the child will live" – per Children's Bureau, U.S. Department of Health and Human Services, "Understanding Child Welfare and the Courts: Factsheet for Families," *Child Welfare Information Gateway*, 2016.

12 *California WIC, Division 2*, Part 1 "Delinquents and Wards of the Juvenile Court," Article 10 "Dependent Children—Judgments and Orders," §361.5, amended 2018.

13 *Los Angeles County*, "2004-2005 Annual Report," 2005, 29

14 *Los Angeles County Department of Children and Family Services*, "Data and Monthly Fact Sheets | Child Welfare Services: Fiscal Year 2003-2004 Fact Sheet," 2004.

15 *Los Angeles County*, "2005-2006 Annual Report," 2006, 93.

16 Andrea Stone, "Both Sides on Gay Adoption Cite Concern for Children," *USA Today*. 20 February 20, 2006.

17 *U.S. Senate Joint Resolution 40—Federal Marriage Amendment*, 108th Congress (2003-2004).

18 Tamara Bortnik, "Let's Talk about Love" ["Pogovorim o Lyubvi"], *Vzglyad*, #750: 12-13, February 9, 2007.

19 Cheryl Romo, "Little Girl's Voice Lost in Bureaucratic Maze," *InLA*, November 1, 2005.

20 Garett Therolf, "County Dithered, Children Died," *Los Angeles Times*, June 14, 2009, A13.

21 *Adoption Questionnaire;* Form AD-4324. (2003). California Department of Social Services.

22 *California WIC, Division 2*, Part 1 "Delinquents and Wards of the Juvenile Court," Article 10 "Dependent Children—Judgments and Orders," §361.5 (8).

23 "A *walk-on report* is a request to submit a report to the court when a hearing is not calendared, but the matter requires immediate court attention," *Los Angeles County "Child Welfare Policy Manual* 0300-503.94: Set-On/Walk-On Procedures," July 1, 2014.

24 Andrea Di Robilant, *A Venetian Affair* (New York: Alfred Knopf, 2003).

25 In 2009, California Blue Ribbon Commission on Children in Foster Care reported that juvenile court attorneys worked on 131-616 cases, with an average caseload of 273 *"far exceeding the recommended 188 clients per attorney"* (87). The statistics on the judges' caseloads were even more shocking: the state's entire dependency court system had fewer than 150 judges, with an average caseload of 1,000 cases. The judge's average length of stay on the job was less than three years. California Blue Ribbon Commission on Children in Foster Care, *"Fostering a New Future for California's Children: Final Report and Action Plan,"* Judicial Council of California, San Francisco, 2009.

26 My translation from Russian.

27 Karl Vick and Sonya Geis, "California Fires Continue to Rage; Evacuation May Be Largest, Officials Say," *Washington Post,* October 24, 2007, A01.

28 Mike Davis, *City of Quartz: Excavating the Future in Los Angeles* (New York: Verso Books, 2006).

29 California provides monthly post-adoption payments to the parents of a child adopted from the state's foster system, along with free medical insurance for the child until he or she turns 18.

30 *California Rules of Court*, "Rule 5.570. Request to change court order (petition for modification); Section H Conduct of hearing, § 388," effective January 1, 2007.

31 From February 12 to March 11, 2004, on the orders from Mayor Gavin Newsom, the City and County of San Francisco issued marriage licenses to approximately 4,000 same-sex couples despite it being illegal to do so at both the state and federal level. On August 12, 2004, California Supreme Court ruled that Mayor Newsom had exceeded his authority and violated state law, and voided all those marriage licenses.

32 Tamara Bortnik, "A Fair Law" ["Spravedlivii Zakon"], *Kstati*, #701: 30-31, September 4, 2008.

33 Tobias Wolff, (1989). *This Boy's Life* (New York: Grove Atlantic, 1989), 121.

34 Karen Grigsby Bates, "18,000 Same-Sex Couples Await Ruling in California," *National Public Radio*, May 11, 2009.

35 Katy Steinmetz, "Obama's 20-Year Evolution on LGBT Rights," *Time Magazine*, April 20, 2015.

36 In 2010, an Arkansas Circuit Court overturned Arkansas Act 1 in *Arkansas Department of Human Services v. Cole*, and the following year, the ruling was upheld unanimously by the state's Supreme Court. Florida's ban on gay and lesbian adoption was ruled unconstitutional in 2010, and was officially repealed in 2015.

37 United States Senate Hearing 112-120, 112th Congress. "Testimony of A. Lane Igoudin and Jonathan D. Clark," in "S. 598 The Respect for Marriage Act: Assessing the Impact of DOMA on American Families: Hearing before the Committee on the Judiciary," *U.S. Government Publishing Office*, 2011, 170-174.

38 "A Brief History of Civil Rights in the United States: Proposition 8," *Howard University School of Law*, 2018.

39 Editors of *Encyclopaedia Britannica*. "Obergefell v. Hodges." *Encyclopedia Britannica*, August 1, 2023.

40 Madeleine Carlisle and Belinda Luscombe, "Supreme Court Sides with Catholic Agency in LGBTQ Foster Care Case—But Avoids Major Religious Freedom Questions." *Time Magazine.* July 17, 2021.

41 The latter is not a remote possibility: in a similar case in 2019, Miracle Hill, a large Evangelical foster agency in South Carolina refused to certify a heterosexual Jewish couple as foster parents, not just its gay applicants. The Anti-Defamation League and Human Rights Campaign fought to overturn the agency's policy, but the Trump administration issued a special waiver allowing Miracle Hill to discriminate in its choice of prospective foster parents.

42 *Catholic Charities West Michigan v. Michigan Department of Health and Human Services* (No. 2:19-CV-11661-DPH-DRG), March 21, 2022.

43 See Carlisle and Luscombe (2021) above.

44 Jeffrey Jones, "In U.S., 10.2% of LGBT Adults Now Married to Same-Sex Spouse," *Gallup.com.* June 22, 2017.

45 "Facts about LGBTQ+ Families," *FamilyEquality.org,* June 2020.

46 Shoshana K. Goldberg and Kerith J. Conron, "How Many Same-Sex Couples in the U.S. are Raising Children?" *The Williams Institute at UCLA School of Law.* July 2018.

47 Lane Igoudin, "Demystifying Child Welfare Policies for Foster-to-Adopt Parents," *Adoption.com*, December 21, 2021.

Acknowledgments

A Family, Maybe owes a debt of gratitude to Jennifer Alessi for guiding it through multiple drafts and, above all, for encouraging me, a first-time author, to persist through the many ups and downs of the submission process. I am grateful to the early readers of the book, Caryn Davidson, Alrica Goldstein, and Craig Loftin, for their advice and feedback, which helped to chisel the story out of so many stories and improved the book's readability. The early enthusiastic reviews from Greta Boris, Betsy Jennings, Jenny Serrano, Reverend Stan Sloan, and Brenda Starr helped to draw attention to this project and find the right press to take it on. And finally, I am deeply thankful to Robyn Crummer, Janeth Hernandez, Jackie Krantz, Alena Rivas, Laura Renckens, and Elaine Schumacher at Ooligan Press, whose professionalism and passion made *A Family, Maybe* happen. I couldn't have wished for a better team.

About the Author

Lane Igoudin, MA, PhD, is a writer, activist, and professor of English and linguistics at Los Angeles City College. He has written extensively on adoption and parenting, and his work has been featured on *Adoption.com*, *FamilyEquality.org*, *Bay Windows*, *The Forward*, *Lambda Literary Review*, and *Parabola Magazine*. As a sociolinguist, he has published book chapters with major academic presses, and was a recent Andrew W. Mellon fellow with the Humanities Division of UCLA. Lane is a member of the LGBTQ and College Creative Writing caucuses of the Association of Writers and Writing Programs. He lives in Long Beach, California, with his husband and their children.

Photography by Robert Gamo

Ooligan Press

Ooligan Press is a student-run publishing house rooted in the rich literary culture of the Pacific Northwest. Founded in 2001 as part of Portland State University's Department of English, Ooligan is dedicated to the art and craft of publishing. Students pursuing master's degrees in book publishing staff the press in an apprenticeship program under the guidance of a core faculty of publishing professionals.

Project Managers
Jackie Krantz
Janeth Hernandez

Acquisitions
Alena Rivas
Angela Griffin
Jenny Davis
Kelly Zatlin
Theo Thompson

Editorial
Kelly Morrison
Jordan Bernard
Sienna Berlinger
Tanner Croom

Design
Elaine Schumacher
Laura Renckens
Eva Sheehan

Digital
Anna Wehmeier Giol
Cecilia Too

Marketing
Sarah Bradley
Tara McCarron
Yomari Lobo

DEI and Online Content
Elliot Bailey
Jules Roth
Nell Stamper

Operations
Dani Tellvik
Em Villaverde
Haley Young

Book Production
Abby Relph
Aspen Ritter
Brenna Ebner
Claire Curry
Emma Wallace
Emmily Tomulet
Kyndall Tiller
Mara Palmieri
Maya Karkabi
Nora Kuyumjian
Savannah Lyda
Shoshana Weaver
Thomas Hernandez